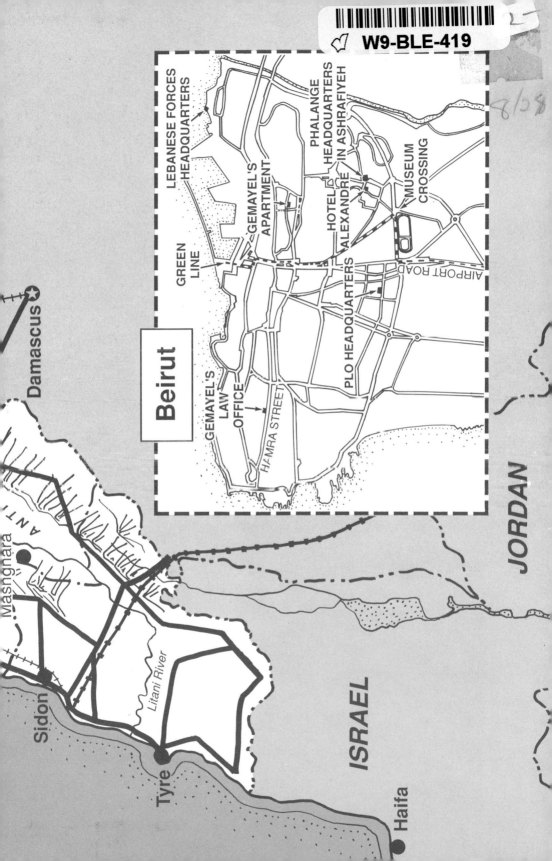

8/58

Beirut

LEBANESE FORCES HEADQUARTERS

PHALANGE HEADQUARTERS IN ASHRAFIYEH

GEMAYEL'S APARTMENT

HOTEL ALEXANDRE

MUSEUM CROSSING

GREEN LINE

PLO HEADQUARTERS

AIRPORT ROAD

GEMAYEL'S LAW OFFICE

HAMRA STREET

Damascus

ANTI

Masnghara

Litani River

Sidon

Tyre

ISRAEL

JORDAN

Haifa

The Covenant

LOVE AND DEATH IN BEIRUT

by Barbara Newman
with Barbara Rogan

CROWN PUBLISHERS, INC.   NEW YORK

Copyright © 1989 by Barbara Newman

Published by Crown Publishers, Inc., 225 Park Avenue South, New York, New York 10003.

CROWN is a trademark of Crown Publishers, Inc.

Printed in the U.S.A.

Library of Congress Cataloging-in-Publication Data

Newman, Barbara (Barbara P.)
   The covenant : love and death in Beirut / by Barbara Newman with Barbara Rogan.
       p.   cm.
    1. Lebanon—Politics and government—1975-
2. Gemayel, Bashir, 1947-1982.   3. Lebanon—Presidents—Biography.   4. Newman, Barbara (Barbara P.)
5. Woman journalists—United States—Biography.
6.   Television journalists—United States—Biography.   I. Rogan, Barbara.   II. Title.
DS87.N48   1989
956.92'044'0922—dc19
[B]   88-38674
                                                            CIP
ISBN 0-517-57215-X

Book design by June Marie Bennett

10   9   8   7   6   5   4   3   2   1

First Edition

To Penelope
and to my parents
B.N.

I wish to thank the following people for their support and encouragement during times when telling the story required more than I thought I could do.

Ambassador Benjamin Netanyahu—for telling me that if I did not tell the truth about Bashir, then no one would.

Ze'ev Schiff—his clarity and brutal honesty in reporting on the war in Lebanon and his friendship were beacons in the night.

Jack Limpert—the brilliant editor of the *Washingtonian* magazine, a longtime friend and colleague who pushed the story out of me.

Joy Harris—my agent, for her enduring belief in this book.

Barbara Grossman—my editor at Crown, for sticking with me despite my unorthodox habits.

Robert Farah and Charbel el-Khoury—in whom the purity of Bashir still shines.

Peter J. Goss—for his constant support and encouragement.

Preface

I kneel beside his grave and close my eyes, but no prayer comes to me. Instead I see his strong face, his stern mouth and smiling eyes. Suddenly his voice speaks to me. "Barbara," he says, in the thick Middle Eastern accent that still reaches to the pit of my stomach . . .

He lies in a stone sepulcher set high on a grassy knoll, an oasis of tranquillity in a land that has forgotten peace. With him is buried the hope of his country. Bashir Gemayel was thirty-four years old when he was elected president of Lebanon. Three weeks later, he was dead.

My daughter presses my arm, looks anxiously into my face. She never met Bashir; her concern is all for me. "Leave me alone," I say, for I can't cry in front of her. Penny kisses me and moves away with our escorts. I am alone with Bashir.

"I told you I'd be back," I say, and there is something unpleasantly accusatory in my tone—a faint, hectoring note. Since his death, this past year has been a nightmare of unanswerable longing and fruitless regret. Apart from grief, there is anger to deal with: How could Bashir do this to me? How could he do it to his country? Why wasn't he more careful? I warned him; his friends warned him. He had no right to get himself killed. And if he had to die, did he have to do it while I was halfway across the world?

But this anger is displaced and I know it. It's not Bashir who is to blame but his murderers, who have not yet been called to account. So what if they caught the trigger man, the one who detonated the 450-pound charge of TNT that crushed the hope of Lebanon under three stories of stone? (When they finally dug Bashir out of the wreckage, the back of his head was gone, his beautiful face was crushed beyond recognition, and all his limbs were broken. But I will not think of this now, not while Penny waits in the car for my return.) In the Byzantine world of Middle East politics, no one acts alone. There are wheels within wheels, and the miserable little man whom they captured was nothing but a tiny cog.

I am not an easy person. You cannot be, in my profession. I'm not forgiving, I'm not sweet, and I'm not easy to get along with. What I am is relentless. From the moment I learned of his death, I wanted to know who killed Bashir Gemayel. Now, as I stand by his grave, I feel that desire harden into a resolve as hard and cold as his tombstone.

I have some ideas, of course. Bashir was no angel. "In Lebanon," he used to say, "you do not rule by hugs and kisses." He was adamant, unswayable, and utterly revolutionary; and though he was adored out of human proportion by the rank and file, he had almost as many enemies amidst his supporters as he did among his Palestinian and Syrian enemies. Even within his own family, for Bashir had quickly been replaced as president by his elder brother, Amin, who had long chafed at his supersession as rightful leader of the nation's Christians.

I knew that his killer must have been close to him— someone who knew his comings and goings, a trusted friend, comrade, or relative. That meant that I almost certainly knew the person, for Bashir and I had been more than lovers. Strange as it seems—for I am a New York–born Jew, an investigative journalist, twice divorced and nobody's fool, whereas Bashir was a militant Lebanese Christian, married, a man of action, not words—I was his confidante. Perhaps it was because of these differences, and the fact that I was a woman, that this very private man was able to be as open with me as he was. Whatever the reason, I believe what he told me—that during our two years together, no one except his mother was closer to Bashir than I.

There is also this: that as different as we were in circumstance of birth, we shared a greater sameness. I am a practical person, no mystic; but when I say that our love was based on deep understanding, I mean an understanding that transcends boundaries of place and circumstance, a kind of recognition. Love is a tempestuous emotion, not a trustworthy one, or so I've found. But I didn't just love Bashir; I cared for him. He was my friend. And for that I owe him something that it may be within my power to give: perhaps not justice, but truth.

Seeking hidden truth is my profession, and I'm good at what I do. Experience has taught me that to discover the truth, one must always begin by going backward. I don't want to take that trip. I came here to bury my past, not to resurrect it. But there is no other way. I had thought to lay Bashir to rest by visiting his grave, only to learn that more, much more, is required of me.

*"If any question why we died,
Tell them, because our fathers lied."*
RUDYARD KIPLING
"EPITAPHS OF THE WAR: 1914–1918"
Common Form

The question is where to begin, and the answer, I find, is not simple. Most love stories start with the lovers' initial encounter, but the genesis of our love—Bashir's and mine—began long before we met. Perhaps it would be more romantic to speak of love at first sight, and it wouldn't be a lie, either, because our attraction was instant and mutual. But the truth is that a whole chain of circumstances and events set me up for Bashir and ordained my descent into a state I had long avoided.

Perhaps our story begins in Jerusalem, on a cold, wet winter day in 1980. The Israelis are terrific soldiers, but they are astonishingly inept at heating buildings. Every Israeli I met owned a thick, lightweight green army jacket, which was worn indoors and out. I kept warm by working and running frenetically.

I had only six weeks to research and produce an hour-length report on terrorism for "20/20," ABC's news magazine program, and I was starting out at a great disadvantage: the Israelis distrusted me. I had already broken two major stories they'd hated and denied, and now they suspected me of planning another.

In my business, one story leads to another, and the connections are important. To reach the beginning of this story I see that it is necessary to go even further back, to follow a tangled thread that leads from Beirut through Jerusalem all the way back to Washington in 1976, when I broke the Karen Silkwood story. This was both a major story in its own right and a watershed in my career; in the aftermath I was honored with the prestigious Ohio State Award for television journalism, the oldest award in the industry. And I was tempted by a lucrative book offer but let it pass to pursue the greatest boon a major break like this provides: information—reams of it, some spurious, some hot and good; new sources knocking at the door, people with secrets looking for the right person to tell them to. I was like a kid let loose in a candy store, only not all the candy was real.

Because of the nature of the Silkwood story, much of the information that came my way concerned atomic regulations and safeguards, or the lack of them. I had learned a lot from that investigation and heard many rumors, not all related to the story. Several of these rumors, from various sources, concerned the alleged cover-up of the theft of U.S. bomb-grade uranium from Numec, a plant in Apollo, Pennsylvania, that processed fuel for the U.S. naval nuclear program.

I had a few loquacious contacts in the atomic establishment who went very quiet when asked about Numec. This was encouraging. I hunkered down and dug in, and after eight months I was able to prove that in the midsixties, the Israeli Mossad had diverted between two hundred and four hundred pounds of highly enriched uranium from the plant, enough for at least a dozen nuclear bombs.

Both the magnitude of the loss and the sensitivity of the

story were amplified by the fact that it was the naval reactor program—prototype of the civilian program that later drew on its resources, personnel, technology, and system of safeguards—that had been penetrated and plundered. Several reporters were working on this story, but I got it first and took it furthest. After my story aired on National Public Radio, it was printed in *Rolling Stone*. All three network news programs picked it up, and I was interviewed by Tom Brokaw and Jane Pauley on the "Today" show.

I didn't get into the story to hurt Israel, though neither was I interested in helping. My angle was the inadequate safeguarding of nuclear material by the Atomic Energy Commission. But my intentions didn't matter to the Israelis, who were outraged at the accusation and vehement in their denials. They had to be: it was embarrassing as hell to get caught with their hands in the cookie jar of their greatest ally.

The most astonishing thing about the Numec story turned out to be the extent of the cover-up. (One story leads to another.) The diversion took place in 1965. In the ensuing years, small leaks had appeared here and there, and several low-key investigations were launched and abandoned. The Atomic Energy Commission claimed that the uranium was never stolen, but it had been "lost in the pipes," their standard response to all allegations that nuclear fuel had disappeared. They meant that during the production process, as the uranium passed through miles of piping, some of it stuck to the pipes—a logical-sounding explanation that never quite panned out, because when the pipes were flushed and the amount of uranium lining them was measured, the quantity found was always a fraction of what was lost. In the case of Numec, with hundreds of pounds missing, the FBI dismissed the AEC's lost-in-the-pipes story out of hand; but when they tried to pursue the matter, they were ordered off the case, ultimately by President Johnson himself.

By that time the FBI had reached the conclusion that a high-ranking official of Numec with close ties to Israel had either aided or allowed the diversion. Although neither Numec nor the AEC has ever admitted publicly that the diversion took place (insisting to the end that the material simply vanished in the process), the company was eventually fined $835,000, an enormous sum in those days.

Given that the cover-up, had it succeeded, would have greatly benefited the Israelis, it was impossible not to wonder about AEC complicity with the Mossad; and if the AEC was complicit, what about its watchdogs in the FBI and CIA? Some of the information I had developed supported the hypothesis of tacit acquiescence within the AEC, and also revealed a remarkably laissez-faire attitude on the part of the CIA toward Mossad operations in its own backyard.

I wrote a series of follow-up pieces about the cover-up of the Numec affair for the *Nashville Tennessean*, a great newspaper known as the *New York Times* of the South. By this time the CIA had also become involved because a foreign country was suspected of illegally obtaining U.S. nuclear material. The CIA concluded in a highly classified report that the diversion of uranium was made possible by an AEC commissioner who was a Soviet mole, and that the KGB was trying through this man to penetrate the Mossad. The publication of these allegations made waves in both the CIA and the Mossad; and, as often happens, some of the ripples splashed onto my shore. The more I learned, the more information came to me, including some fascinating material from a disaffected Mossad agent. Eventually I found that the focus of my attention had shifted from the inadequate safeguarding of fissionable material to the Mossad itself.

The Israeli agency had intrigued me even before I learned of its role in the Numec diversion. Mossad agents seemed to glide with ease and elegance through the murky waters of the underground. They were the barracudas of the spy world—efficient, accurate, and deadly; revered by their friends, greatly feared by their enemies. I respect success; and in such cases as the kidnapping of Adolf Eichmann, the diversion at Numec, and the prevention of an Egyptian nuclear missile capacity in the fifties by the assassination of a number of German scientists who were working on it, the Mossad showed that it could succeed at operations no other intelligence agency would even contemplate.

And these exploits were not even its primary function but, rather, were operational outbursts in the course of what was essentially an intelligence-gathering brief. The Mossad operates in conjunction with special units of the Israeli army, such as the Headquarters unit and the Frogmen, in the same manner as the CIA has traditionally worked with the Special Forces. Together with its counterparts in military intelligence, the Mossad directs the gathering of raw data, analyzes the data, and continually feeds its analyses into the computers of the tactical operations forces charged with the most secret and delicate military options.

Even as I write this, Abu Jihad, chief of operations for the PLO, is being buried in Syria. Abu Jihad was the man the Israelis blamed most for the West Bank and Gaza Strip uprisings; his was also the hand that pulled the strings of most of the terrorists who attacked Israeli civilians at home and abroad. The Israelis want it known, without having to say it explicitly, that they killed Abu Jihad. No one doubts it, and the proof that the experts offer again and again is the elegance, economy, and meticulous planning of the operation. The killers gunned down Abu Jihad, his PLO bodyguards, and his aides; they spared his wife and daughters; and they took the time before fleeing to gather up his papers. The attack had all the earmarks of a Mossad-driven operation carried out by the Headquarters unit, which also perpetrated the 1973 lightning raid on Beirut in which three of the PLO's top brass and seventy to eighty soldiers were killed.

This half-developed story on the Mossad was the main item in the dowry I brought with me in 1977, when I joined the staff of ABC's fledgling news magazine, "20/20," as an investigative producer. At his request, I was assigned to work with correspondent Geraldo Rivera. In 1979, Geraldo and I decided to use the material I had begun to develop on the Mossad to do a story on that highly secretive body.

I went through the form of asking the Israeli embassy for help. They were polite; that is, they did not quite laugh in my face. They used a lot of subjunctive clauses—*if only it were possible*s and *if we could*s—which added up to, "No way, lady."

But a little while later, a certain well-informed Israeli came to me. Still no-go on the Mossad story, he said, but if I was interested in doing a piece on terrorism, they would give me a lot of help, a lot of information.

It was my turn to be polite. I thanked the man. I said we would consider it. I went back to Geraldo and said scornfully, "The Israelis want to use us."

"For what?" he asked, ever the pragmatist.

After some discussion, we decided that I would go to Israel to evaluate what they had to offer. At the same time, I would quietly pursue our secret agenda, the Mossad story. Early in December of 1980, I flew to Israel for the first time.

The country was different from anything I had anticipated, as was my reaction to the land and the people who seemed so much a part of it. I was a stranger, yet I could not shake an abiding sense of *déjà vu*. The arid beauty of the landscape, the lovely, subtle colors of Jerusalem—olive-green foliage, azure sky, white stone buildings that glowed golden in the sunlight—were uncannily familiar. I visited the Western Wall and, to my astonishment, I choked on a surge of inexpressible emotion. It was like coming home to a place I'd never known.

But I had no time to contemplate the mystery of my

personal response, for my days passed in a frenzy of investigation and planning. I focused on people, not scenery.

The Israelis are no fools. They knew what I was up to, but they played it smart. They did nothing to hinder my investigation of the Mossad; they just deluged me with information on terrorism and trusted me to go with the better story. Within the first five days of that trip, I knew that they had the real stuff, a major story that seemed, incredibly, never to have been reported before. Of course, specific, isolated incidents of terrorism had been reported in the United States, but to make the network news they had to be spectacular, with multiple casualties, preferably a hijacking or an airport massacre. What I was after, and what the Israelis seemed willing to provide, was the context of terrorism: I wanted to know how terrorism functioned as a political weapon, who pulled whose strings, and its overall effect on a targeted nation.

I have always been prone to looking gift horses in the mouth. When things go badly, I take action, but when they go well, I worry. In a profession in which you're only as hot as your last story, information is the hardest currency of all. Yet from the start it was clear that the Israelis were prepared to fork over a great deal of previously classified information. Why me? I wondered; what had I done to deserve such largesse?

At the time I thought it was precisely because they considered me hostile, because the story they desperately wanted to get out would carry more weight coming from a critical reporter than from one of the gang. I also flattered myself that the Israeli intelligence professionals respected the job I'd done following their cold traces in the Numec story. But I know now that there was another reason that outweighed any other. I was interested; the others weren't. American reporters stationed in Israel had been covering fragments of the story for too long to see the whole. And even if some brash young thing were to try to burrow deeper, he would quickly be shot down by his superiors. Ever wonder why, with a whole world of events to choose from, the networks always carry the same stories, covered from the same angle, presented in pretty much the same order? Thank the great god of network news, Consensus: devourer of offbeat stories, to whom tribute is paid in full measure, both on the field and in the offices.

When Israelis talk about consensus, they use the English word; there is no equivalent in Hebrew, lending weight to the old saw that wherever you have three Israelis you'll find five opinions. Naturally, not all the Israelis I met were enthusiastic about the prospect of working with me. Many officials wanted guarantees, or at least some indication of where I was going with the information I received. This I absolutely refused to provide. Strangely enough, it was the bureaucrats who strongly objected to cooperating blindly and the intelligence brass who seemed willing to shower me with access.

Although there, too, I started off on the wrong foot.

An Israeli contact had given me a phone number inside the Kirya, a Tel Aviv complex that houses Ministry of Defense and intelligence installations. "If this guy talks to you," he said, "you've got it made. But he's very high up, and very discreet."

"What's his name?" I asked.

The Israeli laughed. "They call him Rafi Hamasriach."

Before I flew to Israel, I called the number to set up an appointment. A man's voice answered gruffly, " 'Allo?"

"Is this Mr. Hamasriach?" I asked.

Silence.

"Say again?" the voice demanded incredulously, in English.

I explained who I was and repeated: "Are you Rafi Hamasriach?"

"Do you know," said the deep voice, "what *hamasriach* means?"

"No."

"Stinker," he roared. "You called me Rafi the Stinker."

I put my head in my hands. "I'm sorry," I said. "I didn't know. Does this mean we're not going to work together?"

A strange howling came over the phone. It took a moment to figure out that Rafi Hamasriach was laughing.

His real name was Rafi Eitan, and he was the prime minister's advisor on terrorism, a top aide with strong links to the Mossad (his alma mater) and military intelligence. His nickname, Stinker, came from the period of mandatory British rule before the War of Independence, when he swam through sewage to blow up a British radar station on Mount Carmel in Haifa, which was tracking shiploads of Jewish refugees bound for Palestine. Though I didn't know it then, at the time we met Eitan was also serving as head of Lekem, the ultrasecret scientific intelligence bureau within the Ministry of Defense. Lekem was responsible for the recruitment of the American spy Jonathan Pollard, who handed over reams of U.S. naval intelligence before he and his wife were caught and convicted of espionage.

Despite our rocky beginning, Eitan was to become an invaluable source and, eventually, a friend. To the worried bureaucrats and officious press secretaries who turned thumbs down on me, saying, "No way, look what she did to us on Numec," Eitan would respond unflappably: "All the more reason to help her now."

I always enjoyed going to Eitan's office in the fenced-in compound known as the Kirya. This was the most sensitive area in Tel Aviv, dominated by the secret offices of the Defense Department and military intelligence. There was always an aura of mystery and beehive intensity in its streets filled with determined young officers, in and out of uniform. Eitan's office, a small townhouse inside the King David Gate, was distinguished by a massive, convex, bulletproof door. It was hectic with activity. Phones rang constantly, and Eitan was usually shouting into two or three at the same time, while half a dozen people milled about waiting to see him.

"Baaaaarbara," he would scream out when he saw me, "come in!" He would wave me in with his right hand while he continued talking into the telephone. A short, stocky man with owlish eyes behind thick glasses, Eitan had lost most of his hearing from injuries sustained during the War of Independence, and his glasses concealed a hearing aid. He was no James Bond, but rather a rumpled version of Alec Guinness's Smiley; and his veneer of casual informality overlaid one of the most creative and effective intelligence operatives of his day. Though most of his exploits are still secret, it's well documented that as a young man he was field commander of the Mossad operation that abducted Adolf Eichmann from Argentina.

I said earlier that the Israelis knew about my secret agenda; it's also true that I knew theirs in having me. Rafi Eitan wasn't helping me out of the goodness of his heart. His agenda was cautionary: he wanted to demonstrate the toll that terrorism takes and to warn that unless the West began treating it more seriously, it would spread.

Because he wanted the story to emerge in the biggest way possible, he gave us a good deal of ground-breaking material that was tangential to his purposes except insofar as it assured more publicity for the piece. Thus, he opened the door for us to find the missing links for which journalists had been searching for years: proof of connections between international terrorist groups and credible evidence of Soviet involvement in the training and equipping of their troops. (Eitan warned me at the time, correctly, that these allegations would meet with widespread disbelief, that I would do myself no good by making them.)

It didn't matter that Eitan had his own agenda, as long as the things he was telling me were true and could be substantiated. If so, I had a story that could change the way Americans think. But I let the government know that I would not be fobbed off with part of the story; it was all or nothing.

Each working day began at seven A.M. and ended at two or three in the morning. Besides Eitan, my main contacts were Dan Patir, Prime Minister Begin's press secretary; journalist Uri Dan; General Zvi Bar, who served as my liaison with the elite antiterrorist unit called Yamam; and Ze'ev Schiff, the best military reporter in Israel and my advisor on the piece that would eventually be aired as "The Unholy War."

My speciality was being a relentless pain in the butt. Over and over, I pushed for filming permissions that had never before been granted. Because I wanted to present an assessment of the threat terrorism posed to Israel, I needed access to military intelligence. To understand the kind of training designed to counteract that threat, I had to meet with units like the Golani Brigade, the Frogmen, and the *Sayeret Matkal*, or Headquarters unit of the General Staff, the most elite, advanced antiterrorist unit in the world. I also wanted to examine a single terrorist operation through a close look at the victims, the perpetrators, and the counterforce.

Except for permission to go along on an actual mission, which was granted but then rescinded, I eventually got everything I asked for. Rafi Eitan in particular gave me hours of briefings. He put the information I was receiving into context and provided documentary evidence of interconnections among such groups as Baader-Meinhof, the Red Brigade, the Japanese Red Army, and the IRA. Through his intervention we were permitted to interview a PLO colonel of Arafat's mainstream Al Fatah group in an Israeli prison. The colonel, Adnan Jabar, had attended a school for platoon commanders in the Soviet Union, just outside of Moscow, where the curriculum included weapons, tactics, combat, military engineering, and explosives. Jabar later put his training to use by killing six Jewish worshipers and injuring sixteen others as they returned home from religious services in the West Bank town of Hebron.

Through the consummate insider Rafi Eitan, the story

started to come together, to make sense to me as a journalist. We all wanted to know what was happening, who was behind all the terror. If today it's standard Middle East orthodoxy that the Soviet Union trained and equipped these groups, this is largely due to the work that Geraldo and I and the rest of the "20/20" team did on this story.

After four nearly sleepless weeks in Israel, I returned to ABC with a detailed shooting schedule and every filming permission we needed. When our executive producer, Av Westin, looked at what I'd gathered, he decided that the piece would run the full hour instead of the usual fifteen-minute segment.

Six weeks later, I returned to Israel to talk to the participants in the story and to choose the ones whom Geraldo would interview on film.

We had decided that one of our main segments would be a close-up look at a single terrorist operation, from the points of view of everyone involved: the victims, the perpetrators, and the Israeli antiterrorist squad that dealt with the situation. I met with many victims of terrorism, some of whom were also Holocaust survivors; their stories were particularly painful to hear. I visited a nursery school on the northern border of Israel and saw bullet holes in the wall where PLO soldiers had fired at babies. I went to the elementary school in Ma'alot where PLO soldiers had thrown children out of windows and tossed grenades down at them. But when I heard about Smadar Hadar, I knew she was the one we needed.

In terms of casualties, the "incident" that cost Smadar Hadar everything she had in the world was far from the worst of its kind. Only three Israelis died in that attack, as opposed to dozens massacred in Ben Gurion Airport and at Ma'alot. But Smadar's tragedy had a resonance that struck to my core; it drew, I think, on the bank of racial memory that Jung said dwells within us all.

On the night of April 22, 1979, four PLO guerrillas from

the Al Fatah group penetrated Israeli waters by small boats. They burst into the apartment of Smadar and Danny Hadar, their four-year-old daughter Yael, and their baby boy, in the seaside town of Nahariya. Waking to the sound of breaking glass, Danny Hadar grabbed his gun and raced into the living room, slamming the bedroom door behind him. With the feeling that she had lived through this before, Smadar snatched the baby from his cradle and hid in a clothes cupboard. Her daughter was beyond reach, on the other side of the living room.

The baby, furious at being woken, gathered himself to howl. Smadar pressed her hand firmly over his mouth to keep him from revealing their hiding place. She heard her daughter scream and her husband cry out in anguish, but she remained hidden with the infant.

The Palestinians panicked. They had made too much noise, the neighbors were already roused, and soldiers were sure to follow. They forced Danny and his daughter down to the shore. As Israeli trackers closed in, they ripped the child from her father's arms and hurled her onto the rock-strewn beach. While three men held Danny, the fourth swung the butt of his Soviet AK-7 machine gun at the little girl's head. Striking with all his force, he missed and smashed the stock on a rock. On his second try he struck the child in the head, crushing her skull like a melon. Only then did they shoot her father.

Then the soldiers were upon them. Two were killed and two—Sammy Kuntar and Ahmed Abras—were captured.

When soldiers entered the Hadar home, they saw no one and assumed that the terrorists had taken the entire family. Half an hour passed before they found Smadar frozen with panic in her hiding place. The baby, now limp and silent, was pressed tightly to her chest. They pried him away, but it was too late: in her fugue state of panic, Smadar had smothered the baby to death.

A terrible story, a mother's nightmare; but the worst of

all was that it seemed so familiar. I had read identical stories about the roundup of Jews during the Holocaust.

I went to Nahariya to interview Smadar. She was a small, frail woman, thin and dark, who sat hunched up on the couch in her apartment. She had remarried and had had another child, a daughter she named Ady for the first initials of her dead family. I asked her why she had remained in Nahariya. Her answer, spoken in halting English, will haunt me forever.

"I was the only survivor," Smadar said. "So I thought that I must stay here and start all over again. And from one survivor to become a family again. And I also felt that I have to show them that they can kill children, but they cannot kill a spirit. They cannot kill a belief. They murdered my family, but they didn't destroy me."

To me, Smadar personified the Jews who survived the Holocaust, came to Israel, established a state, fought for that state, and stubbornly refused to die.

I met the two surviving members of this PLO team in an Israeli prison. Clean-shaven, with closely cropped hair and laundered prison uniforms, they told their story matter-of-factly and without a shred of remorse. Sammy Kuntar, whom Geraldo later nicknamed Bullet Head for his pin-shaped, shaven skull, sat facing us with a complacent gap-toothed smile. Asked if he felt sorry for killing the little girl, he replied defiantly: "Naturally, we consider everybody who got the Israeli citizenship as someone who got something at our expense. So we aspire to get rid of the Israeli citizenship and everyone carrying it. I will kill every Israeli because he came and grabbed my land at my people's expense." I listened until the bitter end, then went outside and vomited.

And I met the soldiers who had captured the terrorists, and other soldiers who fought on the front lines of the unholy war against terrorism. I don't know what I expected—gung ho Green Beret types, perhaps. Certainly not anyone like Giora Inbar, the youngest major in the

Israeli army, who served in the elite Golani Brigade. This brigade had led the Litani incursion into Lebanon, and Giora had fought pitched battles with PLO fighters on that and other occasions. I asked him how he felt about it. "I hate it," he replied. "We are not like the terrorists; we fight only against soldiers, not women and children. Yet every time I kill someone, I lose a piece of my soul." I also interviewed Popeye, the head of the Frogmen unit, so-called because he was little and tough as nails, and he smoked a corncob pipe. This legendary soldier talked at length about the moral cost of killing and how careful they were to avoid killing noncombatants, even at the price of losing some of their own men.

In the years that have passed since Bashir's death, I have looked back in search of the point when this story became a mission. I realize that there was no single turning point, but rather a steady succession of events that led me on, deeper and deeper, until I found that I was an observer no longer, but had become a participant. But at the same time I know that the process had a distinct beginning. My encounters with Smadar Hadar and her boastful assailants triggered emotions I had not known I possessed, as if kindling planted in me long ago had suddenly caught flame and was consuming me from within.

I am a Jew, the daughter of eastern European Jews who emigrated before World War II. I am not religious, and for most of my life I was not particularly pro-Zionist. But I cannot remember a time in my life when I did not know about the Holocaust. My parents often talked about the Nazis, who had annihilated whole branches of their families; and it's not coincidental that I majored in history and wrote my thesis on the Holocaust. I have a capacious memory, and part of it looks like Yad VaShem (the Jerusalem Holocaust Memorial). All my life I had hated both Nazism and the complacence that breeds it with a frustrated rage that until now had not found an outlet. I used to daydream in school about fighting with the French resistance; leading a band of guerrillas in skirmishes against the vichyites and their Nazi masters; and derailing death trains, killing the guards and freeing the prisoners. (Another favorite fantasy was the Scarlet Pimpernel, who in my version turned out to be a woman.)

Something happened to me in Israel; something got inside me. I saw that the victims of terrorism, like the victims of the Nazis, were prey to the power of blind hatred harnessed to a cause. Just as Smadar came to stand in my mind for Holocaust survivors, so too terrorism took on the aspect of a new Holocaust which, like the old one, targeted Jews first. In 1980, the world regarded terrorism as a regional problem, just as in 1938 it had treated Nazi anti-Semitism as an internal German affair. And yet it was clear to me that this plague, spawned in the Middle East, would soon spread throughout the Western world. Thus, not only was the Western media's disinterest in terrorism the moral equivalent of its former willful blindness to the Holocaust, but it was also the practical equivalent of burying one's head in the sand. Every night when I lay down to rest, the faces of the soldiers, victims, and terrorists spun before my eyes; their voices spoke in my dreams. I began to feel I had a mission to bear witness.

But I also had a job to do, so I kept my feelings very much to myself and told none of my Israeli sources how the story was shaping up. They were all parties to the story, and I was determined to keep my emotional distance, even at the price of their continued distrust.

Given this reticence and our history of conflict, the Israelis were extraordinarily open. We were allowed to film inside top-security prisons and to visit the navy's ultra-secret radar scanning room, which sits high on a bluff overlooking the Mediterranean coast.

We met General Mano Shaked, commander of a mobile tactical strike force that works with the Headquarters unit, which carried out the raid on Entebbe and the 1973 assassination by commandos of PLO leaders and troops in

Beirut. He showed us the maps and sequential intelligence photographs used in several operations, and discussed with us the reasons for the unit's success. There were two key elements, he said. The first was planning. Potential scenarios involving the unit were computerized; all the contingencies were worked out in advance and practiced, so that when a crisis occurred, there were no surprises. The other key element, the *sine qua non* of every operation, was intelligence. From Mossad and military intelligence field operatives, information on major operations such as Entebbe and the assassinations of PLO leaders in Beirut in 1973 (and, no doubt, in Tunis in 1988) was updated continually, up to the very moment that the operation commenced. And if this type of immediate intelligence is not available, the general said, the operation does not take place.

We were also allowed to film Soviet arms and documents captured on Palestinian guerrillas, and to interview Palestinian prisoners. By the end of our stay, we had enough footage for a dozen pieces, and my thoughts turned toward home and the monumental task of editing it all.

I was sitting with Geraldo in the lobby of the Tel Aviv Sheraton Hotel when a messenger came over: there was a call for me, he said, from Mr. David Kimche. Geraldo looked at me and raised his eyebrows. "The elusive Kimche," he said.

"Too late," I replied.

For weeks I had been trying to see the director of the Foreign Ministry but, true to his reputation as the former number-three man in the Mossad, he had proved virtually invisible. Kimche, head of Mossad's Beirut station in the seventies, was Israel's top man on Lebanon. I had badly wanted to interview him, but his people kept putting me off: he's abroad; he's back but he's swamped; he's on vacation; he's meeting with the prime minister; he's meeting with the Knesset—unreachable.

I got the message. We did without him. Now suddenly,

just a few days before our departure, he was calling me. Too late, I thought, to impact on our story, but it went against my grain to leave any stone unturned. I picked up the phone, thanked him for calling, and scheduled an interview for the next day.

Kimche's office was one of the cluster of prefabricated buildings near the Knesset that house the Foreign Ministry. We waited for a few minutes in his antechamber, which consisted of two rickety old chairs facing his secretary, before we were ushered in. I looked around in amazement. As director general of the ministry, he had one of the largest offices in the compound, but it wasn't even half the size of, for example, an ABC executive's office. The furnishings were solid, well used, and obviously chosen for utilitarian rather than decorative value. I've been in more government offices than I care to remember, but I've never seen one plainer or less imposing than Kimche's.

David Kimche was born in England and, though otherwise thoroughly Israeli, he retains something of the Englishman's habitual reserve. No doubt this was reinforced by years of service in the Mossad, where he had risen nearly to the top before he was ousted by an office coup. He was, unsurprisingly, well briefed on our activities, and he said with obvious amusement that I'd run his people ragged.

The interview went well; Kimche gave us a very useful overview of the Israeli war against terrorism, but when we pressed him for specifics he eluded every inquiry with unfailing courtesy and skill. Geraldo brought up the subject of counterterrorism. In a country with an indigenous pool of potential terrorists, he said, how do you guard against attacks from within?

"Very, very carefully," Kimche replied.

We laughed politely. "But specifically," said Geraldo, "how do you deal with the threat? Do you have agents among the Palestinians? Informers?"

Kimche spread his hands apologetically. "We're out of my depth, I'm afraid."

"You must know."

"Ah, but you see, the whole game of intelligence is based on as few people as possible knowing; and those who know most talk least."

Later Geraldo said, "You're now the director general of the Foreign Ministry, a powerful position. Are you the original spy who came in from the cold?"

"Heaven forbid," Kimche said strenuously. "I'm a civil servant, nothing more glamorous than that, I assure you."

"Not an ex-spy?"

"Certainly not," Kimche said, denying what everyone in the room knew was true.

Kimche seemed surprised that we would do an investigative piece on terrorism. Until then, he told us, reporters had covered only specific incidents, not the whole picture. He wanted to be helpful. Have you seen this person and that one? he asked us, and to every name we answered yes. "Excellent," Kimche said. "And who are you going to see in Lebanon?"

"We're not going to Lebanon," I said.

He looked puzzled. "Really?" he said, with his most British inflection. "But didn't you say your subject is terrorism?"

"Yes," I said, seeing what was coming and not liking it.

"Then, forgive me, but how can you avoid going to Lebanon? Look," he said, "if terrorism is a cancer, then Israel is suffering from a mild, containable case, but Lebanon is riddled through and through with the disease. Lebanon is to terrorism what the Vatican is to Catholicism: the hub from which it radiates."

I thought of home, and of my daughter Penny, who was expecting me. I thought of our deadline. I sighed.

Geraldo looked at me. "I've got to go to Italy," he said in a noncommittal voice that meant it was up to me. "I could come back."

"I don't have a visa," I told him. "I have no contacts there. I don't know anyone."

"Don't worry about that," Kimche put in helpfully. "If you want to go, I'll see you're looked after."

"Thanks a lot."

Geraldo laughed. "See you in Beirut, Barbara."

I turned to Kimche. "Who should I see there?"

"Bashir Gemayel," he said promptly.

"Who?"

"He's only thirty-two and he's head of the Lebanese Forces, the Christian militia. Bashir leads the fight against terrorism in Lebanon. His eighteen-month-old daughter was killed in a car bomb last year. Extraordinary fellow," Kimche added mildly, "very handsome."

"He might be too partisan for our purposes," I said. "We're not going to spend much time on Lebanon. If I go, I want to go in and get out fast. I need someone who can give an overview, not a frontline fighter."

"Up to you, of course," he said with a show of diffidence. "I'll give you a list of people you might consider. Some very respected people among them. But . . ."

"But?"

"But I think you'll be missing a great story, and a great experience, if you pass him up. Personally, I believe that if there's any hope for Lebanon, that hope is Bashir Gemayel."

"Really," I said, skeptically. "Who is he? Where does he come from?"

"He's the youngest son of the powerful Maronite leader, Pierre Gemayel."

And then Kimche explained Lebanese politics with a clarity that I had never before heard applied to that complicated subject, nor have I since. While he spoke I could see the country with its labyrinth of overlapping feuds and sectarian rivalries laid out like a child's board game, perfectly comprehensible to an adult's eye. Kimche had the gifts of clear sight and clear expression, a rare coupling; what follows is only my own fallen-away rendition.

The Maronites, Kimche explained, were a Catholic sect that was expelled from Syria in the fifth century and found sanctuary in the mountains of Lebanon. Like other minorities in the Middle East—the Jews in Israel, the Copts in Egypt, the 'Alawites in Syria—the Maronites lived in a precarious world where safety and security were never assured.

But in Lebanon the Maronites prospered. After repeated bursts of communal strife, a delicate balance evolved and was codified in the National Pact. Under the terms of this agreement, power was divided among the predominant groups, with the post of president designated a Maronite sinecure; in addition, the Maronites held key positions in the army and the all-important financial community.

Lebanon, too, thrived through this arrangement. Until 1970, the country was an oasis of Western culture leavened with Eastern excess. Arab princes kept villas in Lebanon to escape from the austerity of life as mandated by the Koran; Europeans came seeking a safe exoticism. Beirut became known as the Switzerland of the Middle East, for its bankers were among the tiny elite that financed most of the world's great transactions.

Then in 1970, two events occurred that would forever alter the course of Lebanon's history. Jordan's King Hussein expelled the Palestinian refugees of the 1967 Arab-Israeli war, and Lebanon, in a show of Arab solidarity, took them in. A great number of the refugees settled in the south, close to the Israeli border, while their military and political leadership took up residence in predominantly Moslem West Beirut.

The Christians were slow to perceive the threat to their hegemony. Weakened, perhaps, by decades of unaccustomed peace and prosperity, and plagued with internal rivalry among the three leading Maronite families, they failed to respond with united force to the first, early skirmishes with the Palestinians. On April 13, 1975, the spark that led to full-scale civil war was lit. Like so many major historical upheavals, this one started with a small incident.

A busload of PLO soldiers, en route from Aley to the Sabra Palestinian camp, lost its way and found itself in the Christian neighborhood of Ain Rummaneh. The PLO soldiers were on their way to bury a fallen comrade, and they demanded that the Christian shopkeepers close their shops as a sign of respect. A dispute erupted in which one Christian was shot to death. That man happened to be a bodyguard of Sheikh Pierre Gemayel, the Christian founder of the powerful Phalange party, who was at that moment attending a baptism nearby. The Christian community interpreted this incident as an attempt on Sheikh Pierre's life; a few months later, the Christians responded with a massacre of the PLO in Qarantina, a section of the port in East Beirut, which was followed by the PLO's massacre of Christians in Damour; and so it continued, back and forth.

The fighting spread to other groups and intensified. Alliances were formed, broken, reformed. When the Palestinians wrested control of most of southern Lebanon from the Lebanese army, the Syrians seized the opportunity to occupy Lebanon at the behest of the Arab League. Ostensibly, they came to protect the Christians—who were facing a powerful coalition of Palestinians with Amal, the leftist, predominantly Shiite movement, and rebellious Sunni Moslems. But once the military balance shifted in the Maronites' favor, the Syrians threw their weight to the other side.

As the military might of the PLO grew, it became bolder in launching guerrilla attacks against Israel from southern Lebanon. Israel's swift and inevitable retaliation hastened the collapse of central Lebanese authority.

By 1976, the Phalangists, the predominant Christian militia, were engaged in open warfare with the PLO while also fending off attacks from disaffected Lebanese Moslems. Beirut was torn asunder by sectarian militias fighting to stake out territory. Worst of all, from the Christian point of view, the virus of factionalism had so infected their own ranks that Christians took up arms against their brothers. With the central government powerless and the army dissolved into sectarian factions, anarchy prevailed. Lebanon was like an octopus at war with itself.

And out of this chaotic maelstrom, one charismatic leader had arisen like the great champions of medieval Britain: Bashir Gemayel. Gemayel, Kimche said, had just succeeded in doing what no other man in Lebanon could have done: he united the Christians.

How, I asked him.

"Through political persuasion and, when necessary, a surgical use of force," he said. "Bashir's no saint. He did what had to be done."

" 'He did what had to be done.' Sounds like an epitaph," I said lightly.

Kimche looked shocked, but said nothing. He had spoken with great emphasis, even passion about Bashir Gemayel. It was strong advocacy from a powerful man, and I had to wonder what Gemayel had done, or promised to do, to earn it. No doubt Kimche had his own reasons for promoting this particular sheikh, but I wondered how effective Gemayel would be in the long run if he was, as I now suspected, Israel's man in Lebanon. "He did what you told him to do," I mused aloud.

Kimche looked amused. "Meet him," he said. "Judge for yourself if he's anyone's puppet."

I copied Kimche's list into my notebook, adding a small check mark beside the name of Bashir Gemayel. That night Geraldo and I hosted a party for our Israeli contacts and sources. I left early to go to my room with an Israeli friend, who combed through my belongings and removed every indication that I had been in Israel. The next day, I flew alone to Beirut.

It takes six hours to fly from Tel Aviv to Beirut, which is considerably longer than it would take to drive, though faster than walking. Such is the impact of politics on  transportation; the geographical and political maps of accessibility diverge so widely in the Middle East that, like Alice in the Looking Glass world, one must fly west to go north.

Which was fine with me. I was in no hurry to arrive. I stared out the window into the milky sky, sipping Champagne and trying to find a word other than fear to describe the odd feeling in my gut. I closed my eyes and attempted to rest, but scenes from Israel played through my mind. Over and over I heard the matter-of-fact hatred in the voices of the Palestinian prisoners. I had, during those interviews, been keenly aware of the comforting presence of armed guards just outside the door. What would it be like to encounter such people, whose hatred seemed to encompass not only

Israelis but Jews of every nationality, in a country where *they* held the power and the guns? It was not a prospect conducive to rest.

The last week had been one of the most exhausting of my life. I was so deep-down, bone tired and yet so obsessed with *getting the story out* that I had begun shutting down extraneous systems. People talked to me, and unless it was about the piece I didn't hear them. Israeli journalist Uri Dan took me out for a farewell dinner; I muttered an apology, lay down on the banquette, and went to sleep. Anyway, the Israelis thought I was mad. On my first trip, I had interviewed off-camera the young Israeli Major Giora Inbar. When I learned that he was about to be transferred out of the Golani Brigade, I called Dan Patir and absolutely forbade the move until Geraldo arrived with the camera crew.

I realized that I was acting like a tyrant, but there was nothing I could do about it; the job had to get done. The camera crew walked on eggshells around me, and even Geraldo watched himself. By the time I got onto the plane to Cairo, en route to Beirut, I felt as if I were sitting on a live volcano.

Maybe it was the change in air pressure, or the sudden isolation, but as we rose through the clouds something burst in me; suppressed feelings began to erupt. I felt rage, sorrow for the victims of terrorism, and admiration for the men and women who fought it without losing their own humanity. The piece as I was beginning to see it had to do with survivors like Smadar Hadar—people who refused to behave like victims though they had cause enough to, and who stubbornly persisted in casting themselves as victors. I felt that regardless of cause, terrorism was detestable; it was bullying on a violent, international scale, and this perception increased my sympathy and respect for the victims who did not cave in.

My father had imprinted me with the dual need to be strong and to ally myself with the powerless. The stories I was drawn to investigate had almost always focused on the exploitation of workers or consumers, ranging from carnival fraud and dangerous rides to epidemics of lung disease in West Virginia, from the hazards of chemicals in the workplace to illegal hikes in the Blue Cross rates. In every case I got deeply involved in my story, but nothing I had ever done had moved me, *shaken me*, like this story on terrorism. The fact that I was afraid to go to Beirut meant only that I had to go, not because I was foolhardy but because this sense of danger is a valuable signpost pointing to the heart of a story.

I ordered another glass of Champagne and tried to read. The warring factions of Lebanon were intensely complicated. Just when I thought I had it down as Christians vs. Moslems, or Lebanese vs. Palestinians, or Syrians vs. everyone, the Shiites would start massacring each other or the Christians would assassinate a Christian, and I was back where I started. Journalists view Lebanon as a jungle, but Israelis call it a swamp, and I think they come closer.

I would have preferred a real swamp to Beirut. Wading through muck with alligators snapping at my ankles seemed like a summer picnic compared to the prospect of maneuvering through the crossfire from dozens of warring tribes.

And of course I knew about the roadblocks, what had happened and what could happen. Nine years ago, the kidnapping of Americans and other Westerners had not yet become the Lebanese national sport, but there were numerous unpleasant incidents. Kimche had briefed me on the Lebanese editor Salim el-Louzy, who was abducted at a Syrian checkpoint and found days later, dead from torture; his assailants had put out his eyes and dissolved his writing hand in acid. The torture-murder of el-Louzy had not been random. He had taken a stand against the Syrian presence in Lebanon. I had as yet done nothing to offend the Syrians, but the thought of el-Louzy's fate stayed in the back of my mind, an effective antidote to relaxation.

It added to my anxiety to be flying without a visa, on the strength of a vague assurance from Av Westin, executive producer of "20/20," that someone from ABC's Beirut bureau would facilitate my entrance. I knew no one from that bureau and didn't like depending on strangers, especially because in television there's always a good chance of friction between the local news bureau and news magazine producers. They consider us interlopers, willing to blow their sources for a quick and easy kill while they have to slog through the mud, year in and year out. As I brooded, the possibility that there would be no one waiting came to seem a probability.

We began our approach to Beirut, and I craned out of the window for my first glimpse of the city. The plane banked, and the view suddenly revealed was breathtaking. From above, the city was a pleasing jumble of sand-colored buildings and hotels, bracketed by the sparkling blue waters of the Mediterranean and a range of white-topped mountains, the Mount Lebanon range, running almost the entire length of the country. It is the Christian heartland.

Perhaps it was a measure of my nervousness, but as the plane descended through a milky blue afternoon haze, I thought we'd been diverted to an army base. Soldiers were everywhere, standing at ease, machine guns hung loosely over their shoulders, chatting in small groups, smoking, eating pita. But as we approached the cream-colored, two-story stucco terminal, I was reassured by the sight of other passengers on the tarmac. The men were clad in beautifully tailored European suits; the women wore elegant, sexy dresses and carried fur coats slung casually over their shoulders. Altogether there was an atmosphere of wanton luxury that was lost in the United States when flying became mass transport.

Inside the terminal, I stood transfixed by the Fellini-like vision of stylish, bejeweled ladies who looked as if they had just emerged from a Parisian fashion show, casually mingling with heavily armed Lebanese and Syrian soldiers. In my travel-worn wool skirt, sweater, and old trenchcoat, I felt seriously underdressed and sexless. There was a confusing odor in the air of expensive French perfumes compounded with what I thought was a dash of gunpowder.

I looked around the terminal. No sign of Av Westin's someone. I felt sick. Envisioning arrest, interrogation, summary expulsion, or imprisonment, suddenly I caught sight of my name on a large cardboard sign. I waved and the sign bearer came over—a tall, thin man in his mid-thirties.

"Sean Toolin," he said, sticking out his hand. "ABC radio correspondent."

"I'm Barbara Newman." He looked doubtful. I was used to that. Ever since the Silkwood and Numec stories, my name has been known in the industry, but I'd found time and again that people who meet me are surprised by my five-foot, one-hundred–pound frame. Toolin looked me up and down, grinning. Then he stepped aside, and for the first time I noticed he had someone with him.

"This is the manager of the Commodore Hotel, who was kind enough to come to fetch you."

We shook hands. I thanked him for his trouble but said I wasn't staying at the Commodore.

"Would you excuse us for a moment?" Toolin said, very politely. The hotel manager bowed. Toolin took my arm and led me away. "What do you mean, you're not staying at the Commodore?"

"I don't want the Commodore."

"We all stay there. They've got all the facilities."

"I'm staying at the Hotel Alexandre."

"That's in East Beirut," he said, as if explaining to a child. "That's the Christian side. Plus it's a dump. Why would you want to stay there?"

"It was recommended by a friend," I said blandly, not about to tell him my business in the middle of the Beirut airport.

"It's *his* car," said Toolin. "*He's* not going to East Beirut."

"Presumably there are taxis." I was getting mad and didn't mind showing it.

Toolin stared. He shrugged. The side of a divided city that the press chooses to live on is a sure indicator of its slant on the story; both of us understood that by refusing his suggestion I was stepping outside the consensus. "It's your funeral," he said, and pressed his lips tightly together. He went back and apologized to the manager, who gave me a thoughtful look, then bowed again and departed. Toolin and I got my bags—battered leather veterans—and walked out of the building into a blast of cold, harsh light and a deafening cacophony of blaring horns, whistles, sirens, and wailing car radios.

Inside the taxi he turned to me at once, his face gray and tense. "What are you playing at?" he said. "What are you doing here?"

"A piece on terrorism," I said, softly, with an eye on the driver. "We've got the Israeli side, now we want to develop the Lebanese story. We want to interview Arafat. Can you make that happen?"

"Why stay on the Christian side if you want to interview Arafat?"

"They don't have to know. Keep the room at the Commodore in my name."

It wasn't the answer he wanted. He tried again. "You've never been here before, have you?"

"Nope; first time."

"Let me fill you in. No one stays on the Christian side. The Palestinians don't like it if you do. The whole press corps uses the Commodore."

Which, I had heard, had ties to the PLO. I considered telling the truth—that I needed to stay at the Alexandre because David Kimche had arranged for a contact to meet me there—but I heard myself say, "I'm not here to see the press corps."

"And you're not here to see Arafat, either," he growled. We had a short stare-down. Toolin turned away with a shrug. "I can't help you if I don't know what you're doing."

This was true. It was also true that I didn't want to tell him. Part of my reluctance was habitual closeness. Part of it wasn't. Toolin had come through with the visa, but he still didn't feel like someone I'd tell my life story to.

On the other hand, Geraldo was coming in a week and I needed all the help I could get. I opened my spiral notebook to the list of names Kimche had given me and handed it to Toolin. "What can you tell me about these people?"

His eye skimmed the page, then rose to my face in dismay. "Phalangists!" he said incredulously.

This, of course, was nine years ago, an eternity by Middle Eastern standards. Then, the Christian Phalangists were untouchables, perceived by the Western press as fascist stormtroopers fighting to retain positions of privilege over the Moslem masses. The image stemmed from their origin: founded in the late 1930s by Pierre Gemayel, Bashir's father, after a visit to the 1936 Olympics in Munich, the nationalist organization outwardly resembled the fascist youth groups of the era, with its emphasis on military training, political indoctrination, and competitive sport. This resemblance was bolstered by the Phalangist uniform, pith helmets, and straight-armed salute.

But the difference was proved when, in the forties, the Phalangists took upon themselves the security of Lebanon's waning Jewish community, whom they saw as a minority like themselves, only weaker and more in need of protection. In 1967, when the Six-Day War erupted, the Phalangist militia surrounded the Jewish neighborhood in Beirut to protect the residents; when the fighting got hot, they spirited the Jews to safety.

Despite these actions, the fascist image stuck with the Phalangists. Although the press likes to claim that it is neutral, most reporters are sympathetic to Third World anticolonialist and nationalist aspirations. In the case of Lebanon, they perceived the country as belonging to the homeless Palestinian people. This bias colored initial perceptions and reporting of Lebanon's civil war. Since that time, however, a decade of militant Moslem fundamentalism and hostage-taking has shifted our alliances—and so our perceptions—180 degrees.

"In Israel," I said, "intelligence people told me about massacres of Lebanese Christian men, women, and children in Damour and the Shouf Mountains. They were very certain about it, yet I've never heard that story reported on American news."

"We've covered the Christians," Toolin replied, instantly defensive. "They carried out a massacre in Tel Zaatar, for example, which we reported."

"But have you reported the slaughter of the Christians?"

"I've never seen proof."

"Have you looked for it?"

He glared at me. Just then we reached the airport exit. A roadblock was stretched across, manned by five soldiers whose uniforms marked them as Syrian. Unlike the Lebanese troops at the airport, these soldiers held their guns at the ready. They were backed by a formidable array of tanks, armored troop carriers, and automatic weapons.

A young soldier stuck his face in Toolin's window. "Passports," he said in English.

Toolin took mine and passed it over with his own. The soldier carried them to a man in plain clothes—"Syrian military intelligence," Toolin murmured—who studied the documents leisurely before sending them back. The soldier spoke in Arabic to the driver, who got out and opened the trunk. Then we were allowed to proceed.

"Do they do this to Lebanese citizens?" I asked Toolin, as we sped away.

"Of course." He laughed contemptuously. "The Lebanese have nothing to say here."

People who knew Lebanon had told me that Beirut, nestled between the Mediterranean and the mountains, was a beautiful city before the fighting began. Little sign of that beauty remained in the Moslem sector. As we drove past dozens of bombed-out buildings and vast shell craters, Toolin pointed out disaster sites like a tour guide. Syrian and PLO soldiers strode purposefully through streets that were almost empty of civilians; only the children were out in force, playing hide-and-seek amidst piles of fallen concrete and twisted steel girders.

Twice more during the twenty-minute drive to the Hotel Alexandre we were stopped at roadblocks. One, of sturdy-looking cinder-block construction, was manned by Syrians; the other, built of sandbags, by PLO. Each time, I felt a tightening inside, a twinge of fear duly noted but dismissed as irrelevant. I smiled at the soldiers, who smiled back and waved us on. We were crossing the so-called Green Line, which divides Moslem West Beirut from Christian East Beirut. Christian East Beirut looked like a different city. There was no sign of the military presence that permeated West Beirut; here the streets were full of strolling families.

Our taxi pulled into the circular driveway of the Hotel Alexandre, which looked as if it had seen better days but couldn't quite remember when. Toolin got out with me and we went to have a drink at the bar. Just as he was leaving, a tall, distinguished-looking man with light-colored hair and startling green eyes came into the bar. He greeted Toolin, but looked past him at me. Even before Toolin introduced us, I knew that this was Kimche's contact.

"Pierre Yazbeck . . . Barbara Newman," Toolin said, and he gave me a baleful, knowing look. "Pierre is Bashir Gemayel's press liaison."

"Welcome to Beirut," Yazbeck said. He shook my hand firmly. "I thought perhaps we might talk over dinner. But if you'd like to freshen up first . . ."

I took the hint. When I came down from my room, Toolin had disappeared and Yazbeck was waiting in the lobby. He rose to greet me.

We dined in a beautiful French restaurant with stark white walls and plate-glass windows that overlooked spotlighted trees outlined against the darkness. Black-tied waiters hovered round, serving wine and suggesting dishes. We were the only patrons that night.

Pierre Yazbeck was an impeccably dressed cosmopolitan with European manners and Middle Eastern verbosity, a great contrast to the rough-and-ready Israelis. He looked more like an assistant to David Rockefeller than a warlord's *aide de camp*. We talked about the situation in Lebanon, and I asked him to give me a rundown on the people on Kimche's list, which I had learned by heart. When he reached Bashir Gemayel's name, I expected passionate partisanship; but Yazbeck said, with no discernible change of tone, "Bashir is the commanding general of the Lebanese Forces, which includes all of the Christian militias fighting the PLO and Syrian troops in our country. It was he who united all the Christian factions. I don't know if you realize how astonishing that is, in Lebanon."

"How did he unite them?" I asked.

"By sharing his vision of a new Lebanon," Yazbeck said, "a nation free of the sectarian violence and corruption that now poison our lives."

"And by killing off his rivals," I suggested equably, for Kimche had told me in some detail about Bashir Gemayel's unification operation. On July 7, 1980, Gemayel's forces had staged a surprise attack on the Phalangists' largest Maronite rival, the "Tiger" militia run by Danny Chamoun. It was a surgical strike; they killed eighty men and succeeded in disbanding the group. Two other, smaller Christian militias took the hint and joined the united front of Bashir's Lebanese Forces, along with many of Chamoun's men.

Yazbeck gave me a keen look. "Bashir Gemayel is the one man who could have united the Christians, and he did only what was necessary to accomplish that. Without unification we haven't a chance of survival. He's an extraordinary man, and an exceptionally complicated one. You know," he said, "that he is only thirty-two, the youngest in his family."

I must have looked blank. He expanded. "You must understand that in our culture, the custom of political primogeniture is very strong. The eldest son inherits the mantle of leadership—always, without exception. By rights, Bashir's brother Amin should have followed his father as leader of the Christians; but Bashir usurped him, not through force but through sheer strength of character." He hesitated, then leaned toward me and said in a low voice, "I suppose you know about his daughter."

"Only that she died," I said. "David Kimche told me."

"Last year," he said, "early one Sunday morning, three of Bashir's bodyguards took his daughter, Maya, to drive her to her grandmother's house. The car exploded and all four were killed. The child was only eighteen months old."

I thought of my own daughter, safe at home with her father but missing me. My work did not imperil Penny, but it did deprive her. Adults do what they have to do, I thought, and children suffer the consequences.

"Who did it?" I asked.

"We don't know for sure," Yazbeck said grimly. "Maybe the PLO. Maybe Bashir's Christian enemies."

"What did Gemayel do?" I asked, meaning what retribution did he exact; for this was, after all, the Middle East, cradle of *an eye for an eye*.

"He went on television that night to call for calm and to tell his followers that he would tolerate no reprisals. He sent his own bodyguards to escort some Palestinian prisoners we were holding to a safe haven, to save them from being lynched."

"And then what?"

"He buried his daughter and went on with his work."

I put down my pen and my spiral notebook and caught Yazbeck's eye, thinking that I had to nip this nonsense in the bud. "Look, Pierre," I said sternly, "I have a daughter, too."

"I know."

"If anyone ever hurt . . ."—I could not even *say* killed—"my daughter, do you know what I'd do?"

He said, "You would seek revenge, as any normal person would. But Bashir is not a normal person."

"What is he?"

For once Yazbeck seemed at a loss for words. He spread his hands. After a moment he said, "Politicians all talk about putting country before self. Bashir is the only man I know who lives it."

"He doesn't care about his family?" I prodded.

"He adored that child," Yazbeck almost shouted. I saw the waiters draw back and huddle, whispering. He said, more quietly, "Bashir is a passionate man. Maya was everything to him. I assure you, you could not love your daughter more than he did his."

Yazbeck's hands were trembling. He noticed and put them in his lap. "Judge for yourself," he said.

I asked, "Will he see me?"

Yazbeck lit a cigarette and, as if on cue, waiters rushed forward to clear the table. "Bashir has been expecting you," he said, inhaling deeply. "He'll see you tomorrow."

By the time I got back to my room, it was midnight, which made it five P.M. Washington time. Penny would be home from school. I called her at her father's house. Penny was angry with me, curt and uninterested on the phone, as if I were calling from around the corner. She made a point of not asking when I was coming home. "I love you," I told her, and Penny said, "Got to go now, Mom."

It hurt. I did what I always did when something hurt: I plunged into work. I decided to review my notes and clippings about Bashir Gemayel, in preparation for our meeting.

He was a contradictory man on paper: a lawyer who led an army, scion of a powerful, aristocratic family who espoused a populist program of democratic reform. I read in briefing material that Gemayel had spent some months in the United States in 1972, attending a postgraduate course on international law in Houston, where the family had wealthy connections, and had worked briefly for a Washington law firm.

A man being groomed, then, for a position of power in the family empire, which happened to be Lebanon. Not a position of primary power, however; his was to be a chief councillor's role. Bashir had an older brother, Amin, his father's chosen and traditional successor, who was already a representative in Parliament with strong backing in the heavily Christian Metn mountain region of Lebanon.

Clearly, the expectation was that Bashir would come back from the United States in a few years, groomed to assume his position in the Maronite elite.

It didn't work. The Washington firm specialized in corporate law, a field that bored Gemayel silly. He was restless and homesick and longed to be back in what was, for him, the center of the world. Bashir Gemayel abruptly packed his bags, closed his apartment, and returned to Beirut.

His father, Sheikh Pierre, was privately displeased but publicly supportive. Bashir dutifully continued at law from an office on prestigious Hamra Street, but he also returned to his first love—politics—and took up a position as deputy head of the important Ashrafiyeh branch of his father's Phalangist party. Within months of his return, he began meeting with a group of young Christian dissidents who bitterly opposed Syria's presence in Lebanon. Bashir argued, loudly and in any forum that would give him a platform, that although the Syrians had entered Lebanon by invitation, they would not leave as amicably, but needed to be expelled as expeditiously as possible before they became firmly entrenched. Delay, he said, would create a fait accompli for the Syrians, who would grow ever more intransigent. Syria, which had never accepted Lebanon's sovereignty, had proved itself far more willing to send an army than an ambassador to Lebanon.

But the first obstacle faced by the dissidents was not the Syrians but their own Maronite elders, Sheikh Pierre Gemayel among them, who had welcomed the Syrian army as a buffer against the Palestinians. The basic conflict between father and son was that the old guard was willing to suffer the indignities of Syrian occupation in exchange for security, while Bashir argued that Syria was an inherent destabilizer of Lebanon and that it would form coalitions against any faction that was becoming too strong. Bashir and his father also disagreed vehemently about the 1969 Cairo Agreement. This accord, which Pierre Gemayel had voted for in Parliament, gave the PLO license to attack Israel from Lebanon's southern border. Bashir argued that the accord violated Lebanese national integrity, amounted to *de facto* partition of Lebanon, and invited Israeli retaliation on Lebanese soil.

Bashir Gemayel was, then, a young Turk, a revolutionary. An interview I read said that as a child he had admired and envied his father's leading role in expelling the French from Lebanon and had despaired of ever having such an opportunity to test his own mettle. I thought it interesting that when the test finally came, it was his father whom he needed to overcome. Bashir preempted the Maronite power structure and the Phalangist establishment by leading his small band in partisan anti-Syrian harassment. The Syrians, the Israelis had told me with evident respect, hated Bashir.

Sheikh Pierre did not, at first, credit reports of his son's activities. Ever since Bashir was a schoolboy, stories about his exploits had filtered back to the family. The boy's reputation as a political firebrand had attracted more blame than he could rightly lay claim to. Still, Pierre never dismissed anything as impossible where Bashir was concerned. He asked his son point-blank if he was responsible for the harassment of their Syrian guests.

Bashir admitted it with alacrity.

Furious, Pierre ordered him to desist. Henceforth, he decreed, Bashir was to concentrate on his law practice and leave politics to his elders and betters, particularly his older brother, Amin. Bashir refused, with respect. "Your childish impulsiveness will ruin us," Sheikh Pierre raged, and he threatened to expel Bashir and his friends from the Phalangist party. But Sheikh Pierre knew his son, unruly from birth; and when he saw he could not move Bashir, he stopped short of breaking with him.

In 1975, long-simmering disputes among Lebanese Christians, Moslems, and the increasingly powerful and well-armed Palestinians erupted into civil war. The first victim of the fighting was the national Lebanese army, torn asunder by sectarian loyalties. With the Christians left with no protection but their own militias, Bashir Gemayel forsook his law practice and took up arms with the Phalangists.

I had more material on Gemayel, but my eyes could no longer focus. I closed them for a moment's rest and woke hours later to the shrilling of a phone. Disoriented, I reached out blindly.

Sean Toolin's excited voice came over the line. "I have to see you."

"What's up?" I peered at my watch: half-past two.

"Can't tell you over the phone."

"Where are you?"

"Commodore. It's important enough for me to cross over. I'll be there in half an hour."

"Come on over," I said, but the phone was already dead.

I fell asleep again and put my trenchcoat on when I heard his knock.

Toolin came in and carefully locked the door behind him. He looked disheveled and something else—a little drunk, perhaps, though I didn't smell liquor.

"What is it?" I asked. "Did you get me the Arafat interview?"

He laughed. "No way. The PLO won't touch you with a ten-foot pole, and I'm not getting caught in the middle."

I was disappointed, not surprised. Arafat would have been a plum, but we didn't need him; Geraldo's interviews with the PLO prisoners in Israel had covered the ground nicely. "So what's so important?" I asked Toolin. He stumbled over to the bed, sat down, and patted a spot beside him. I stayed where I was.

"I have some great hash," he said. "Want some?"

I thought I was dreaming. Two-thirty in the goddamn morning and this maniac is offering me hash? "I don't smoke," I said.

"When in Rome . . ." he wheedled. "Just a taste?"

"You crossed over from West Beirut for this? How many roadblocks did you pass?"

"Just two," he said modestly. "You've got to know the back roads. If you're not into hash, we could do something else."

"Such as?"

He grinned up at me. "I noticed your black leather boots. I'm into that scene. I'd like to stick pins in you."

"Pins," I echoed, more fascinated than outraged. "Where?"

"In your breasts, but with love. I can tie you to the bed."

"Out! Get out!" I screamed, pulling him up and shoving him out the door.

I never saw Toolin again. Shortly after "The Unholy War," our "20/20" piece on terrorism, aired in April 1981, Toolin was shot to death in West Beirut. His murderer was never apprehended. People at ABC were shocked, and some whispered that he was killed because of the piece.

Management called me in. George Watson, now ABC's Washington bureau chief, tried to make the interview informal, but I felt more discomfort sitting in his office than I had facing Syrian blockades. "What can you tell us about this?" Watson asked.

"Nothing," I said. "I had very little to do with him."

"Didn't he help you with your piece?"

"He picked me up at the airport and dropped me at the hotel."

"Do you think he was killed in retribution?"

I didn't want to believe that. "Toolin had some personal problems," I said. "It may have been a personal crime."

"What personal problems?" he asked.

I told him about Toolin's drug use and his offer to stick pins in my breasts. Watson didn't blink or speak or move a muscle. His face revealed neither surprise nor disbelief. It was as if I were telling him that Toolin was a Boy Scout leader.

When I finished there was silence; and then he stood politely, thanked me for coming, and ushered me out.

I don't like to think Toolin was killed because of my story, but I know it's possible. We'll probably never find out. I guess the one thing we can be sure of is that Sean Toolin died of Lebanon.

I had the rare good fortune to work at a job that precisely suited my temperament. Being an investigative reporter and producer afforded me a transient intimacy—the best kind of intimacy as far as I was concerned. I could get passionately involved with a story and a group of people for weeks or months, and then, when it was over, I could walk away. After especially grueling stories I would rest for a while, spend some time with Penny, then plunge into my next project.

That's the way my father raised me. He taught me that work is happiness, and gave me to understand the corollary: anything that interferes with work is bad. Especially love.

I grew up in Riverdale, New York, in comfortable circumstances. My father was a Jewish immigrant, son of intellectuals from Vilna, who put himself through law school and rose to become a top New York trial lawyer;

my mother came from simpler Russian stock. My father was a good provider and a loving parent, but he gave nearly all his time, energy, and attention to his work and consequently had little to spare for my sister and me. When we did spend time together, he loved to regale us with historical tales, especially about courage. One of my favorites was the story of Leonidas of Thermopylae, the Spartan king who challenged the Persian hordes of Xerxes, choosing death with honor over a life of servitude.

Not only did I grow up determined to demonstrate my courage to my father and the world, I was also programmed to respond to that quality in men. I guess that, in a way, my father set me up for Bashir Gemayel.

Pierre Yazbeck returned the next morning to bring me to Gemayel. I hadn't slept much since the scene with Toolin. I had a miserable headache and replied curtly to Yazbeck's cheery greeting.

It was a clear, crisp Sunday morning, and the din of traffic had finally died out. We sped through narrow, deserted streets, Yazbeck gunning his beat-up jalopy as if he were trying out for the Indianapolis 500.

From afar, Gemayel's building looked like an ordinary six-story apartment house, but when we got closer I saw that it was a fortress. Dozens of heavily armed soldiers with rifles on their shoulders and machine guns in their hands stood at alert behind piles of sandbags eight feet high. The soldiers kept us waiting outside, shivering in the cold, while an officer scrutinized my identification and face. At last he nodded to Yazbeck, and we were allowed to enter. Inside, the lobbyless building was dark and dingy. A small hall led to an ancient elevator with a wire gate, which carried us with stately leisure to the top floor.

A pretty, plump woman of about thirty opened the door. Yazbeck introduced me to Bashir's wife, Solange Gemayel.

"Come in, Barbara," Solange said in lilting, schoolgirl English. "Please sit down. I will get Bashir."

As soon as she left, I prowled around the room. On one end of the living room was a small dining alcove, on the other a balcony pockmarked with bullet scars. Several undistinguished prints hung on the wall. The furnishings were simple and modern, and the only concession to wealth or status was a platter on the coffee table piled high with every brand of American cigarettes. Though comfortable enough and pleasant, the apartment was not even remotely close to what I imagined for an Arabian sheikh; later I would learn that in the context of a Levantine society, Gemayel's abode was indeed radically modest, a purposeful demonstration of his political ethos.

I was studying a small photograph, framed in silver, of a little girl with smiling eyes and a daredevil look when a door burst open behind me. I spun around.

Bashir Gemayel walked into the room, barefoot and dripping wet, clothed only in a terrycloth robe. He strode up to me, coming so close that I had to stop myself from stepping backward. "Sorry to keep you waiting," he said, thrusting his hand out, looking straight into my eyes. "I was up all night."

"Bashir," Yazbeck murmured, half in introduction, half in remonstrance.

I had seen pictures, but they didn't prepare me. Bashir Gemayel was simply a beautiful man. He was of medium height, with thick, pitch-black hair. His mouth formed a firm, even line, but his eyes dominated his face. Arresting, passionate, they seemed to smile, tease, and challenge. In no way were they the eyes of a stranger. I knew that he was thirty-two years old, four years my junior, but he looked even younger. Beneath his robe his body was heavily muscled.

I shook his hand and muttered something, I don't remember what.

Gemayel took my arm and led me to a sofa. There was a shyness about his touch, yet his behavior was extremely self-assured. Surreptitiously drying my hand on my skirt, I thought, "This guy can't be all bad." I tried to imagine an American politician appearing for an interview half naked and dripping wet. Jimmy Carter, for example? Ronald Reagan? Lyndon Johnson?—now, that was at least conceivable.

"I'll be right back," Gemayel said. He returned moments later dressed in a dark suit. A maid served coffee and withdrew. Gemayel sat on a couch near me and began talking as if we had known one another for years, as if I had been away on a short trip and we were catching up with each other. There was no ice to be broken, no boundaries to be staked out. He wasn't aggressive. He was direct and without ploy.

"What do you want to do here?" he asked.

"I want to find out what's been happening here with the PLO. I want proof of the connections, if there are connections, between the PLO and other terrorist groups. And I want to learn about you. Who are you, and what do you represent?"

Gemayel nodded and said briskly, "Then it is good that you have come to us. We have been fighting the PLO for twelve years. We know them better than anyone, even the Israelis. The PLO don't care who they have to destroy to achieve their goal. They came here and established their own state on our soil, and they swear they will never leave Lebanon until they march into Israel. *We* know," he said, clearly meaning he and I, "that that will never happen. And we have been fighting not only the PLO and the Syrians but also the Japanese Red Army, Baader-Meinhof, the Italian Red Brigades, who all train at the PLO camps in Lebanon. Every time there's another atrocity and the West discovers some new terrorist leader, we laugh and say, 'We knew him when.' "

"When did the fighting begin?"

"The *battering* began twelve years ago, when the PLO moved in; the *fighting* began five years ago, when we

Christians realized at last that we had lost sovereignty over our own country," he said with a slight sigh. "Our government and institutions are empty husks. Nobody takes responsibility. Our leaders are feudal warlords, not national statesmen. We went to sleep in a civilized country and woke up in a jungle."

"Jungles don't spring up overnight," I said.

"There are viruses," Gemayel said, "that invade so quickly they can paralyze a man within hours. The Palestinians are carriers of such a virus: wherever they go they bring violence and death. They have crippled Lebanon, but we are not dead. We are fighting back."

"An eye for an eye."

"*No*." His dark eyes blazed. "That is *not* my way. We fight anarchy with order, destruction with creation. The Lebanese Forces are far more than a militia, Barbara. We have become the intelligent arm of a state that has no head. We have established structures to fill the vacuum—hospitals, courts, orphanages, youth centers, programs for the elderly, radio stations—did you know that the Lebanese Forces run a classical music station? Because we alone envision a future for Lebanon. We will win this war, and we will force the Syrians and their stooges, the Palestinians, out of our country; and only then will the real work begin, the job of reconstructing Lebanon."

"In what form?" I asked, thinking that Gemayel was right about one thing: he was the only person I'd talked to so far who envisioned a sovereign Lebanon any time in the future.

"As a parliamentary democracy," he said with great emphasis. "This land is not only for us, the Christians. This is something we must make clear." Again that *we*; he was drawing me in, making assumptions. "The Western press portrays us as an elite caste, clinging to our privileges. This is completely false. We detest elitism; we are fighting for sovereignty over our own country, not to monopolize power but to restore dignity, freedom, and democracy to all the people. No more 'special arrangements' and privileges; Lebanon has had enough of the kind of justice that goes to the highest bidder. We are sworn to create a state in which the Druze, the Shiite, the Sunni, and the Christian can live together in secure and peaceful coexistence."

Freedom and democracy, peaceful coexistence—if I had a nickel for every time I'd heard a politician utter those words. . . . But Gemayel's eyes lacked the usual politician's glaze of disingenuity; he was vibrant with contagious passion.

He jumped up and paced about, then halted in the middle of the room, facing me with his arms folded across his chest. "When we met," he said, "I apologized for being late. But really it is you who are late, years late."

I knew he meant you Americans, but it felt as if he were talking to me personally. And he was waiting for an answer. "We're here now," I said.

His eyes flashed. "*Now*," he said. "Now, after a hundred thousand men, women, and children have died. Out of a population of three-and-a-half million. Do you know how much that would be in America, proportionately? About six hundred and fifty thousand dead."

I couldn't believe this. The Israelis had talked about heavy civilian casualties in Lebanon, but were vague about the figure. So many deaths could not have gone unnoticed. Peering into my eyes, Gemayel read my skepticism.

"You didn't know that?"

"No," I said evenly. "No such figures have ever been reported in our press."

"Why not?" he challenged, and answered himself. "The Americans choose not to know, while we hold the line against worldwide terrorism. And at what a price." He pointed to his dark suit. "After this I go to a memorial service for my three friends who died in the car with my daughter. Later this week is the service for Maya. We are not alone. There's not a family in Lebanon that hasn't lost a son, a father, a brother; and that is not the worst. Do you know how many funerals of women and babies I've attended?" He crossed the room and sat close beside me. He touched my hand to stop me from writing. "You can bring the truth about Lebanon home to the people," he said. "But perhaps your American public is not ready to hear the truth."

"Say what you want," I told him. "Say whatever's true."

"The truth is that your President Carter encourages terrorism in Lebanon."

"How so?"

"The PLO kills the former American ambassador to Lebanon, Francis Meloy, in 1976 and tosses his body into the garbage. Later they dig it out and send it back to the United States. And what does your President Carter do?" Gemayel said scornfully. "Does he punish the killers? Does he, at least, denounce the PLO? No—your President Carter writes the PLO a thank-you note! Addressed to 'President Arafat,' no less. What does Carter think Arafat is president of—Lebanon?"

I was astonished by his directness. The politicians I knew would turn themselves inside out for the kind of exposure "20/20" could give them. But Gemayel answered every question I asked with a directness and candor unprecedented in my experience. He seemed entirely without artifice, determined to speak the truth as he saw it without regard for its effect on me.

Solange came into the room. "It's time to go," she told Gemayel. He did not seem to hear her. He brought his face close to mine.

Solange said, "Bashir."

He stood up. "After the services we are going to lunch at my sister's house," he said. "Will you come to lunch?"

I noticed that he had not looked at his wife before issuing the invitation. She, however, looked at him, and said something in French. "Speak English," he told her.

"Madis will be there," she murmured.

"All the more reason," he answered without taking his eyes off me. "Will you come?"

I said that I would.

The family had gathered for cocktails in a beautifully proportioned and appointed salon of Abu Halka's penthouse. Through floor-to-ceiling windows a sprawling Beirut lay at our feet. Silent servants circulated with trays of drinks and hors d'oeuvres. As in Bashir Gemayel's apartment, platters full of assorted American cigarettes were prominently placed, but here the platters were silver and gold, and the furnishings magnificent antiques. Joseph Abu Halka was a businessman.

Pierre Yazbeck brought me to Abu Halka's home while Bashir and Solange Gemayel attended memorial services for the men who had died in Bashir's place. Like most upper-class Lebanese, the family spoke French among themselves and Arabic with the servants. Their Arabic dialect is unique, infused with many French words and phrases; they call it Lebanese. The family seemed perplexed by my presence, though extremely polite and gracious. Jacqueline Abu Halka told me that Bashir had never before invited a stranger to a family gathering— "but," she added quickly lest I be offended, "we are very glad you have come." I was not offended; *stranger* was the operant word in this room charged with an intimacy born not merely of kinship but of some shared knowledge from which I was excluded.

The room was lively with chatter and the tinkling sound of crystal and silver. I was talking with my host when suddenly an absolute silence fell over the room. Conversations broke off. Those who were sitting stood up. Abu Halka stiffened to attention. I turned around. Bashir Gemayel had entered the room.

All attention was on him. I was amazed to see his family, all of them his elders, defer to him as if to royalty. The men waited for him to speak before answering respectfully; the women brought him food and drink with their own hands. I remembered what Pierre Yazbeck had said the night before about the primacy of the eldest son, and my wonder grew.

Gemayel came directly to me, took my arm, and introduced me to his two sisters and brothers-in-law, explaining that I was an American television producer.

"She has taken the time to come to Lebanon to see for herself what has happened to us," he told them. Turning his face and bringing it very close to mine, he asked, "How are you feeling? Have you had enough lessons for the day?"

"No, I'm fine," I mumbled, flustered by this sudden intimacy.

There was one woman in the room who had not risen when Bashir Gemayel entered, who, when he greeted her, turned her head away. Unlike the other women, who were elegantly attired, she wore a plain black dress. I had watched her smoke cigarette after cigarette, hunched in her chair alone in a corner.

"My sister Madis," Gemayel whispered in my ear. "Her son was killed in the fighting. Nineteen years old. She has never recovered." He crossed to her side and put his arm around her. She shrugged it off without looking at him.

We went in to lunch. I was placed close to the head, on Joseph Abu Halka's left; Gemayel was in the center. Plates of vegetables, including radishes the size of lemons, hummus, chopped eggplant, great tureens full of chicken soup, roast chicken, and platters of ground beef mixed with pine nuts, or *kibbeh*, covered the table. It was my first taste of Lebanese cuisine, and I found it delicious; but I had little time to eat, for my host peppered me with shotgun questions.

I was expected, as Americans abroad so often are, to speak for my country. Why was the United States so obsessed with Israel yet so indifferent to Lebanon? Why did Americans talk so much about terrorism yet never lift a finger to help those who fought it? "Lebanon has become the cradle of international terrorism," Abu Halka said. "We Lebanese Christians stand alone between the West and this growing nest of vipers. What would happen to you if we should fail? Do you want another Libya, another Iran?"

"Most Americans," I said, awkward in the role of spokesperson, "believe that Lebanon's problems should be solved by the Lebanese people, with as little outside interference as possible."

"Pious muck," he answered with a grimace. "The truth is that you do not care. You Americans are content to sit and watch in silence while we die by the tens of thousands, fighting a battle that is as much yours as ours. To you, we are only Arabs."

"How could that be, tens of thousands? If it's true, why hasn't it been reported?"

"The press sees what it wishes to see and reports what it wishes to report."

"Are you saying that there's some kind of conspiracy against the Christians of Lebanon?"

"A conspiracy of silence, yes, I say that. A turning away. It would not be the first time in history," Abu Halka said, with a telling glance. I wondered if they knew I was Jewish.

"What you say is not true of Barbara." Bashir Gemayel's voice rang out protectively, from halfway down the table. I had not known he was listening. "She has not turned her back," he said. "She has come all the way from the United States to learn. She is sitting at our table."

There was a subtle directive in his tone, something almost territorial, and I saw Abu Halka take it. He drew back a little, and his face assumed a bland, social cast.

I dreamt that I was alone in a rowboat in the middle of a boundless red lake. The boat was shot full of holes in the bottom, and I was bailing water with my shoe because I had no bucket. All around me I heard voices calling my name: "Bar-ba-ra!" they cried, in an accent either Hebraic or Arabic, "Bar-ba-ra!" but I didn't look up, because I knew that if I stopped bailing for one moment, the boat would sink. Suddenly I heard a cock crow. Impossible, I thought; I must be dreaming. I woke up and the rooster was crowing still, in the darkness just outside my window.

I peered at my watch—five-thirty. No sign of dawn yet, but the moon shone bright into my hotel room, which looked even worse by moonlight than it did by day. Peeling, off-white walls showed their age, and the only furniture was a single chair covered in threadbare material, the bed, and a battered, splintered wooden desk. The radio, my link to the world, was set in a huge block of wood and looked like a Marconi reject.

I closed my eyes and tried to will myself back to sleep, but it was useless; my mind was already awake and hard at work, gnawing at logistics, trying to figure out how to cover the story in the short time I had left. I knew I wanted Geraldo to interview Bashir Gemayel, but that was only the tip of the iceberg, because before I would allow Gemayel to use my program as a platform, I needed to make damn sure his claims were true; if they weren't, I needed to arm Geraldo.

I also had to connect with the PLO, to give them an opportunity to answer the accusations of the Israelis and the Lebanese Christians. I had seen the underbelly of the PLO in our chilling encounters with their rank-and-file killers in Israel, and was very interested to see if the PLO brass would express the same fierce, unmitigated hatred of all Israelis. Somehow I had to put the story together by the time Geraldo arrived, in five days. I had no one to turn to for help, because ABC's bureau chief, Jerry King, was out of Beirut, and I sure as hell wasn't calling on Toolin.

The Phalangists claimed that 100,000 Christian and Moslem civilians and 4,000 Christian soldiers had been killed so far, an enormous figure. They also claimed that some Christian villages had been forcibly evacuated, while others had been abandoned after the PLO and their leftist Moslem allies tortured, raped, and murdered innocent civilians in the villages of Damour, Aicheah, Kaa, Achach, and Chekka.

I listened at first with numbing disbelief. Although I was beginning to realize that what was horror to us was commonplace in the Middle East, these stories seemed too awful to have gone unreported. Whatever a reporter's ideology—and we all have our opinions and beliefs—the bottom line is getting the truth out. I had to wonder if Gemayel and his people were not attempting to perpetrate some great fraud, because the only alternative was that the journalist community had turned its back on the Lebanese Christians. But all the evidence I'd been able to develop tended to confirm the accuracy of Gemayel's statistics, if not his point of view.

I have rarely been the fortunate recipient of "over-the-transom" stories, so-called from the days when sources would slip stories under the doors of leading journalists without identifying themselves. My kind of journalism was more akin to method acting. I developed my stories through assiduous research and tedious checking of facts, comparing information from different sources for inconsistencies. Once I had absorbed all the available facts, I would confront witnesses, pit one against another, let them think I knew more than I did, and sometimes, I'm afraid, bully them. I absorbed each of my stories, eating, drinking, practically living with my sources until I knew all their expressions and how their eyes went when they were lying. I worked on them until I could write credible scripts in my head—scripts that generally turned out to be pretty close to the way things actually happened.

Breaking a story that becomes a national media event, like Silkwood or Numec, is the most exciting experience in the world. One feels like a crusader with the grail in sight or an explorer discovering virgin territory. Is it truly possible, one asks, that no one has been here before? But in Lebanon I felt no exhilaration—just a cold, hard knot of anger in my gut—because what I was seeing looked very much like a cover-up by the press.

Such things have been known to happen, of course. They're not even that unusual. It happened in the late 1930s and early 1940s, when the Western media refused to credit photographic evidence and eyewitness reports that the Nazis were systematically exterminating Jews and other minorities. It happened again in the 1960s, prior to Mylai, when the establishment press ignored persistent reports of American atrocities in Vietnam. It was Seymour Hersh who broke the story of Mylai for a small news agency after major news organizations turned it down. He staked his career on the story, and it was only after he was proved right that he was hired by the *New York Times* and the rest of the American press establishment began to shift its stand on the war.

It's easy to forget now, after Silkwood and Three Mile Island, that there was a time in the fifties and sixties that nuclear energy was touted as a savior of mankind, a perfectly safe, 100 percent failproof source of limitless cheap energy—even, through the irradiation of food, as a hedge against famine. Skeptics then were voices crying in the wilderness, and they were treated with the contempt accorded all true prophets. This is how public perceptions evolve: in fits and starts, with jolts and occasional regressions, like an infant learning to walk.

Though I was, for me, unusually tactful, I had been appalled by Sean Toolin's reaction to the prospect of my interviewing Bashir Gemayel. Like his consternation about my choice of hotel, it was a clear warning that I was taking the "wrong" side. He intended, I think, to be helpful; but any time I am advised not to look into some aspect of a story I become uncommonly interested.

That may sound like boasting, but in fact what I am confessing is a certain kind of stupidity. Smart producers heed the kind of advice Toolin was dispensing. I'm not smart, not in that way. I like going my own way too much, and by temperament I would rather lose outright than compromise. The result has been some big stories and the satisfaction of knowing that without my work they might never have come out. My independence has cost me dearly, however. I have been too direct; my corporate skills have stunk. Instead of building up my business contacts with judicious socializing, I have made friends on the outside, often with sources, because these tend to be the kind of active, engaged people who attract me. In the business, I am regarded as special, but also as a special pain in the ass—a maverick, talented but no team player.

It was possible that Toolin and his colleagues had closed their eyes to what was happening to the Christians in Lebanon. It was also possible that Gemayel's people were lying. I would take nothing at all on faith; I demanded documentation for every allegation, great or small.

The evening after my lunch at Abu Halka's penthouse, Pierre Yazbeck phoned my hotel. "I am at your service," he said fulsomely. "My people are your people, Bar-ba-ra. Use them as you will. Bashir himself has ordered full cooperation," he added.

"Fine," I said, perhaps a bit ungraciously, and because I knew just what I wanted, I launched into a no-nonsense, nonstop recital. "I'll need a couple of hours with you tomorrow, and you'll have to get me photographs of the massacres, details, dates, copies of police and military reports. I'll need to talk with eyewitnesses, and if you've got any film footage documenting the attacks, I'll need that, too. Also a translator. And background on Gemayel: copies of speeches, interviews by foreign and local press, translated into English, of course."

"When do you want all this, Barbara?"

"Yesterday, Pierre."

In the silence at the other end I could hear Yazbeck rolling his eyes and grimacing, but when he spoke it was with his habitual politeness. "Is that all? If there is anything else we can do to help? You have only to ask."

"I will," I promised.

The next day I stayed in my hotel room, and all the misery of Lebanon beat a path to my door. Simple people, bearing boxes of photographs, clutching albums to their chests as if they were precious souvenirs. I thought of my own family albums, filled with images of my daughter's birthday parties, my parents' anniversaries, weddings, holidays, graduations, trips to Disney World and the beach. . . .

These people had memories of a different order.

I saw bodies of men, women, and children shot in their

own homes; dead women with their skirts around their heads, raped and mutilated. Priests were singled out for special attention: one picture showed an eighty-year-old priest who'd been tied to the rear fender of a car and dragged through the streets until he died. Another had been hung in his vestments alongside the crucifix of his church. The bearers of these family death albums were villagers who survived the massacres in the mid-seventies, in the southern Lebanon city of Damour, the Shouf Mountains, and the northern Lebanon villages of Beitmellat and Achach. Through my interpreter (who started off chipper, but as the day wore on showed signs of strain and deep emotion), they told me what they had witnessed. I also saw films taken by the Christians showing, in bloody detail, the massacres at Damour and other villages. One, which still haunts me, showed a little girl's body being used for target practice by soldiers in PLO uniforms.

It seemed dreadfully wrong that these people should have to line up at my door like petitioners, parading their bereavement, baring their lives to a stranger. One woman showed me photos of her three children, saying their names with tender maternal pride. She was like any other mother showing off her babies, except that in this case the children in the photos were bloody corpses. I covered my eyes; but then I thought that if she had the courage to go on living after such a loss, the least I could do was to look.

In Israel I had visited Yad VaShem, the Holocaust Memorial in Jerusalem. The same sense of knee-bending sorrow assailed me now as then. I felt shattered—awed, almost—by the immensity of suffering and the depravity of the killers. And, strangely, I also felt a sense of shame. At one point during the day I excused myself and went into the bathroom to study my face in the mirror. They are human, I thought, the ones who did these things. And I am human. Am I capable of doing what they did? I thought, "There but for the grace of God go I"—and it wasn't just the victims I meant, but their torturers as well.

No one can appreciate the value of political order who has not experienced the terror of anarchy. I knew that the Christians, and in particular the Phalangists, had also been accused of carrying out massacres. That side of the story had been fully reported in the Western press. But not a word had ever been heard outside of Lebanon on what had been done *to* these people. It did not diminish my pity for these survivors to know that some of their own had struck back. When people can't turn to government for justice and protection, they must choose between retribution and despair.

Of all the things my work has taught me, nothing came harder than the realization that civilization is but a thin, fragile layer of skin—that under certain circumstances everyone is capable of shedding that skin and reverting to savagery. And when civilized people run wild, there is no limit to the cruelty human ingenuity can devise. We call such cruelty inhuman or bestial only to hide from ourselves the fact that we are the only creatures on earth capable of it. Dante's words speak to a reality that I know well: "O human race, born to fly upward, wherefore at a little wind dost thou so fall?"

The photos, the stories, and the faces of the survivors were painful reminders of things I already knew. They made demands on me, both as a person and as a reporter. Bashir Gemayel also made demands, with his compelling expectation that I was on his side, that for some inexplicable reason we were allies in his people's struggle. So, too, had Abu Halka challenged me with his claim that the Western press was as purposely blind to the slaughter of Lebanon's Christians as it had been to Germany's Jews.

I believe—and this may be either a result of my profession or the reason I chose it—that no sin is worse than apathy. Dante also said that the hottest place in hell is reserved for those who in times of moral crisis do nothing. To me, the "good Germans" who pretended not to know who was going up in smoke were even more repulsive than the "bad Germans," who had at least the courage of their evil convictions. So I looked at thousands of pictures, listened to one horror story after another, and refused to heed the small queasy voice inside that whispered, "Enough, enough already. Not your war; not your fight; not your problem."

There came a point during that first terrible day of immersion that the flow of people miraculously slowed; there was a lull. I sent my translator out of the room and lay down on the bed, grateful for the sudden silence. My eyes burned with fatigue and the effort to hold back tears. I rubbed my temples.

The telephone rang.

" 'Allo, Barbara." Husky, intimate voice. I knew it at once, found I had been anticipating his call.

"Hello, Bashir," I said.

"How are you feeling?"

"Do you know what I've been doing today?"

"Yes."

"Then you know how I'm feeling."

He commiserated silently, which was more than I deserved for complaining. "Tomorrow you must see another part of the picture," he said. "What are your plans? Who is coming to get you?"

"Why, Bashir?" I teased. "Do you want to be my guide?"

I realized even as I spoke how inappropriate this was. I was speaking to Gemayel as if he were an old friend or lover, not the head of the Lebanese Forces and the strongman of Lebanon.

Far from objecting, Gemayel replied in the same tone. "Sure. What do you want to do? What time should I pick you up?" Spoken for all the world as if he were asking me out on a date.

Ten to one he's kidding, I thought. He must be—men in his position don't squire reporters around; they have aides do it. But what if he's not? On the off chance that he meant it, I didn't want to blow the opportunity.

"I realize you've got a lot more on your plate than me," I said carefully.

"Educating the West about Lebanon is essential to our cause," he said, and by his emphasis on *our*, I had, again, the distinct impression that he meant his and mine. "After all, there is much to teach."

Precisely at nine the next morning, as I sat in the hotel dining room eating the Lebanese breakfast of yogurt with honey and pita and scribbling pages of questions in my reporter's notebook, a heavily muscled, cleanly groomed young man made his way to my table. His dark blue Mercedes was waiting just outside the hotel entrance. The young man held the back door for me, then took his place behind the wheel. Beside him on the front seat was an M-16 machine gun.

The War Council headquarters of the Lebanese Forces was a three-story concrete bunker in a heavily guarded area known as Qarantina, near Beirut's port. Ancient-looking armored vehicles stood in state about the entrance to the headquarters. I recognized them as the same sort of fortified jeep that stood along the road leading into Jerusalem, memorials to Israel's War of Independence. Later I confirmed my guess that these were indeed Israeli vehicles, supplied in the late seventies when Israel first began arming the Christians. For the first time I noticed that the uniforms of the Lebanese Forces were identical to Israeli uniforms, except for the Arabic Lebanese Forces insignia and their symbol, the cedar and the red circle, inscribed over the left breast pocket. My driver pointed to an adjacent low-slung building—the military command center of the Lebanese Forces.

There was a briny smell in the air, and the winter light was diffused. In the center of the compound three flags snapped in the wind, silhouetted against a powder-blue sky broken by billowing clouds: the cedar flag of Lebanon in the center, flanked by the flag of the Lebanese Forces—on which the cedar of Lebanon was encircled by a red band on a field of white—and the Phalange party flag, a large triangle split in three parts in the shape of a tree, symbolizing God, family, and country.

Westerners tend to dismiss as "mere" symbolism matters that to Middle Easterners have great practical import. The positioning of these three flags meant that just as the Phalange party, a factional Christian militia founded by Bashir's father, Pierre Gemayel, had been subsumed under the united Christian front of the Lebanese Forces, so too would the Lebanese Forces be subsumed under the banner of a sovereign Lebanon.

As we entered the headquarters, I was struck by the reverent hush and the incongruous but somehow touching sight of Bashir Gemayel's tough, hardened fighters scurrying about on tiptoe so as not to disturb the great man, who was, incidentally, younger than most of them. As I tried to keep up with my escort, who bounded up two flights of stairs in his haste to deliver me to his master, the clatter of my sling-backed heels broke the general quiet like a staccato of automatic gunfire. The driver spoke in a quiet voice to Gemayel's secretary, who did not look at me but opened a double door and disappeared inside for half a minute. Re-emerging, she stood aside and let me in.

Gemayel's office, a large, rectangular room that took up one whole wing of the building, was decorated as simply as his home. A color photo of Beirut being shelled at night hung on the wall over a tan leather couch. It was a striking picture: the white streaks of the shells illuminating the dark sky, in apposition to the night lights of the city. Next to it was a photo of Gemayel with his law school graduating class. On another wall hung a large relief map of Lebanon. Bashir's desk was at the front end of the room, opposite a big conference table. His desk was immaculate and orderly, completely uncluttered—an astonishing sight in the middle of a civil war and a state of general anarchy.

Gemayel, wearing slacks, a blue tee-shirt, and black loafers, stood to greet me. We shook hands, then he walked over to take a chair while I sat on the couch.

"So," I said, "where are we going?"

"I want you to see the spirit of the people. We are going to the funeral of one of my men."

Great, I thought. A funeral. Just what I need.

"Then," he continued, "we will go to a restaurant owned by a friend of mine, where you can ask me any questions you want."

"Good. I have a few."

Gemayel grinned. "Pierre complains you are driving his people crazy. He says that no sooner do they fulfill one outrageous demand than you issue another."

"What did you say?"

"I told him it's good to find a woman who knows what she wants."

The telephone rang incessantly; each time, Gemayel got up and went to his desk to answer it. As he spoke—very softly, just a few words—he picked up a wooden map pointer and switched it from hand to hand. Once I saw his face constrict to a tight mask; his voice remained low but the smooth flow of his melodious Lebanese gave way to syncopated blasts. Bashir grasped the pointer in both hands and suddenly it snapped in two. He threw it down, ended the conversation, and returned to his seat. In all the time I knew him, I very rarely heard Bashir Gemayel raise his voice, yet he ruled his unruly men with iron control. I later learned that his secretary stocked boxes of identical pointers for him.

We left his office and walked downstairs to a waiting Jaguar. Gemayel changed cars four or five times a day for security reasons. He drove himself, he said, because he found the constant presence of bodyguards suffocating, and because, "If I am destined to be killed, I prefer to die alone. The three who were with Maya," he added softly, looking at the road, "were my friends."

He drove skillfully and fast, frequently checking his rearview mirror. I reflected that despite his aura of practiced authority, Bashir Gemayel was still young enough to enjoy the feel of a good, fast car. Every time we stopped at a light or passed another car, the drivers would glance over and recognize Gemayel. Some stopped dead in the middle of the road, some waved and threw kisses, others simply gawked. I thought it miraculous that he didn't leave a trail of auto accidents in his wake.

There was little opportunity to talk with the car phone ringing every few seconds. When we arrived at the church, the priest and the parents of the dead soldier hurried over to shake Gemayel's hand. The Lebanese Forces' honor guard saluted Gemayel as he walked past. Hundreds of people had crowded into the church, which was filled with the high, preternatural keening of people lost in pain. During the service, priests walked down the aisle swinging silver chalices filled with incense. Little puffs of smoke rose upward toward the vaulted ceiling. The children's song "Puff, The Magic Dragon" came into my head, and I clung to it, humming under my breath, to block out the overwhelming pain and misery around me. When Gemayel rose to speak to the mourners, a friend of his took his place beside me and translated his words in a whisper.

"If they kill ten thousand," Gemayel told them, "or fifty thousand, or one hundred thousand, they will never kill our cause. They cannot, because our cause is just and our goals are honorable. We cannot fail."

He spoke with passion and energy, chopping at the air with his right hand. He used no notes. His jaw was rigid, and his eyes blazed.

"This is our country," he said. "We are not Bedouin, to steal away with our tents on our backs. We are the bearers of traditions that go back fourteen centuries. No force in this world can deprive us of our dignity or make of us petitioners in our own land. We are a proud people, we are an ancient people, and we have deep roots in Lebanon. We will not be forced out of our home by intruders. It is our sacred duty to ensure that not one death shall be in vain. By the soul of our fallen comrades I swear that while I live there will be no compromise of the principle of sovereignty for which our people laid down their lives."

As he spoke I saw determination set into the faces of the listeners. The dead boy's mother, who at the beginning of the services had been prostrate, rose at the end to shake Gemayel's hand.

At last Bashir pried himself away from the crowd and inched his way toward the car. I stayed close to him. Once in the car he relaxed completely and continued our previous conversation as if it had never been interrupted. Though the emotion I'd seen in him during the funeral had been unmistakably genuine, he appeared to shed it like a coat once he emerged. I thought that there was something of the performer about this man—for I was still trying to be analytical, to resist the intimacy implicit in his unselfconscious relaxation in my presence. But if he was an actor, then surely it was his life he was acting out, and what he gave was of his essence.

Perhaps because Bashir treated this peculiar intimacy between us as natural and right, I found it disturbing. I was a reporter, not his friend, not his colleague, not his lover. I liked him—I liked him a lot—but I wasn't going to let that get in the way of my story. I was going to distance myself from Bashir until I was certain of the facts.

"What does it cost you," I asked him as dispassionately as I could, "to go to these funerals?" I had been told that he went to all of them, as well as to an astonishing number of christenings, weddings, and baptisms.

It was the most personal question I had ever asked him. He replied distractedly and a bit coldly, "I don't ask the price. It's the way things are. I have no choice."

Gemayel's answer was a direct equivalent of an Israeli expression I had heard so often during my stay there that by the end I was using it myself: *ein breira*, no choice. *Ein breira* was the all-purpose explanation of why the Israelis fought so many wars, how they won, what made their air force and intelligence agencies so superior, and why they put up with the highest tax rate in the world and two months of reserve duty each year. *No choice*, David Kimche had told me, was the secret of Israel's martial success, for Israel had only to lose one war never to fight another. Having met his enemies and seen their handiwork, I understood him well; but I would have understood anyway, for the phrase bypassed personal experience to speak to racial memory. History has impressed upon us the knowledge that vulnerability is an invitation to involuntary martyrdom, and that if we can't defend ourselves, no one will do it for us.

A lot of baggage for a few words, and Gemayel was laying claim to all of it. I looked directly at him. He was a young man, but thirty-two years in the Middle East is nothing like thirty-two in the United States. He looked stern and cold and determined, and though I had not seen the expression before, it somehow seemed characteristic and revealing. I felt again the force of his absolute expectation that I would understand him. But for the first time, I realized that part of that expectation was derived from the fact that I was a Jew.

The restaurant he chose was a simple place with wooden tables barely covered by small, worn, linen cloths. Plate-glass windows shed light on the front tables, but the back was darker and more intimate. The restaurant was crowded, but as soon as Gemayel was spotted, every person in the room fell silent. He took my elbow and led me to a quiet corner table in the back. Slowly conversations around us were resumed, but I could hear an electrical undercurrent in the hushed voices. Bashir, who seemed to accept this envelope of reverential awe as natural, downed a Coke in short order. I was far more self-conscious than he, as if I'd strolled into a neighborhood joint with a winged and haloed angel on my arm. I ordered white wine, opened my notebook, and switched on the tape.

The ubiquitous Lebanese hors d'oeuvres, called *mezza*, appeared: eggplant, hummus, falafel, pickled beets, olives, feta cheese, and *baba ghannough*, a delectable blend of chopped eggplant with oil and garlic. There was so much food that plates were piled one on top of another. I took notes while Bashir ate with gusto, talking so much that I couldn't stop writing to eat. He noticed me looking wistfully at the quickly disappearing food and said, "Should we stop now so you can eat something?"

"No, thanks. I can always eat, but I don't know how much time I'll be able to spend with you. You're a busy man."

He gave me a very direct look. He said, "Don't worry, Barbara. You can have as much of me as you want."

I think I blushed. I saw him smile as he turned back to his plate. The innuendo was very clear, and I felt an answering surge of desire that shook me to the core. But I had reached a point where I needed to ask some hard questions, and I would not be distracted by extraneous feelings.

"You complain about an unfair press," I said, "and clearly there are gaps in our coverage of Lebanon. But you're not saying, are you, that the Christians are entirely blameless for what has happened here?"

He took his time answering. I watched him closely. His dark eyes were so extraordinarily revealing (especially for a politician, who must master the art of concealment) that he gave the impression of thinking aloud. At last he said, "No, we are not blameless. But you must distinguish between the Christian leadership and the people. You must understand that in the midst of civil war we are also waging a revolution. We have thrown off the yoke of the old Levantine, mercantile, elitist attitudes, and in their place we are building a democratic, nationalist mentality. What the West fails to comprehend is that the heart of Lebanon's conflict with our Arab neighbors is politics, not religion. Egypt, Libya, Iraq—they're all socialist countries. Our identification is with the Free World."

"Come on, Bashir," I said impatiently, and to my surprise his first name just slipped out, as if I were arguing with a friend. "You say you answer anarchy with order, yet the Christians have been blamed for some of the bloodiest massacres of the civil war."

Gemayel laid down his fork and again I saw his face grow hard and very grave. "Terrible things have been done on all sides," he said. "I do not condone this. I am working to make such acts unthinkable among us. But the provocation is very great, and Lebanon is not America. One does not rule here with hugs and kisses."

He brought his face close and fixed his eyes on mine. "My goal," he said, "my destiny, I believe, is to unite all of Lebanon's Christians under one banner. And then to bring in the Moslems and the Druze. And that will not be the banner of the Phalangists or the Maronites or even the Lebanese Forces; it will be the flag of Lebanon."

"When we first met," I said, "you told me that you believed in answering chaos with law and order. And yet I've read reports of your men running wild through the streets of Tel Zaatar and other Palestinian areas, slaughtering civilians."

"This lawlessness is the disease of Lebanon," Gemayel said. "To my sorrow we are not immune from the general sickness. The viruses of terror and anarchy have also infected our ranks. Our own soldiers shoot each other over *women*! Women," he repeated, inviting me to share his amazement and contempt.

"But you must understand this, Barbara." He put his hand over mine to stop me from writing. "If you had a baby, and strangers broke into your home and they took your baby, and before your eyes they tore it limb from limb, then you would feel what we feel. Lebanon is our beloved child, and we are maddened by her agony."

I thought—how could I help but think?—of his daughter Maya, and also of the way Smadar Hadar's daughter had been slaughtered like a pig before her father's eyes. And though I pitied him his loss, I hardened myself and said, "Pierre Yazbeck told me that when your daughter was killed, you went on television to forbid your people to carry out reprisals."

"Yes, I did." He spoke slowly, with an effort. "Because

even though it hurt me terribly, I understood that Maya was just one more victim of our powerlessness, one more martyr to the cause. And if the blood of our martyrs is ever to be redeemed, it cannot be through more bloodshed, but only through a true solution to our problems."

"But that's not all you did, is it, Bashir?"

He looked at me.

"Wasn't it shortly after Maya's death that you installed Elie Hobeika as your chief of security?"

His face underwent an extraordinary change. Once again I glimpsed the cold steel beneath the boyish surface. He did not answer. I had been told that Hobeika was a ruthless murderer.

"Elie Hobeika," I read from my notes. "Bright boy, poor family. Uneducated but cunning. History of cocaine use and arms smuggling in Lebanon's Bekáa Valley. A friend of Rifat Assad, notorious brother of Syrian President Hafer Assad, a leading figure in the Middle East drug industry. Joined the Phalangists in 1975 with the outbreak of civil war. Undistinguished service until the Black Saturday incident. Five Phalangists were found murdered. Hobeika led a group of Phalangists to the Beirut highway, where they set up a roadblock, pulled Moslems out of cars, and slit their throats in full view of their families. Over one hundred murdered." I looked up.

Bashir's face was grim. "He did it on his own, without sanction, while my father was out of the country. The five murdered were friends of his and of mine. But there is no justification."

"Hobeika had found his calling," I read. "Afterward he set up a group of twenty-five men as a hit team. Fled south with band when Syrians entered East Beirut in 1976. Terrorized Moslem Shiite villages until the Israelis kicked them out, then returned to Beirut, where he continued as leader of a mobile hit squad."

"Unsanctioned," Bashir said.

"After Maya was killed, you put him in charge of security."

"I brought him under my control. I put him on a leash."

"You grabbed a tiger by the tail."

"Better than letting him run loose."

"Is he your Iago, Bashir?"

He did not answer. I looked at him. He did not speak.

Every night for a week, sometimes very late, I saw Bashir. A car would come to fetch me from wherever I was and take me to his office. It was the end of my day, the middle of his, though the late hour precluded all but urgent interruptions.

A photograph of Maya stood on a small table near his desk, flanked by two bookcases set into the wall. One of them held a photo of his sister Madis's son, who was killed in action. I noticed it particularly because it was beautifully set, off center in a large silver frame. When I admired it, Bashir impetuously took it in his hands and held it out to me. "Take it," he said. "It is my nephew."

Whenever he looked at Maya's picture a fleeting wave of sorrow broke over his face, and I marveled each time at his childlike openness of expression. But his daughter also reminded me of mine, who had expected me home a week ago and had been disappointed, again.

I carried a load of guilt about my eleven-year-old daughter, Penny. Whenever I went away she lived with her father, who took good care of her, but I knew that my daughter missed, resented, and anticipated disappointment from her mother. I never looked into her eyes without seeing the unspoken question: "When are you leaving me this time?"

There was no good solution. Sometimes I thought of leaving my profession, finding something in a related field that would allow me to live more at home. But that meant quitting a job I loved and was damn good at. From childhood I had hated quitting anything, even ballet lessons, at which I was awful. Having Penny, loving Penny, gave my life a dimension it would otherwise never have had, but part of the price was living with a constant undercurrent of concern. Where was she? Who was she with? Was she all right? Were *we* all right?

There was a corollary to this concern. If I was sacrificing a portion of my daughter's happiness to my work, then the work I did had to be worth it. It had to be morally compelling, equal to her sacrifice and my own. I knew that this story was all of that, which made it more urgent to get it right, to get it across, and to get it through. It had become an obsession. When I wasn't thinking about doing the piece, I was planning how to ram it through the ABC bureaucracy. I expected opposition, because the pieces of the Lebanon puzzle were falling into a shape that could be perceived as embarrassing by news organizations, including ABC, since they had failed to report the story earlier.

Each night I would come to Gemayel's office agitated and nervous, angry at him for dumping his struggle in my lap. One night my eye fell on Maya's picture, and I snapped at him: "Don't you feel guilty for Maya's death?"

I was ashamed almost as soon as the words left my mouth. He looked at me and almost without pause said very quietly, "No."

Decency demanded that I drop the subject. I persisted: "How can you answer so quickly?"

He gave me a sad smile. "Because I thought about it when it happened and many times since then. No, I don't feel guilty."

No rebuke. I would have felt better for one. As it was I was struggling to hold back tears. Bashir had stopped talking. I didn't speak, either. Very gently, he was guiding me into the pain of his world, and reluctantly but ineluctably, I had begun to follow.

Our meetings sometimes lasted only an hour, sometimes till dawn. Occasionally I sat in on meetings of the Lebanese Forces High Command, which could take place any time between seven A.M. and three the next morning. Not only did Gemayel work a twenty-four-hour day, he expected the same from everyone around him.

Bashir provided a translator on those occasions, but I found myself as fascinated by form as by content. Gemayel had absolute control over the meetings, which were conducted with a decorum highly incongruous with both the urgent life-and-death matters under discussion and the quarrelsome natures of the councilmen, most of whom had been at each other's throats until Gemayel's July 7 unification of the Christian factions.

Bashir would introduce a topic of discussion and ask who wished to address it. Whoever wanted to speak would hold up his hand, while Bashir wrote their names on a little white pad. He called on them one by one. Each speaker was limited to five minutes. Gemayel would listen in silence, his face unreadable, until the last person spoke. Then, very softly, he would announce his decision and the topic was closed.

Once I said to him in amazement, "They act more like a college debating team than a war council," and he replied, "I make them. But don't be deceived. None of us sits behind a desk. Every one of us is on the ground. We're fighters all."

It was at one such meeting that I first laid eyes on Elie Hobeika. He was by far the youngest man on the council, only twenty-four at the time, though the harsh lines on his face belied his chronological age. He had a menacing look, was muscular in build, wore his black hair closely cropped in the shape of a helmet: This hairstyle was an insignia of the Lebanese Force's intelligence service. He carried himself stolidly and, except for the dark, wary eyes that darted restlessly, his face was perfectly immobile. There was nothing light about him, not his brooding gaze, not his calculated banter. We spoke briefly after the meeting. Most of the councilmen took their lead from Bashir and treated me with courtesy and openness. Hobeika alone was curt and suspicious. He struck me as a careful man, not impulsive, and unwilling to leave anything to chance.

But most of these late-night meetings with Bashir were spent alone in his office, talking. We were both keenly aware of the intimacy of the setting. To say I was attracted to him is both pallid and irrelevant; rather, I felt that what was going to happen between us was as certain as if it had already happened—which in a sense it had, the moment we met. All I could control was the timing, and it was clear to me, though not entirely to Bashir, that I could not allow my feelings to distract me from my work. When the piece was wrapped up and in the can, then and only then would I be free to act on what I already felt.

Geraldo's arrival was a welcome relief, pulling me back into my own world. Geraldo has one of the highest "Q" ratings in broadcasting, which means that a very large number of viewers know who he is and will tune in specifically to watch him. Many journalists resent this, charging that Geraldo is more showman than journalist. But we had worked together for several years and I knew him for a quick study, extremely intelligent, and an excellent writer. He never panicked in tight situations, and I could count on him to bring out the best in a story.

I had booked us into both the Commodore and the Alexandre, to keep travel across the city to a minimum.

Since Geraldo was eager to set up meetings with the PLO, and we still hoped to interview Chairman Arafat himself, as well as other PLO commanders, we planned to meet in the bar of the Commodore Hotel. It was the first time I'd visited the Commodore, and the differences between the two hotels were telling.

The Alexandre was a drab and sleepy place, almost as quiet at noon as at midnight; its clientele was mostly European travelers and Lebanese visitors to the capital. The Commodore was located just off Hamra Street in Moslem West Beirut, the most elegant shopping and strolling street in the Middle East. Large and rather plain, the Commodore boasted an oversized bar that was the central meeting point for all the journalists in Beirut. The ground floor could have served as a set for Greta Garbo's *Grand Hotel*, but the ambience was déclassé, more like Rick's place in *Casablanca*. People of all nationalities darted around, a great many of them agents of various countries and interests and no one precisely who he claimed to be. It was here that the foreign press, the diplomatic corps, and spies came together to milk information from one another. Like all such places, it was well protected.

The Commodore was controlled by interests close to the PLO. Unlike at the Alexandre, the staff were extremely accommodating to the press. There was no service they would not provide: safe passage through dangerous areas, introductions to PLO leaders, help with story ideas or execution, telex services (which they monitored), hashish, women, or boys. If you let them, they would organize your every waking hour, and somehow there would never be time enough to make the dangerous crossing over to the other side.

I was sitting in the bar when Geraldo and the "20/20" crew walked into the lobby with Jerry King, ABC's Beirut bureau chief, who had picked them up at the airport. Rivera spotted me and came over. "So, Babsy," he said, "how's the beach?"

"Terrific," I replied. "I've lined up a dozen beauties for you, Geraldo, all stewardesses."

"Good work, kid," he said. "So," he said, "what's it all about?"

I lurched into a rundown of what I had been doing and how I saw the piece. "This Christian story is really unbelievable. Everyone has them down as ruthless fascists, because no one's ever spent the time to get their side. The Christians feel that their country is being stolen from them. Thousands have been displaced, thrown out of their houses after PLO massacres in their villages. I've seen the most grizzly photographs you can imagine."

Geraldo listened intently. I could see him assimilating the material. He said, "Who have you got lined up to speak for them?"

"Bashir Gemayel," I said, and nothing more. Geraldo raised his eyebrows. I said, "Judge for yourself."

"That's it?"

"He's something else. That's all I'm going to say until you meet him."

"When's that?" he asked.

"Dinner tonight. But where are we staying? We can't cross the Green Line at night."

"Why not?"

I saw it coming. Geraldo and I were going to make the crossing, despite warnings from every side.

The manager of the Commodore approached us, gave me a cold bow, and asked to speak privately with Geraldo. A few minutes later I saw Rivera sitting in a chair next to an over-the-hill, puffy-faced blonde. He walked back with a hand-caught-in-the-cookie-jar look.

"So?" I said.

"They offered me Miss Holland," he said.

"Miss Holland, 1903," I added.

I noticed our cameraman and crew in an intense huddle. The management had presented them with a sizable block of hashish, like the complimentary flowers and Champagne bestowed by more traditional establishments. I was offered nothing, and I wondered if that was because I was staying on the Christian side or because I was a woman.

Jerry King joined us at the bar. A tall, friendly man, he seemed eager to help and sorry that he had been traveling when I arrived. Geraldo told him that our story was about terrorism, that we had been to Israel and filmed PLO prisoners there. He explained that we wanted to meet Yasir Arafat, to get the other side of the story. King disappeared and returned a few minutes later, saying that Arafat was out of town and that first we had to go through Mahmoud Labadi, Arafat's press chief. We were to go at once.

We piled into Jerry's car for the ten-minute ride to PLO headquarters, a nondescript, rundown office building in a working-class neighborhood of Beirut. The Israelis had always assailed the callousness of the PLO in locating their installations in residential neighborhoods, but for a long time it proved an effective ploy; the Israelis, they had discovered with contempt, were queasy about bombing civilians.

Labadi saw us right away and immediately drew blood. "We know where you've been. We know you have come from Israel."

Geraldo ignored his antagonism and answered in a level tone, "That's right, and now we're here to give you time to tell your side of the story. The Israelis showed us their elite fighters and allowed us to talk to their commanders; we were also able to interview your people who are being held in Israeli prisons. We ask the same from you."

"We'll cooperate to this extent," Labadi immediately replied. "We will take you into areas where Israel has bombed civilian populations, and you will film the hospitals and the victims. You will show the world the true face of Zionism."

"If that is your answer to the charges made against you

by the Israelis, then we will include it. But not as the whole story. We want the opportunity to show the PLO training, just as we did the Israeli, and to interview your elite commanders, as we did theirs."

"Unacceptable," Labadi shot back.

Jerry King tried to intervene on our behalf, arguing that our presence proved our intention of doing a balanced story. He recounted instances in the past of ABC's fairness in presenting PLO positions, and mentioned an hour-long documentary, very sympathetic to the PLO, that had appeared on ABC's "Close Up" series. Labadi, who had obviously made up his mind not to work with us, brushed this aside. Take it or leave it, he told Geraldo.

"You're trying to censor us, Mr. Labadi," Geraldo said. "And that's something we didn't let the Israelis do, and we won't let you do. If you change your mind, we would like the opportunity to tell your side of the story."

We shook hands perfunctorily and left. Labadi was a very sullen and rigid man. Revolutions and causes attract a good number of psychopaths as well as true believers. I put Labadi in the first group. A few years later, Labadi would denounce Arafat as a traitor for being too moderate, and join the Popular Front for the Liberation of Palestine— General Command, one of the most radical groups of the rejectionist front.

It was already dark when King dropped us off at the Commodore. We went up to our rooms, washed, and returned to the lobby in record time. I had left all my clothes in my room at the Alexandre; Geraldo carried an overnight case. It took some doing and a large amount of cash—U.S. dollars—to find a taxi driver willing to risk the trip from West to East Beirut and then back again. When I saw the cabbies' fearful reactions I really began to wonder how I let Geraldo talk me into this insanity.

"Turn on the interior lights," Geraldo ordered the driver. "It will be easier to see that we're unarmed."

We were stopped at a Syrian army checkpoint at the

Green Line, manned by six soldiers standing behind sand-bags. One came over and asked for our passports. The road was virtually untraveled at night, and the soldiers looked bored.

Our American passports got us through safely. As soon as we arrived at the Alexandre, I called Bashir, who sent a car to bring us to his office.

I had been looking forward to this first meeting between Geraldo and Bashir. Geraldo was the original macho man; he loved to cover wars, and he loved tough guys. Bashir was the real article. I couldn't wait to see the chemistry. After brief introductions, Geraldo plunged in.

"The world community thinks of you as an outlaw, someone who's making peace in the Middle East more difficult," he said.

Bashir relished both the question and its directness. He looked Geraldo in the eye. "What we are saying is precisely what no one wants to hear. We are the wheel they cannot oil."

"What are you saying that we don't want to hear?"

"You know," Bashir said, "there is an extra nation in this part of the world, and that is the Palestinian people. Our friends in the West want to settle the Palestinian problem in order to win the support and blessings of the oil producers. They decided that the people of Lebanon would pay the price. They are selling their friends to please their enemies."

"Are you bitter toward the U.S. for not giving you more support?" asked Geraldo, who'd snapped to attention and was regarding Bashir with puzzled intensity. I knew my colleague well enough to recognize this sudden, bloodhound-type engagement. I felt a moment's satisfaction in knowing that I was not alone.

"Because of the cowardice and lack of moral leadership of the West, we don't have the strong leadership we need to face the blackmail and extortion of the PLO and the leftist extremists. Right now we are paying, but you are also paying a hidden cost; because we are the only pro-Western regime among the Arab states."

Geraldo blew out sharply and gave a small laugh. He looked at me and I could see what he was thinking. It's very rare for a political leader, especially one who wants support from the United States, to be so candid. It was astonishing, coming from this baby-faced boy of thirty-two who, despite his youth, had succeeded in uniting and controlling the greatest indigenous force in Lebanon. Geraldo and I walked out of Bashir's office in silence, as the three of us went to dinner.

Early the next morning, Geraldo and I met for breakfast. The crew had stayed in West Beirut and came over to meet us. It was our first day of filming.

To his obvious though unspoken relief, Pierre Yazbeck had been replaced as our liaison by Fadi Hayek, an aide close to Bashir. An attorney by profession, Hayek was a plain-spoken man, very intense and uncomfortable with small talk. Unlike Yazbeck, who dressed in European suits, Hayek wore a military uniform that looked slept in and cracked, worn boots. With only two weeks to shoot, we had a hectic schedule. Hayek drove us in a large jeep at breakneck speed over narrow mountain passes. In my innocence, I had thought the Israelis reckless drivers.

It was a brilliant, sunny day, but freezing in the Metn mountains and drafty in the jeep. Bundled in two or three sweaters, I buttoned my raincoat so tightly around my neck I felt I was going to choke. The scenery was breathtaking. As we wound our way up along mountain roads, waterfalls appeared out of nowhere. Higher up we stopped to gaze down upon a wide, verdant valley. Unlike the sparse pine forests of Israel, these woods were deciduous, with foliage ranging from gold to emerald to deep forest green. Every few miles we passed a roadside crucifix or pietà, well tended and covered with offerings of fresh flowers. We were in Christian territory now, and we were going to meet its defenders.

They weren't professional soldiers, but volunteers who, like Bashir, had put their lives on hold to meet the emergency. In real life, as they liked to call it, they were doctors, dentists, lawyers, engineers, farmers, and accountants.

Though I had been told that the Metn mountains were the stronghold of Bashir's brother, Amin, the first thing I saw on entering mountain headquarters was a giant poster of Bashir in uniform. His arms were crossed across his chest and his face wore a look of defiance, perhaps because the sun was shining in his eyes and he was squinting. As I walked about the camp with a translator, speaking with men I picked at random, it struck me that Bashir was no older than most of these fighters. Yet whenever they spoke of him, it was with awe. Though I already knew the sudden, dramatic hush that fell over every gathering as Bashir entered, I was still astonished to see these hardened, unkempt fellows turn misty-eyed when they talked about him. "Why do you treat Bashir like this?" I asked one officer. "He's the same age as you, yet you act like he's a god. Is it because he's a Gemayel?"

The officer laughed. "Amin's a Gemayel," he said, with the air of having produced an unanswerable refutation.

"Then what is it?"

"Bashir is our martyr," he said.

A shudder ran through me. Though he had spoken very clearly, I thought one of us must have misunderstood. "What do you mean?"

He shrugged uncomfortably.

Hope came to me. "Do you know what 'martyr' means?"
Oh, yes, he sighed. He knew what "martyr" meant.

"Do you think Bashir is going to die?" I demanded, staring into his eyes. I thought of the bullet marks that scarred Bashir's balcony, and of the two car bombs he'd survived—one in 1979, defused before it could explode, and a second whose detonation had killed Maya.

"We will all die for the cause if we have to," the officer said curtly. He looked away. The conversation had ended.

We wanted footage of Bashir's men as they faced the Syrians across a narrow valley, but as soon as we got our cameras into position, the soldiers sprang together with their guns in their hands, posing stiffly as if for a nineteenth-century daguerrotype. "Stop it!" I ordered them, and we tried again. And again. Each time the cameras began to roll, they struck their fighter's pose. Finally I couldn't stand it anymore.

"Cut it out!" I hollered. I rushed over to the soldiers, pulled their rifles out of their hands and pounded their backs, trying to force them to relax. They looked embarrassed, these hard-bitten types, to find themselves being pummeled by a screaming five-foot harridan, but it didn't do a bit of good. Geraldo was no help, either, howling with laughter on the sidelines.

"Watch out, Babsy," he yelled. "Treat them like you treat the crew, they're liable to shoot you."

We traveled on to a Christian village that had been so often attacked by the Syrians it had finally come under the protection of the Lebanese Forces. The soldiers assigned to the village provided not only security but also whatever semblance of order and normalcy the village possessed. A few years earlier, when the situation had been critical, the local schoolteacher had fled. Now some of the soldiers doubled as teachers, and we watched them giving lessons. It was a strange but moving experience to see these rugged, swarthy men tending so gently and diligently to the little children. They themselves, however, found it a natural extension of their duties. One soldier-teacher told me, "It's for these children that we're rebuilding Lebanon. From us they learn what we are fighting for, and why we must never compromise our national integrity."

I was reminded again of the Israelis, who also used their army to provide teachers in out-of-the-way or dangerous areas. They, too, had an army-owned and -run radio station, clinics and hospitals. It seemed to me that Bashir was deliberately patterning his Lebanese Forces after the Israeli Defense Forces.

Behind schedule by about two hours, we rushed to a lunch appointment with some of Bashir's regional commanders. The setting was extraordinary: an enclosed gazebo in a mountain clearing, surrounded by a leafy forest, beside a clear and rapid brook. The air was fresh and mountain sharp. We sat at a round table as soldiers served the typical Lebanese *mezza* and freshly baked, aromatic pita bread. Bashir's commanders were very polite. They spoke softly, they ate slowly, as if they had all the time in the world.

The only exception was Fadi Hayek. Hayek fidgeted, looked at his watch, and muttered under his breath, clearly frustrated at his inability to do what he wanted, which was to throw us into the jeep and take off for Beirut. We were scheduled to shoot Bashir addressing a weekly meeting of the Phalange party in Beirut. On the way back, Hayek allowed himself a single outburst when we complained that he would kill us all with his insane driving: "Bashir is waiting for us," he cried, with a kind of horror that it should be so.

The meeting was just breaking up as we screeched to the curb just outside Phalange headquarters in the wealthy Ashrafiyeh section of East Beirut, where Bashir had served as deputy head of the branch since the early seventies. One would have thought that after such a long time the people would have grown used to him, but as we pulled up, I saw him standing outside, surrounded by a three-deep throng of admirers.

Bashir Gemayel, Commander-in-Chief of the Lebanese Forces, in 1978.

Bashir with the two elder statesmen who ran Lebanon before him—on the left, former President Camille Chamoun; in the center, his father, Sheikh Pierre Gemayel—in front of the headquarters of the Lebanese Forces in East Beirut.

Chamoun with Bashir at a meeting of the military council of the Phalange in 1979, days before Gemayel's forces overwhelmed Chamoun's Tiger Militia.

Barbara Newman with her camera crew on the Beirut Airport road. Several Western hostages were abducted here.

The Command Council Room, hub of the Lebanese Forces intelligence and military operations. Bashir sits under a photo of his father.

A narrow, congested street in the Shiite-controlled suburbs of South Beirut where Western hostages are held.

A 1982 meeting of Lebanese leaders at the Presidential Palace. *Clockwise from Bashir:* Nasri Malouf, Minister; Chafik Wazzan, Prime Minister; Elias Sarkis, President; Fuad Boutrous, Foreign Minister; Nabib Berri, head of Shiite Amal Militia; Walid Jumblatt, head of the Druze Militia.

Above and top right: Women and men of the Lebanese Forces in training.

Part of the small
force of Bashir's
soldiers who
successfully resisted
the Syrian Army in
Zahle in April 1981.
This encounter
established Bashir as
a major geopolitical
player in the region.

The Gemayel brothers; Amin succeeded Bashir as president upon his younger brother's death.

Bashir and the people of
Ashrafiyeh in front of Phalange
headquarters, where he was killed in 1982.

The Gemayels pose for a family portrait at the celebration following Bashir's election to the presidency July 23, 1982. *Clockwise from Bashir:* his wife, Solange; his mother, Genevieve; Sheikh Pierre; Amin, and his wife, Joyce.

Bashir's wife, Solange Gemayel, and their daughter Youmna at their beach home near Junieh.

Bashir tosses his beloved Maya into the air a year before she died in a car bombing meant for her father.
(BASHIR GEMAYEL FOUNDATION)

He spotted us immediately and came straight to me. I apologized for missing the meeting. Bashir shrugged. "I knew you'd never make it in time." There was a red mark on the left lapel of my raincoat. He took it in hand, drawing me near. "What is this? Not blood?"

"Lipstick," I said, flustered at his closeness.

"Are you exhausted?" Bashir asked softly.

"I'm okay."

Then others came between us, elbowing me back, and I was borne off to dinner with Fadi Hayek, Geraldo, and the crew. We talked over the day's work and planned for the next.

As I opened the door to my hotel room, the phone began to ring. I picked it up. Bashir's voice said, "Would you like to have dinner with me?" I was certain he knew that I had already eaten; he kept track of everything we did.

"Of course," I said. I threw off my muddy clothes and quickly showered. For the first time since I had arrived in Beirut, I put on a dress and made up my face. The dress was one of my favorites, a raspberry-colored wool with a black sweater midriff. Dousing myself with Chanel No. 5, I rushed down the hall to the elevator. One of Bashir's bodyguards was waiting for me. In the car I saw him sniffing the air. Maybe I've overdone it, I thought, and opened a window.

Bashir's headquarters was deserted, except for his secretary and a few soldiers. "Thank you for coming," Bashir said. "Do you mind if we eat in the office?"

"Not at all," I said.

Bashir's secretary, Isis, set out a pretty floral tablecloth, plates, and silverware on his conference table at the end of the room. I felt a little uncomfortable, unsure of whether I should help her. But since she didn't seem to expect it, I stayed put. Bashir was on the phone, surrounded by his guards. Within a few moments everyone left, and we sat down to eat.

"You must be exhausted," he said, as if he'd spent the day at the beach. "Why do you look so good?"

"Because I was looking forward to seeing you."

His eyes were laughing, warm, intimate. He reached out toward me. I said, "Bashir, something happened today."

"What happened?" he said, in a teasing voice.

"This is serious," I insisted. "One of the soldiers called you their 'martyr.' What did he mean? I asked if he thought you would be killed, and he wouldn't answer. How much danger are you in?"

He shrugged. "It's not something I think about. What will be, will be. In the meantime I do what I have to do."

I did not like that "in the meantime."

"It's strange to hear you sound so fatalistic," I said. "I've watched you operate. You *make* things happen. Kimche said you were the only man capable of uniting the Christians, and from all I've seen so far, he was right."

"That's because it is my destiny. What the end will be, I cannot control."

"You believe in destiny," I said.

"As do you," he said. "I know because you've met yours."

"What is it?"

"To tell the truth about Lebanon." He grinned mischievously. "What did you think I meant?" We stared at one another until I felt that to go on another moment would be dangerous. Then he said, "In 1970, when I was twenty-three years old, I met Gamal Abdel Nasser. His son was my friend, and he invited me to Cairo. Nasser stood for everything I opposed, for Arab pan-nationalism and tyranny of the Moslem majority. I detested his politics but I respected the man as a great patriot. My friend took me into his study and introduced me to his father. Nasser shook my hand and stared into my eyes as if he were reading my soul. For a long time he said nothing, nor did he let go my hand. I began to wonder what I had done wrong. Finally he spoke to me. 'I see in your eyes that you are destined to lead Lebanon to freedom.' And that's all he said."

"And you believed him."

"I believe it because I know it's true. Only I don't know how much time I have."

"You mean you don't know how long you'll live," I blurted.

He inclined his head. "Which of us does? That's one reason I push so hard."

"What's another?"

"Maya," he murmured. "Two things marked me, Barbara. Maya's accident"—he could never bring himself to say her murder—"and my kidnapping. Those things released the force in me. They focused my attention. They turned me from Lebanon's naughty boy into a leader."

"Your kidnapping?" I heard myself say.

He looked at me. "It happened in Tel Zaatar, in 1969. I was the first Lebanese to be kidnapped by the PLO. Some honor, eh, Barbara?"

I didn't smile back. I said tensely, "What happened?"

"I was stopped in my car and taken by a bunch of PLO thugs to a house in Tel Zaatar. They beat me up a little, nothing terrible. But then a man I had not seen before came in, and he had a hatchet." He fell silent. His face was rigid except for an almost imperceptible twitch of his mouth.

I said, "What did you do?"

"Nothing," he said, and his voice was very soft. "I looked at him and he looked at me. I saw that he meant to kill me. He brought the hatchet to my head slowly, measuring the distance, and then he swung it back. And suddenly another man burst into the room, seized the hatchet, and threw it on the ground."

I sagged a little in my chair. After a moment Bashir went on.

"They'd found out who I was, you see, and they were afraid. In those days the PLO didn't have nearly the strength they do today, thanks to our negligence. About ten people rushed into the room where I was being held.

'You will follow us,' they told me. 'You will put your hands in your pockets and walk casually, as if you were one of us. You will not cause a disturbance.' 'Fine,' I said. I walked among them to a car, and they drove me first to a PLO office on Hamra Street, then to a spot several miles from my home in Ashrafiyeh, where they dropped me off. I walked home. As I turned onto our street, I saw a mob in front of my house. They were waving weapons, crying, shouting my name. As soon as I was spotted they were all over me, prodding and poking to see if my fingers were all there, my ears, my nose."

"Then what happened?" I asked.

"I telephoned my father. He was a minister in the government then. His office was in an uproar. They told me that he was at an emergency meeting at the Presidential Palace. I called the palace and asked to speak to Sheikh Pierre Gemayel. The fellow who answered shouted, 'I can't call him now. Don't you know what's happened?' and hung up on me. I called back and said, 'This is Bashir. May I speak with my father?'

"Silence; then the man yelled, 'Really? Really? Where are you?'

" 'At home.'

" 'Really at home?' He turned away from the receiver and I heard him bellow, 'He's back! He's back!'

"My father came on the line. His voice was so taut it vibrated like a string. 'Who is this?' he demanded.

" 'Father, this is Bashir.'

" 'Are you hurt?'

" 'I'm fine,' I told him, and he caught his breath."

Bashir looked at me. I was taking notes, but I stopped.

"I wasn't, though, you know. I was deeply shocked. I was," he said, "humiliated."

"The thing you hate the most," I said.

"Yes—but the humiliation was not just for myself, but for my people, that we whose country this is should be subject to arbitrary arrest by *foreigners*." He was gripping the table so tightly his knuckles were white.

"Shortly after my release," he said, "I locked myself in my house and refused to come out for a week. I saw no one, spoke to no one. I needed time to think. . . . It was necessary to understand what had happened to me."

"And did you?"

He nodded. His eyes never left mine. "What happened to me was precisely what has happened to my country. Before, all that I did was based on theory, fueled by a childish need to be in the thick of the action. Now it was as if my ideas had taken on flesh, my flesh, which had felt the scourge of occupation. *I lost sovereignty over my own body.* It was," he said, watching me quizzically to see if I understood, "a kind of rape."

My food had gone cold, but I wasn't hungry anyway. "You said it marked you. How? Did it make you hate Palestinians?"

Bashir shook his head impatiently. "It taught me to look past the symptoms, to go for the root of the problem. It showed me that it's neither the Palestinians nor the Syrians who are the real danger to Lebanon, but our own lack of unity. I had already figured out that our social and political structures—the system of *baksheesh,* the awarding of high-paying government and military posts on the basis of family and religion instead of merit—reinforced our internal divisions. But now I realized, I was absolutely convinced, that unless we unified, we would never regain our sovereignty."

"So you set out to unify the Christians," I said.

"Not just the Christians," he replied very earnestly. "Also the Moslems and the Druze."

"Just like that," I said, laughing.

He spread his hands. "I was the one who saw what had to be done," he explained simply, almost apologetically. "So I was the one who had to do it."

"*He is our martyr,*" the officer had said.

And Bashir had said, "*I don't know how much time I have.*"

They came together in a vision of the future that made

me cry out in horror. Bashir leaned forward, cradled my face in his hands. And the telephone rang.

Bashir muttered under his breath but went immediately to answer it. He spoke impatiently into the receiver, watching me all the time. But the intrusion had awakened me to reality. I couldn't do this. I didn't care, at the moment, that he was married. This thing that stood between us had nothing to do with that. It had to do with professionalism. I couldn't. Not for anything could I compromise this story.

Yet I still felt the smooth warmth of his hands on my cheeks, his breath on my face.

The moment he hung up the phone, I told him that I could not keep my eyes open and wanted to go back to my hotel.

"I'll drive you," he said at once.

"No," I answered firmly.

In a few minutes one of his bodyguards appeared. Bashir walked me down to the car. When I kissed him good-bye on each cheek, my bright red lipstick left clear imprints on his face. I said nothing. I wanted to leave my mark on him.

As I entered the lobby of the Alexandre, I heard a car pull into the circular driveway. Glancing back, I saw Bashir at the wheel. He had followed me.

I turned away. The elevator door slid open and I rushed inside, shutting the door behind me.

We spent our last day in Beirut filming Palestinian refugee camps. Labadi never budged, so Geraldo went around him. He paid several hundred dollars for protection and a tour of a refugee camp to a member of the rejectionist Popular Front for the Liberation of Palestine—General Command. This PLO faction adamantly opposes any negotiation with the "Zionist entity" Israel.

Supplied by the ever-obliging staff of the Commodore Hotel, our guide came heavily armed with side arms, a pistol, and a machine gun. He and a friend drove us around the Bourj el-Barajneh refugee camp; they were jittery bodyguards, ever alert for trouble. They rushed us through our shooting so we could get out before word spread that we were filming the camp.

The camp, one of a chain of camps in West Beirut encircling the airport, was a teeming, bustling place. Children ran past, intent on mysterious errands; women carried squawking chickens and great basketfuls of fresh produce home from the open-air market; and soldiers loaded on open trucks sped about the area, looking very busy but oddly aimless. Though I noticed no difference in uniform or insignia, my escorts knew at a glance which faction each group belonged to. There was a pervasive, dispiriting smell of chaos about the place, of lawlessness and anarchy. We felt we had to rush in and out, because in such a place we could sink and disappear without a trace.

Peace prevailed in the camp, but it was a palpably uneasy peace. Like the Lebanese Christians before the advent of Bashir, the Palestinians were deeply divided. As the commander of the mainstream PLO faction Al Fatah, Yasir Arafat was nominally the chairman of the PLO as a whole. However, the PLO comprises many factions, including some sponsored by Syria, Iraq, and Libya, that are much more militant than Al Fatah regarding Israel. Periodically, tensions among these factions, whose differences remain ideological rather than practical so long as Israel retains its hold on the land, erupt into bloody battles, often at the behest of the various factions' sponsors, who find it convenient to do battle by proxy. Under the pressure-cooker conditions of the camps, these outbreaks seem to take place with the regularity and inexorability of lava flowing from a live volcano.

Indeed, at the time of this writing there is fighting in Bourj el-Barajneh between soldiers of Al Fatah and the Syrian-backed Fatah Uprising. Bashir's predictions about the Syrians have indeed proved prophetic. They keep conflict alive in Lebanon by constantly shifting their own weight to balance the sides.

In the late afternoon, we crossed the Green Line for a parting dinner with Bashir, Pierre Yazbeck, and Fadi Hayek. Bashir had chosen the restaurant, which was set in an underground cave, dimly lit, very attractive, very crowded. Pierre and Fadi were there when we arrived, but

Bashir, they told us, would come later. We sat on a leather couch built into the cave wall and ordered drinks. Geraldo and the crew were elated, for we knew we had a damn good piece. But I couldn't join in the celebration.

The shoot was over and, despite all the problems, it had gone well. I was leaving Beirut tomorrow, flying home to Penny. I ought to have been ecstatic. Yet all I could think of was getting up the next morning, and the next, and the next, knowing that I wouldn't be seeing Bashir that day.

I tried to put him out of my mind. But knowing that the piece, though not yet edited, was essentially finished raised all kinds of alarming possibilities. I conjured up all the other barriers—his wife, his child, my child, the aura of danger that enveloped him constantly—but nothing was enough to stem the tide. Other images intruded. His speaking eyes. His openness with me. His hand touching the back of mine. Don't write, it meant. This is not a story; this is your life.

The longer we waited, the deeper I sank in longing to see him. I wasn't worried or anxious; I knew that Bashir would never let me leave without saying good-bye.

It was one A.M. when Bashir came. We were just being served our main courses. I moved over, and a place was set for him beside me. Bashir acted as if we were alone. He sat very close to me, pressing his left thigh to my right. I took his hand in mine under the table. Hayek engaged the others in loud conversation.

"Tomorrow you are leaving us," Bashir murmured.

"Tomorrow I am leaving Beirut," I corrected him.

"I'm going to miss you," he said, unsmiling.

I looked into his eyes and then I couldn't help myself. I put my mouth next to his ear. "Pierre Yazbeck warned me not to fall in love with you," I whispered.

"Don't listen to him," said Bashir.

"I haven't," I said. I shocked myself more than Bashir. Fool, I told myself. Fool, where are you going? But I couldn't feel sorry. I had said what needed to be said.

Bashir drew a sharp breath. He squeezed my hand

painfully. "I will see you very soon. In a few months I will come to the U.S."

Outside the restaurant he took me in his arms and held me. We kissed. Then Geraldo took my arm. We left Bashir and drove back to the hotel.

The airport was swarming with Syrian and PLO soldiers. Our precious tapes needed to be carried, not sent. There were no copies. If those tapes were confiscated or destroyed, all our work would have been in vain. Not to speak of the consequences to whoever was carrying them.

Geraldo decided that I would carry them.

I didn't argue. I didn't even ask why. It was as obvious to me as it was to them that, in this place, a woman has a far better chance of escaping scrutiny than a man. I thought it was the right decision and, coming from my macho friend, a gutsy one. I still think so, despite what happened later.

The morning dawned, cold and clear. Pierre Yazbeck had arranged for the private inspection of our box of tapes, away from the airport, by a customs official who was one of theirs. Pierre picked me up very early and drove me to a government building. Carrying a box with about thirty ¾-inch cassettes and some posters of Bashir, I walked up a few flights of stairs to the office of the customs official.

The man told me to open the box. He reached into the opened box and pulled out a picture of Bashir. "No," he said, shaking his head. "No, no."

I felt a cold tingle inside. "Why not?" I said. "This *is* the final inspection, isn't it?"

"Hopefully, lady," the official said and sighed, as if he knew something I didn't. He closed and sealed the box with red wax, then gave me a typed document in Arabic, which stated that the box had been inspected by customs and need not be opened at the airport. "Good luck," he said, with the clear implication that I'd need it.

I walked down the steps on legs that seemed to have turned to rubber. Fatigue, I told myself. Downstairs a jeep was waiting. I got in and was immediately surrounded by four burly Lebanese army soldiers, each concealing a rifle in his lap. No one spoke to me. The driver switched on a flashing red light atop the roof, and we careened through the streets, almost sideswiping half a dozen cars. The ride to the airport was harrowing but mercifully short. But instead of stopping at the terminal, the driver swerved onto the tarmac and screeched to a halt about three hundred feet from the jet I guessed was my flight.

"Now wait a minute, guys," I said. "I need to check in first." No response. I tried in French.

The soldier beside the driver turned around. I had never seen him before. For that matter, I had never seen any of these guys before. "Give me your passport," he said.

"What for?"

"And your ticket."

Reluctantly, I handed over my passport and ticket. He left the car. Fifteen minutes later he returned with sandwiches, the long, thin tubes I had seen before at the Beirut airport. He offered me one. I couldn't eat a thing.

"Well," I said, trying to glance nonchalantly at my watch, "it's about time."

The four soldiers chewed stolidly, staring out the windows at the same mix of overdressed travelers and military uniforms that had startled me on my arrival. It seemed odd that I had never seen these four before.

We sat on the tarmac. I remonstrated. After a while it became clear that talking was useless, so I shut up. A quarter of an hour passed. Busloads of passengers passed us on the way to the plane. Half an hour passed. I saw Geraldo and the crew board the last bus from the terminal.

"We're late," I told the driver for the twelfth time, pointing at my watch. *"Nous sommes en retard."* He shook his head.

So this is it, I thought. I felt a mounting panic. Penny

came into my mind, and Bashir, and the tapes sitting near my feet, and Geraldo on the plane. That was distressing but better than thinking about the editor Salim el-Louzy.

Suddenly a soldier raced over to the jeep and shouted rapid-fire orders at my escorts (or guards, or whatever they were). The driver jerked into gear and we took off like a jet, weaving around the tarmac, finally screeching to a halt in the path of my plane. Suddenly Geraldo appeared on the platform just outside the open cabin door. He froze for a moment, staring down at the jeep. My escorts got out and one ceremoniously held the door for me. I slid out, clutching the precious box of film. The soldier who had sat beside the driver handed me my passport and a boarding pass.

"Have a nice flight," he said.

Geraldo hurtled down the steps to the tarmac. We didn't say a word, just looked at one another. He picked up the box of tapes, put it on his head, and walked back up to the plane.

The pilot, an Englishman, came down to meet us. He said he would not take off until that box—he pointed to Geraldo's head—had been opened and inspected. My soldier-escorts showed him the customs authorization and argued convincingly, with rifles over their shoulders, that an additional inspection was unnecessary. The pilot looked from them to me and finally relented. "Get on board," he growled.

I sat next to Geraldo in the small first-class compartment. One by one the cockpit crew came out to stare curiously, but I avoided catching anyone's eye. We didn't talk. The ABC crew, also seated in first class, didn't even glance in my direction. No one wanted an incident on the ground. After we reached cruising altitude, Rivera turned to me and whispered, "What happened to you? I was on my way off the plane."

I finally turned my head to look at him. He looked strange, pale around the lips. It crossed my mind that I had never seen Geraldo scared before.

"I thought you'd been kidnapped," he said.

"I thought so, too," I said. My voice sounded strange to me—not the tone or timbre, but hearing it at all. Sitting in that jeep as time ticked by, I had not believed this moment would come. Now that it had, it seemed unreal.

"I made them stop the plane," he said. "I was getting off."

I just nodded. I didn't feel like talking. I needed time to decompress slowly, to begin the long process of forgetting by remembering.

I rested my head against the window and closed my eyes.

"I would never have left you there alone," Geraldo said after a while. With that he put on his earphones, and we flew the rest of the way home without speaking.

Geraldo gave me a ride into Manhattan in his limousine. "It's been a great shoot, Babsy," he said, quite recovered now from my harrowing experience. "Everybody's going to be jealous of you when you get back. How many of them could do a story like this?"

I wasn't thinking about anyone at ABC. I was still in Beirut, and I wanted the feeling to last.

I checked into the Essex House on Central Park South, called Penny, and fell into bed. My body was still on Middle Eastern time, seven hours ahead of New York. I woke up in the middle of the night and could not get back to sleep. At dawn I dressed to go running in Central Park.

It hurt. Before I left for Israel, I had jogged four miles a day through Rock Creek Park in Washington. But for two months I had done no running. Despite the early hour, I passed a parade of no-nonsense joggers. They wore the same purposeful look as had Bashir's soldiers when they posed for our cameras.

"20/20" was housed in its own building on the corner of Sixty-sixth Street and Columbus Avenue. Besides Geraldo, the show had two other on-air correspondents, each with his staff and suite of offices. Other producers who worked for the show were rotated among the correspondents and the program's host, Hugh Downs. Although these jobs were not the most prestigious (because if you were hot, a correspondent wanted you exclusively), they tended to be the longest lasting. Free-agent producers struck alliances with executives, who protected them when correspondents couldn't.

Geraldo arrived early in the morning dressed in his working clothes: khaki fatigues with a Swiss Army knife in his belt, combat boots, and a black tee-shirt. He was in great shape because he worked hard at it. He had trained as a boxer and still kept up the conditioning and the diet. No matter where we were, he always exercised, either jogging or skipping rope.

"I told Av we have a great piece here," he said as soon as he saw me. "They're definitely giving us the whole hour. We see him later this morning. How fast can you do an outline?"

Av Westin was the ABC vice-president in charge of "20/20," a highly controversial figure and as talented as he was ambitious. Years ago he had been fired by the ABC News president, Roone Arledge, for his habit of writing memos criticizing his bosses. After wandering a while in the desert, he returned; the same thing happened again a few years later.

Westin dropped by Geraldo's office at the appointed time. "What do you have?" he asked us.

He might have but didn't need to add, "in twenty words or less." Most network executives credit viewers with the attention span of a parakeet. If you can't hook them in twenty seconds, they say, you've lost them for good. Usually I could perform this necessary trick of the trade without difficulty, but this time I was flummoxed. How to sum up in a single sentence an experience that I already knew had changed my life forever?

Geraldo, however, had no such problem. He crossed one khaki leg over the over and said, "It's your basic Geraldo-goes-to-war type piece."

Westin blinked at him. I swallowed hard. After a while Westin turned to me and repeated the question.

"Mossad documents," I said. "Photos. Maps. Operations against the PLO in Europe. Commando training, PLO prisoners, Menachem Begin interview, Lebanese Christian situation."

Westin repeated the list word for word and smiled like the cat who'd got into the cream.

We set up an editing schedule and I took the shuttle home to Washington. I couldn't wait to see my daughter, though there was, as always, trepidation mixed with the anticipation. The closer I came to Penny, the closer I came to Penny's anger. When she was younger, she used to call me when I went away and say, "Mommy, why don't you love me?" I would reassure her and hide my own hurt. Lately she had outgrown the saying of it, though not, I suspected, the feeling.

I was divorced from her father, a law professor in the D.C. area, when she was six years old. We agreed on joint custody, regarded then as a progressive, innovative arrangement. Penny's week was split between our houses.

But what seemed modern and fair to us turned out to be brutal for a six-year-old. From day to day she was unable to remember which school bus she was supposed to take to reach the appropriate house.

Though I yearned to see my daughter, I flew homeward with a sense of deep sadness, even hopelessness. Leaving Bashir with everything between us unresolved, mutual desire spoken but not acted upon, was one of the hardest things I had ever done. Being hard didn't make it right, however. By controlling my life to such a great extent, I had lost control of my own desires. All my energy went into my work, and it had paid off professionally. But for that payoff I had mangled my own feelings: I had walked away from the man I wanted and I had injured the person I loved most.

It came to me how strangely like my father I'd turned out. I was involved with the great issues of the day; I did work that mattered. But the price was the total sacrifice of my personal life.

I took a taxi home from Dulles Airport. My home is in a very staid, middle-class section of Washington, an area with lots of children and a wooded park nearby. The houses are comfortable and unpretentious, and if the neighborhood is a little dull, that suits me fine. It felt good driving up the block to my house. I paid the taxi and carried my bags to the front door.

As soon as she heard me come in, Penny bounded through the house and into my arms. I lifted her in my arms and hugged her tightly. "Oh Penny," I said, "I missed you."

She mumbled something against my sweater. I put her down and looked at her, my beautiful princess. "What did you say, Penny?" I asked, brushing her light brown hair back from her face. It had grown long in the six weeks since I'd seen her last.

"When do you have to leave again?" my daughter asked.

The telephone rang. Penny picked it up. "Yes? Who? Wait a minute."

"For you," she said, "again," and handed me the receiver with a reproachful look.

 " 'Allo, Barbara." Bashir's voice sounded as if he were next door, and I wished he were.

"Bashir, where are you calling from?"

"Beirut. I just wanted to know that you arrived safely and everything is okay."

"Everything's fine. It's so good to hear you."

There was so much more I wanted to say, but Penny was eyeing me balefully, arms crossed, waiting. I faltered. Then I launched into a rundown of our production schedule.

Bashir interrupted. "When am I going to see you again?"

"Mom, what are we going to do today?" Penny said in a loud voice. "Or are you just going to stay home and work all day as usual?"

"Shhhh." I put my finger to my lips.

"Barbara, are you there?" called Bashir.

"It's just like all the other times," Penny complained. "You say you're glad to see me, you tell me how much you love me, you give me presents, and then you get on the phone and all you do is work."

"When will I see you again, Barbara?"

"Let me survive this week, Bashir, and then we'll talk about that."

"I'm sending someone to help you. If you need me, Alfred Mady can always reach me immediately. He'll get you anything you want from us." Mady was the director of the Lebanese Information and Research Center, a registered lobby for the Lebanese Forces. As such, he was Bashir's representative in the United States, charged with developing support in the Congress, the administration, the Pentagon, the media, and the CIA, which for the past few years had been training some of Bashir's operatives, including Elie Hobeika. It was also Mady's job to develop and maintain ties with the large Lebanese-American community. Since the Lebanese Forces had taken over most of the functions of Lebanon's paralyzed central government, Mady performed the functions of an ambassador without possessing the title or receiving the perks.

I hung up and followed Penny into the den, where she sat pouting opposite the television. I sat beside her.

"That was Bashir Gemayel," I said. "He's an important man to a lot of people."

"Not to me," my daughter retorted. "Just like I'm not important to you."

I wasn't angry. I knew how hurt she was that even when I was home, my attention was drawn away from her. As a child I had suffered similarly from my father's constant preoccupation. I had promised Penny that this week's interlude before I had to return to New York would be just for us. What a wishful, hopeless promise: the only way to keep it would have been to disconnect the phone. Sometimes Penny took it off the hook without telling me. I felt too torn to protest. I knew that she was going to get the short end of the stick, again. At the same time I felt an overwhelming responsibility to tell the stories I had investigated, the stories of Lebanon and terrorism.

It was five in the afternoon but midnight by my internal clock. I had had no rest in either Israel or Beirut. The whole trip, but especially my departure with the tapes, had been harrowing. The arrangements with ABC went on nonstop. I was ready to collapse. But an eleven-year-old girl whose mother has been away for six weeks feels rejection, not comprehension.

I forced myself to sit next to Penny while she watched television, but I kept slumping over. Finally she nudged me. "Go to sleep, Mom. It's okay, really. I'm used to it."

I went to bed, and got up at three in the morning, ready to start my day.

The house looked like Mother Hubbard's cupboard. I had to do a mammoth shopping spree for groceries. As soon as the stores were open, I drove to the supermarket.

Here was another jolt back to reality, or unreality. Four days ago I had been selecting shots of massacres. Today I was picking fruit from a bin in a supermarket in Washington. On the checkout line a woman turned to me and complained bitterly about the lettuce. "And the prices!" she moaned. "The prices go up and the quality comes down. And you think they care?" I made, I think, the appropriate noises. But it all seemed absurd and empty.

There is for me, and I suppose for many reporters, a period of disorientation and distress, when a story I've been working on for months is finally finished and out of my hands. I expect it; I've learned to deal with it. But my feelings about leaving Lebanon and Bashir were of a different magnitude altogether. I saw with double vision. Everything reminded me of Lebanon, everything referred back. I dreamed every night that I was there, and no matter how frightening the dream, I was always crushed to awaken safe in my own bed, in my own home.

That afternoon Alfred Mady appeared at my door. He looked like the opposite of Bashir. While Bashir was most comfortable in a tee-shirt and slacks, Alfred wore a dark silk suit, white silk shirt, red-patterned Hermès tie, black silk stockings, and a dark navy overcoat, which he draped European-style over his shoulders like a modern-day Phantom of the Opera. I couldn't prove it, but from the way he moved, I'd bet his underwear was silk, too. Alfred looked as much like a fighter as Liberace. I had trouble picturing him together with Bashir.

We sat in the living room. I called Penny in and introduced her.

"Hello," she muttered and vanished immediately.

"I've heard a lot about you," Alfred said, looking me over curiously. "Bashir was very impressed. He talks about you a lot."

He meant to flatter me, but I didn't need to hear from him how Bashir felt about me, and was mildly offended at the presumption. Alfred went on: "We have a tie line from Beirut to Washington. When Bashir calls, I'll patch him through to you. Anything at all you need for the piece, you ask me and I'll get it for you right away."

A short while after he left, Bashir called.

"What's with this guy Alfred?" I asked him. "He looks like a fop."

"A what?"

"You know, dressed in silk from head to toe."

Bashir laughed. "It doesn't matter, Barbara. He's a very good guy. He will help you with anything you need. I've told him to take care of you."

"Take care of me? What do you mean?"

"To make sure you're okay. I am not there to do it."

"Bashir, I don't need anyone to take care of me; and if I did, Alfred is the last person I'd pick. Are you worried something will happen because of the piece?"

"I *know* something will happen. I just want to be sure it doesn't happen to you. You mean a lot to me," Bashir said.

One week later I flew back to New York. We were at the stage of editing where I would write a draft, Geraldo would edit it, and we would then record a scratch track. Later on we would rerecord the script in a sound studio.

I started working on the last segment of the show, the Bashir portion. In that cramped and airtight compartment called an editing room, I felt as if I were looking into his very soul. It's difficult to cheat a television camera, especially under conditions of stress and fatigue, and in unguarded moments. Watching Bashir close up on the monitor, I saw clearly the power and the passion that galvanized a nation.

Bashir was a modern man born into an ancient world, the ancient world of Lebanon, unchanged from the time of the Ottoman Empire. It was a world of feudalism and privilege, where advancement depended not on one's efforts, but on the circumstances of one's birth; where the sole use of power was the aggrandizement of its holder; where blind, feudal fealty was due the local *seigneur*, not the national leader.

By demanding that individuals be judged according to merit, and by working to replace loyalty to a sheikh with loyalty to the state, Bashir was acting against the immediate interests of families like his own. In a sense, he was trying to saw off the branch on which he sat. Bashir was not simply a phenomenon of the moment, I thought; he was a historical force created by the needs of the region and the dynamics of his own character.

Of course, neither of these forces was disposed to produce a peaceable man. Lebanon was a land of everyday violence and brutality, a country wracked by the fevers of the region. Bashir was deeply, almost religiously loved in Lebanon, but he was also feared.

From infancy, I knew from his sisters, he had had a wild streak, a pugnacious disrespect for authority and a dangerous impulsiveness. As a child, he was in constant trouble at school because of his restlessness, which would not allow him to sit still in a classroom. In the mid-1970s, while the Syrians were shelling the Christian sectors of Beirut, Bashir demanded that the Voice of Lebanon station broadcast a condemnation of the Syrians for killing civilians. When no such statement was read, he sent a group of his soldiers to surround the station. The station director, Joseph Hashem, went down to see what was happening. Hashem was a close friend of Pierre Gemayel's and had known Bashir from his birth.

Bashir strode up and screamed in his face: "I told you to tell the truth about the Syrians. Now look what they've done to our people!" Then, in front of a large group of people, he slapped Hashem hard across the face.

Hashem telephoned Pierre Gemayel, who hurried to the station, grabbed Bashir, and ordered him to apologize publicly. As Hashem approached, Sheikh Pierre thrust Bashir forward and told him to shake hands and kiss, as part of the Middle Eastern ritual of reconciliation. "Okay," Bashir said, "I'll shake his hand. But I won't kiss him."

It is said that power corrupts, and from what I've seen with my own eyes, I'd say that it's true nine times out of ten. But power didn't corrupt Bashir; it made him better. The young Bashir had slapped and humiliated an older man in a fit of self-indulgent rage. The Bashir I knew never raised his voice, struck out, or lost his temper. As a boy, Bashir had been too hyperkinetic to sit for a half hour in a classroom; as a man he spent half his days in long, tedious meetings without ever betraying a sign of impatience. Achieving this degree of self-mastery under conditions of unrelenting stress must have been a Herculean task, but Bashir did it, I believe, because he saw that he could not lead others until he had learned to rule himself.

By the age of thirty-two, Bashir had achieved an astonishing degree of control over the world around him. His expanding reach was mirrored in the growth of the Lebanese Forces. Before he created the Lebanese Forces, the defense of the various Christian communities was an ad hoc affair, with every village for itself. Not since the start of the civil war in 1975 had there been a functional national army, nor was there any unified Christian command to succor beleaguered communities. The Lebanese Forces started out as a mobile task force of about fifty hand-picked fighters loyal to Bashir, who operated on "personal initiative" outside the auspices of the sedentary Phalange leadership. Bashir would dispatch his men to any place that Christians were attacked, and, though few, his fierce fighters made all the difference. Within a few years the Lebanese Forces had become the military arm, first of the Phalangists, then, after the July 7 operation, of the Christian community as a whole.

By 1980, Bashir's Lebanese Forces were also the leading civilian authority in Lebanon, more powerful and pervasive than the government. To develop a sense of community, Bashir established a television station and two radio stations, including a classical music station, so that people could forget about the war. (He himself loved classical music and used it as a respite from tension.)

Bashir's reach extended even to controlling inflation. He imposed price controls. Every day the radio would announce prices for one hundred leading items, and merchants who violated the price controls were jailed.

To deal with the horrendous traffic in East Beirut, the Lebanese Forces set up parking garages, manned by disabled soldiers, which charged minimal parking fees.

Bashir scheduled trains and mediated labor disputes. He seemed tireless. He was driven. He was, when necessary, ruthless.

"You don't unite Lebanon with hugs and kisses," he liked to say. A true child of his region, Bashir used the weapons at hand. I first met him six months after he had united the Christians with his July 7 surprise attack on the Tigers, the militia controlled by President Chamoun's son Danny. It was a bloody, brutal operation, with many killed and injured. But Bashir told me that it was the most important thing he had ever done.

"It was a zoo here," he said. "Each faction had its own fighters. The militias terrorized the villages with constant gun battles. Just to get a sandwich they would take a tank, drive to a village store, buy some food, and drive back again. Families were divided, brothers buried each under a different flag. After one battle, Danny Chamoun was pictured on the front pages of the Beirut papers, toasting with Champagne the death of our guys. They wouldn't even let us bury our dead honorably. This chaos was like a gangrene attacking the body politic, and I was the surgeon who had to cut it out."

"But your men committed terrible excesses. I heard that they threw men out of windows and off of towers."

"I didn't want that. It showed me again how important it is to get to the root of Lebanon's problems: our lack of unity. But what do you expect when these men have seen their own fathers and brothers killed by the very group they were fighting against? You in the West don't understand. Men become animals under such circumstances. This is just what we are trying to end. But to change the mentality we have to do hard things. There's a price to be paid for civilization, and we are willing to pay it."

Harsh as the July 7 operation was, there were mitigating factors. The targets had been military men. The attack had been an effective, perhaps even a necessary, route to unification. Very knowledgeable Israelis told me that Israel had been trying for years to convince the Christian leaders with whom it had contact that unless they unified, they had no hope of prevailing over the Palestinians and Syrians. It was only after Bashir went against his own father to forcibly unite the Christians that they decided to support him.

I had seen Lebanon with my own eyes. I'd seen the victims of terrorism, the bombed-out cities, the madness that passed as normalcy, the wildness of the fighters whom Bashir held in such tight check. Not even Gandhi could have unified Lebanon without force. Gandhi? God himself couldn't have done it. I am not a pacifist, and would not condemn out of hand a military operation designed to end a state of anarchy.

After Maya's death Bashir had installed Elie Hobeika as his chief of security, knowing full well who the man was and what he'd done. I wondered, watching him over and over on the monitor as I picked sound bites and visuals for the segment, how I felt about that dark side of Bashir.

I still do wonder. Yet I am convinced that by the time we met, Bashir had conquered the rage that made him lash out in revenge, had subdued that passion and bent its energy to constructive uses. Bashir was not an angel sent by God to rescue Lebanon; he was a man of vision and restless energy, born and bred in a violent land, who needed to outgrow himself and who had to an extraordinary degree succeeded in doing so.

Had he lived, Bashir would have led Lebanon to nationhood in fact, not just in name. (And that, I've since learned, is why he did not live—but I will come to that later.) The strength of his cohesive force can be seen in the disintegration of Lebanon after his death. Lebanon today is like Humpty-Dumpty, irreparably shattered. But there was a time when the possibility existed that Lebanon could be made whole; and that time coincided with the brief ascent to power of Bashir Gemayel.

Our piece aired on April 3, 1981. On the night of the broadcast, I watched the program with my parents. During the entire hour they were very quiet. Even during the commercials they sat still, waiting in silence. When the program ended my father stood up. He walked over to me and kissed my cheek. "I'm proud that you're my daughter," he said.

I was shocked. It was by far the nicest thing he'd ever said to me. But I felt enervated and strangely depressed. The enormous burden of work had been lifted from me, but not the burden of concern and what I could only call my obsession with Bashir.

I went to bed without waiting to see the 11 o'clock news, so it wasn't until the next day that I heard the news from Lebanon. On the same day as our program was broadcast, Bashir's men had fought the Syrians in the Christian city of Zahle, close to the Syrian border. Zahle was the capital of the eastern part of Lebanon—the Bekáa Valley—which was completely controlled by the Syrians. Because of its strategic location and size—it was the third largest city in Lebanon, with a population of about 200,000—the struggle over Zahle had turned into an elaborate chess game for three players: the Phalange, the Syrians, and the Israelis. Bashir was trying to cast the Israelis as the backers of the Christians in Lebanon.

Bashir, of course, knew full well that his force alone could not oust the mighty Syrians from the Bekáa Valley—unless he could persuade or inveigle the Israelis into getting involved. In several previous meetings with Israeli Prime Minister Begin, Bashir had succeeded in eliciting an emotional if operationally vague promise that, "We will never allow the Syrians to perpetrate genocide in Lebanon." In order to win control of Zahle, Bashir embarked on a series of maneuvers designed to activate that Israeli promise.

He infiltrated about ninety Phalange fighters into the city through Mount Senin, and he broke ground on a road to connect Zahle directly to Christian East Beirut. When the Syrians did not immediately respond to that act of defiance, Bashir upped the stakes: his forces shelled Syrian sentries guarding a bridge on the vital Beirut-Damascus highway.

The response was swift. Syrian commandos surrounded the city, using helicopters to penetrate the Mount Senin region and cut off the dirt roads that linked Zahle to the Christian hinterland. Artillery rained down on the city. Bashir had gone much too far, and the Syrians did not expect Israeli intervention. To preempt that possible intervention, President Assad of Syria telegraphed his intended response: his troops dug, and then left empty, emplacements for the SAM-6 missiles that had until then by tacit agreement between Syria and Israel been kept out of Lebanon.

The Israeli Cabinet met to discuss the fighting in Zahle. A fierce argument developed among those ministers, including Prime Minister Begin and Minister of Defense Ariel Sharon, who wanted to intervene, and others who warned that the whole purpose of Bashir Gemayel's exercise was to draw Israel into a conflict with Syria. The result was stalemate, a policy of wait-and-see.

The siege continued. The Phalange held fast, despite constant artillery barrages on Zahle and Mount Senin. In mid-April, Bashir traveled to Israel with former Lebanese president Camille Chamoun. They met with Begin and warned him of catastrophic consequences to the Christians if Mount Senin and Zahle were to fall.

It would not happen, Begin promised.

Frustrated by its inability to rid Zahle of a few score Phalangists, and encouraged by Israel's lack of response, Syria stepped up the pressure, attacking the Christians with helicopter gunships. On April 28, the Israeli Cabinet met in an extraordinary session whose only agenda was the Syrian attack on the Christians. The cabinet divided along the same lines as previously, but this time, the Christian position seemed more hazardous. After heated debate, the cabinet sanctioned a limited air strike.

So eager were Arik Sharon and his chief of staff to intervene that the air strike was carried out even before the meeting adjourned. The Israelis shot down what they thought was a helicopter gunship, but which turned out to be a troop carrier. In return, Syria carried out its implied threat and installed surface-to-air missiles in the Bekáa Valley emplacements. Syria and Israel had each taken a giant step closer to war.

The only winner was Bashir, but he was a big winner. Simply by leveraging a few dozen fighters, he had managed in one stroke to involve the Israelis, embarrass the Syrians, and establish himself as the undisputed champion of Lebanon. Political leaders, especially in the United States, took note of this impressive and precocious display of realpolitik. Bashir's stock climbed sharply.

Our "20/20" piece also impacted strongly on Bashir's improving image in the United States. Reactions to the program were polarized. It received many excellent reviews, the *Wall Street Journal* in particular hailing it in a special column on the editorial page. But, as I had predicted to Av Westin, a number of ABC producers and executives who felt they had a stake in the former canon on the Problem of Lebanon were outraged. While Bashir was busy fighting his battles, I was fighting my own.

I had realized while we were still in Israel that the story emerging would not be a popular one. Terrorism up close is utterly repugnant, frightening far beyond its actual capabilities because it reaches to our primeval fear of random and meaningless evil.

It's hard to reconcile pity for the homeless Palestinian people with the kind of emotions aroused by a close-up view of the PLO's terrorist tactics. And the media as a whole, and many of my colleagues in particular, were deeply sympathetic to the Palestinian cause. Once Israel had been the focus of their compassion, when the fledgling nation was viewed as fragile and endangered. But since Israel's 1967 defeat of four massed Arab armies in only seven days, the media had changed its view, and the same country that had been hailed as a brave, pioneering, egalitarian nation was recast as an imperialistic co-opter of Palestinian rights and land.

Most of the ABC producers who disliked my piece had never been in the Middle East. Their only contacts with the PLO were with that organization's slick U.S.-based propagandists, who would at the click of a pen quote poetry about their diaspora and who were so adept at feeding back to the media what the media wanted to hear. Terrorism to these colleagues was like a boil on the face of a sufferer, an unfortunate eruption from which it was only decent to avert one's eyes.

Living in Washington insulated me from corporate politics. I was rather surprised not to have had any feedback from those colleagues whom I'd expected to be most upset by "The Unholy War." The first indication that I had a problem came when Av Westin's secretary phoned from New York to summon me to a meeting about the piece. What about the piece? I asked. She said there had been mail. Of course there was mail, I said, what did they expect? I asked who was coming to the meeting. Representatives of Arab-American organizations, she told me. Oh, and a few "20/20" producers who'd expressed reservations about the piece.

It's unusual but not unheard of for producers to meet with disgruntled viewers, especially if they represent powerful interest groups. But as far as I knew, it was unprecedented for other producers to join in. There are other forums for professionals to express opinions of each other's work, and the best one is face to face, one on one. But that was not my colleagues' choice.

The meeting took place in a conference room in the ABC News Corporation headquarters on West 66th Street. Av Westin introduced me to half a dozen representatives of the Arab-American organizations who had complained about the piece. Among them sat four or five of my fellow producers from "20/20," the very people whose silence I'd wondered at. One person was conspicuously absent: Geraldo. I was a little surprised, but I shouldn't have been. That's the way the system works: the producer takes the heat to protect the talent. In any case, I had no problem defending the piece, with or without Rivera.

Av Westin chaired the meeting and did most of the talking. The gist of the complaints was that the report had been unfair to the PLO by presenting their use of terror in isolation, rather than in the context of Israeli oppression of the Palestinian people. The theft of the Palestinians' land, they said, was an act of state terrorism far more virulent than anything the PLO had ever done.

Westin defended the story. He pointed out that its subject was terrorism, not Middle East politics, and that this had been clearly stated at the start.

The representatives then complained about ABC's broadcast of a new mini-series called "Masada." That the first part of the series aired the same week as our "20/20" piece was clear evidence to them of ABC's Zionist slant. They met with scorn and disbelief Av Westin's explanation that the "Masada" series was scheduled months before the "20/20" piece was even conceived.

Eventually I was called on to speak. With full confidence in the validity and integrity of our piece, I defended it calmly but strongly. The pens of my colleagues made feverish scratching sounds, but they did not speak; they kept their eyes on their notebooks and away from my face.

Later, Av Westin thanked me for coming and I thanked him for his support. We parted cordially, both of us knowing that my days at ABC were numbered.

Not all Arab-Americans objected to our piece. Several weeks after "The Unholy War" aired, I learned that the American Lebanese League was giving me its award for journalism.

"I'm honored," I told the official who called to tell me, "but I'm not familiar with the award. Who else has received it?"

There was an awkward pause.

"Last year," the man said reluctantly, "it was Salim el-Louzy."

"The *late* Salim el-Louzy?"

"He was alive at the time."

"Thank you so much," I said bleakly.

The ceremony was held in the banquet hall in Crystal City, Virginia, across the Potomac from Washington. Penny and I sat together at the round table closest to the podium. I felt strange. The only person I knew there was Alfred Mady; my only real link to Lebanon was Bashir. Just before the award was presented, Charles Malik, a senior Lebanese statesman, former foreign minister, and president of the United Nations General Assembly, made a speech in which he praised Bashir highly. Then it was my turn.

I don't much like giving speeches. I walked up to the podium and looked down at a sea of strange, expectant faces. Then Penny caught my eye, beaming encouragement. She looked very proud.

I talked about Bashir. I tried to be careful. I didn't want to say too much, but I felt as if my feelings were written on my face. I said that I thought Bashir was that old-fashioned thing, a hero; that he had the courage to march to his own drumbeat and to accept the consequences. I spoke for only a few minutes and ended with a quote from Emerson that seemed to me a perfect description of Bashir. "If a man holds his place and there abides, defying all odds, then the whole world will come around to him."

These words electrified the room like a bolt of lightning. The audience jumped to its feet, cheering and applauding—not for me, I thought, but for Bashir. Alfred rushed up to me and told me he was going to telex Bashir with the Emerson quotation.

The story was over, and as far as ABC was concerned, it was back to business as usual. I was developing a story about how Muammar Qadaffi of Libya, using Soviet support and his own troops, was fighting a rebel army in the neighboring country of Chad. The leader of the revolution in Chad had CIA, Sudanese, and Israeli intelligence support. The story was compelling to me as a living example of the way the great powers fight wars by proxy, using surrogates. But for one reason or another, I could not give it my full concentration.

I have never worked a story that is "just" a story. They all absorb me totally. Necessity has taught me to let go when the story is over, to step back and return to myself. Only this time I couldn't let go. Lebanon had got its hooks in me.

One of the hooks was my feeling for the Christians of Lebanon, who were to my mind the ultimate victims— scapegoats for all the troubles of a deeply troubled region. Had they been passive victims, though, they would not have moved me as much as they did. But under Bashir's tutelage they were organizing and fighting back to regain their country. Lebanon was a drama more riveting than any I'd ever experienced.

The other hook was Bashir.

The story was over and I needed to get on with my life; but every time Bashir called me, which was nearly every day, I went all weak-kneed and girlish at the sound of his voice, like the heroine of a book I would have scorned. The feelings for Bashir that I'd battened down during my watch were now freed, and their unleashed force was frightening. Nothing in my life compelled me as this man did. Nothing came close, except Penny—and they were each pulling in opposite directions.

It scared me. I was on the verge of a fateful commitment to a man who, however he loved me, would never be mine.

Unable to see or touch one another, Bashir and I compensated with long, intimate talks on the phone. We grew very close. Bashir cared for his wife and was adored in return, but he did not feel free to open his heart to Solange as he did to me. To his wife, as to his people,

Bashir had to appear always strong, always self-confident, always resolute. He felt he owed her that. He told me: "I don't want to be ugly with Solange. She doesn't deserve that."

I didn't want to hurt Solange, either. But that little drop of sisterly concern was lost in the turbulence of my feelings for Bashir. I thought about him constantly, fantasized like a schoolgirl, compared nearly everyone to him and found them wanting.

And on the day Bashir called to announce jubilantly that he was coming to Washington, I made plans to go abroad.

It was pure funk. I was scared

The piece had been a barrier between us. Without it I had no protection from Bashir, or rather from that unknown part of me that he seemed to call forth. I felt something uncontrollable in my attraction to Bashir, which was like a moth's reckless impulse toward flame, only this was worse, because I could clearly see the madness of my way. Bashir was a warlord whose life even the most benevolent insurance company would never underwrite; he was also a husband, a father, and a Catholic. My life, my daughter, and my work were all here. If there was a man that conventional wisdom would deem wrong for me, Bashir was that man. And I was falling in love with him.

I didn't like the feeling. I certainly didn't trust it. My parents' world views seldom coincided, but their voices in me were united in warning: never let feelings interfere with your life, my father whispered, and my mother clucked in agreement and sighed, "What's the matter, you don't have enough trouble already?"

So I flew to Paris to gather information for my story about the surrogate war in Sudan. For five days I met with sources from Libya and Chad—intelligence operatives, journalists, and academics—who spent hours with me, laying out the scenario, the issues, and the players of that little-known war. During those days of hard work I remembered who I was; then, reinforced, I returned home to Washington and Bashir.

Within an hour of my return, Alfred called. "Bashir's here," he said excitedly. "He wants to see you. When can he come?"

We set a time for later that afternoon. I bathed and put on a gray suit I'd bought in Paris for the occasion. Bashir had known me mostly under battle conditions; he'd seen me dirty, smelly, cold, and bedraggled, with windblown hair and smeared lipstick. I looked forward to seeing his eyes when he met the other me.

I sat in my study and tried to work, but had no patience. Instead I watched the clock and wondered how Bashir would find my house. No doubt Alfred would give him directions.

Precisely at the appointed hour, I heard an uproar on my quiet suburban street. I looked out the window and saw a cavalcade of five black sedans pull up in front of my house. By the time I got to the door, the sidewalk was full of men in dark glasses, carrying walkie-talkies. Then I saw Bashir. He was talking with one of the Secret Service men.

I threw open the door. "Bashir!" I shouted. He looked up and a broad smile came over his face. He walked very quickly to the door, grabbed me, and gave me a kiss. Over his shoulder I saw the startled faces of his escorts and the curious eyes of one of my neighbors who was walking to her car.

Alfred Mady followed him into my house like a shadow.

I was so excited to see Bashir that I neglected to say hello to Alfred. He laughed in an offended way, and said, "All she sees is you, Bashir." Then he walked into the kitchen and started making telephone calls.

Bashir's eyes were warm and mischievous. He kissed me again. I said, "What are all those men doing here? I expected you to come alone, not with half the U.S. Secret Service."

Bashir laughed. "They insisted. But I wouldn't let them come in; I told them it was a private visit."

"But isn't the whole trip a private visit?"

He seemed surprised that I hadn't known. "Your government invited me," he said. "It's official." Then he laughed. "Last year when we came to the U.S. we went to the State Department. No one wanted to talk to us, so we left and went around the corner and bought an ice cream cone. This time, they sent a nuclear submarine for me."

I brought him into the den, a bright room with a wide picture window overlooking a wooded area. Bashir sat beside me and held my hand. Nervously, I launched into a barrage of questions about politics. Bashir replied in monosyllables, with laughter in his eyes. Then he stood up. "Let's go upstairs," he said. "You can show me the rest of the house."

"But what about the Secret Service?"

"They'll wait," he said.

We went upstairs.

This moment had been building between us since the day we met. When it came at last, the pent-up force was explosive. It seemed so good and so right that our bodies were at last doing what our spirits had done long ago.

When we came down, we found Alfred in the kitchen, eating fruit with a knife and fork. He glanced up sullenly as we came in, then went back to peeling a peach. I brought a plate and fork and knife to Bashir, who helped himself to a huge serving of fruit.

Wishing Alfred on the moon, I whispered to Bashir, "Can we spend the night together?"

"Yes," he said, and said something in Lebanese to Alfred.

"No," said Alfred, then he switched to Lebanese and spoke vehemently for several minutes. Bashir shrugged in resignation.

"Alfred's afraid it will look bad to the Americans. Come over to the hotel tomorrow afternoon at about two. We can spend some time together then."

It was beautiful and warm the next day. I put on blue brocade slacks and black lizard sling-back heels and went to the Four Seasons Hotel; Bashir had been moved there from the Madison after threats against his life were received, and was now sharing a two-bedroom suite with Alfred. The Secret Service had the rooms across the hall. I was very tired from a sleepless night, so instead of sitting on the couch in Bashir's room, I lay down. Alfred ran over to me. "Sit up, sit up," he hissed, looking back at the open door to the corridor. I sat up.

In a few minutes Bashir came out of the bedroom. He put his arms around me and began to kiss me. The door was still open, and I could feel Alfred's nervousness—but then I forgot all about him.

I noticed a silver pin in Bashir's lapel. It was embossed with a cedar tree; underneath the tree was the word *Kataeb*, or Phalange, in Arabic. "That's a beautiful pin," I said. He took it off his jacket and handed it to me, showing me the inscription with his name in Arabic. "Keep it," he said, closing my hand around it. I put my arms around him and rested my head on his shoulder. Alfred yawned loudly and announced that he was going to take a nap. He went into his bedroom and closed the door.

Later, Bashir asked me when I could come back to Beirut.

"Soon," I told him. "Very soon."

"It will be better for us there. No Secret Service, no Alfred. At home I can come and go just as I like. There will be plenty of time for us to be together. You can stay in Alfred's place outside Beirut, and I can stay there with you."

I was very quiet. The thoughts that had kept me up the night before returned to me now. I understood and accepted that Bashir was married, and that in his position and his world he would never get divorced. For a Maronite there is no divorce. Bashir used to tell his young soldiers this over and over lest they rush into marriage. And even if he were single, I could never leave my daughter; nor could I bring her to live in Beirut.

I knew the end would be sad. But it seemed hard that the beginning should be, too. We ought to have gone away together, spent a leisurely weekend alone in a beautiful place. But Bashir was suddenly a V.I.P. in Washington, with a schedule that left no time for love. All we had were stolen hours.

Bashir noticed that I was very quiet. "You will come, won't you?" he said shyly, touching my face. "I need you. You know that I can't talk freely with most other people. It's different with you. You're not like other women. You are very important to me."

"Nothing could keep me away," I said, putting my hand on his.

Later the conversation turned, as it usually did, to politics. Bashir was very pleased with his reception in the United States. "Suddenly the Americans are very interested in us," he said. "They are beginning to understand the region better and to realize that they are not getting anywhere playing the Arab card."

"What do you mean?"

He began to speak rapidly and very intently. "The Saudis made a deal with the Americans that they would pressure Arafat to be more moderate if the Americans would pressure the Israelis not to help us and not to antagonize the PLO. The Americans thought that this would work, since the Saudis hold the purse strings for the PLO, as the U.S. does for Israel. They didn't realize that the plan was doomed from the start, because the Saudis and Arafat never keep their word. Arafat breathes sixty times a minute, and lies a hundred and twenty times. An agreement with him means nothing. The Americans are naïve and they have dug their own grave in the Middle East. But now times are changing. The Israelis have asked the Americans to give us financial support, and the Americans are going to do it."

I reached instinctively for my notebook, but of course it wasn't there.

"Things are changing fast," Bashir said. "Israel is going to take some tough action against the PLO and change the balance in the region."

"But Bashir," I said. "You don't really think the Israelis would move their army into Lebanon?"

With a big smile in his eyes, he said, "Just watch, Barbara. It will come soon."

I didn't believe him. I thought he was expressing his hopes more than the realities. But I didn't have the heart to tell him.

By September, my story on the surrogate war in Chad had reached the point where I was ready to go to the Sudan to film Hussein Habrè. Habrè is now president of Chad, but  at that time he commanded rebel forces who fought the country's Libyan-backed regime. There were Soviet and CIA advisors and intelligence agents on the ground; Libyan soldiers fought in Chad; and Habrè's rebellion was backed by the CIA, Israel, and the Sudan, which allowed Habrè to base his forces on Sudanese territory, just over the border from Chad. His band of several hundred fighters was a thorn in Libya's side.

Bashir had asked me to come to Beirut, and I wanted very much to see him. Instead of going straight from Paris to the Sudan, I made a detour to Lebanon.

The flight was smooth, but I was keyed up and not only with excitement about seeing Bashir again. Alfred and I had discussed a project, and I didn't know how Bashir would like it. The plan was for me to do a feature film about Bashir. At the time, I told myself it was to help the cause I had come to identify as mine, and to tell the truth about a man who had been so unjustly maligned by the Western press. But in my heart I knew that I had another, overriding consideration; I thought the movie would bring me closer to Bashir.

Perhaps it seems a strange way to get close to someone, surveying his life through a camera lens, interviewing friends and family, selling Bashir in treatments and proposals. But for me it was the most natural way, using a medium at which I excelled—and given our circumstances, it was the best chance Bashir and I had to be together.

The film would allow me to do something I yearned to do anyway: to contact his intimates, the people who knew him before he was powerful—his mother, father, brother, childhood friends. There was more to this hunger than the usual lover's desire to speak of his or her beloved. As much as I loved Bashir, I did not fully understand what had shaped him.

For all his openness with me, Bashir was an intensely private man, and I did not know if he would tolerate this degree of exposure. Alfred Mady had preceded me to Lebanon by about a week, and we had agreed that he would put the proposal to Bashir, to give him time to consider it before my arrival.

I didn't apply for a visa because I didn't want my name appearing on any official list. Alfred had assured me that it wouldn't matter; he would pick me up at the airport and spirit me through passport control.

"You'd better," I told him. I've done a lot of dangerous things in my job, but I do them because I need to, not because I like it. I'd been nervous the first time I flew to Beirut (also without a visa; some people never learn!), but then I was an unknown quantity to Syrians. Now that our "20/20" piece had aired, I was not likely to be their favorite journalist. I felt that Bashir would not let any harm come to me; but Bashir had no control over the Syrians, and his "territory" did not extend to the airport, which was in Moslem West Beirut.

The plane began to descend and then it banked. As I gazed down at Beirut, set like a jewel between the blue sea and green mountains, I felt the quickening sensation of coming home.

We landed. I looked out the window of my first-class seat, which faced the terminal. No sign of Alfred, but waiting on the tarmac was a great knot of soldiers who were holding what looked like a photograph and were scrutinizing the disembarking passengers. Though I didn't recognize their uniforms, I knew the airport was controlled by Syrian and Palestinian troops. Thirty soldiers seemed a bit large for a welcoming party; perhaps they were there to arrest someone. Still no sign of Alfred. But he had promised to be on the tarmac, and I had found that despite his popinjay appearance, Alfred was a reliable man.

I stayed in my seat until all the other passengers had deplaned. The soldiers were still waiting, but now they were talking among themselves in an agitated manner. The captain came out of his cabin and looked at me. A stewardess approached. "Are you all right, Miss?"

I said I was fine and walked to the first-class door. Most of the soldiers were still congregated around the tourist-class exit. I went down the steps and without looking at the soldiers, walked as casually as I could past them in the direction of the terminal. What I would do without a visa once I got there, I had no idea.

I never made it. A soldier spotted me, cried out, and ran over waving a photograph. He held it out to me. "Is this you?"

The photograph was one taken last time I was in Beirut, before I had my hair cut short. I hesitated. It wasn't a very good likeness and I looked different enough now that I could conceivably deny it. But what then? And the picture was one taken by a friend of Bashir's. How would the Syrians or Palestinians have acquired it? More and more soldiers were coming over, looking from the picture to me.

"Yes," I said at last.

At once the soldier grasped my arm and began hustling me away from the terminal. I set my feet and resisted. He pulled; I pulled back. "Come on!" he said, nearly desperate.

"Where to?"

"Your plane was late," he said. "You were the last one off. The sheikh is waiting."

Still I did not move. "What army are you with?" I asked politely. (And never, until this writing, stopped to think what a strange and telling question it was.)

"We're Lebanese army," he said.

Which meant nothing, since the army was as factionalized as the country. There was a Shiite Brigade, a Sunni Brigade, a Druze Brigade, and a Christian Brigade, each loyal only to its sect. We stood and stared at one another for a few moments, and then he reached inside his shirt and pulled out a silver chain with a cross and a religious medallion.

I doubt if any Jew has ever been so glad to see a crucifix. I felt like kissing him, but he wouldn't have understood. Another soldier asked for my baggage claim check, and I handed it over. The thirty soldiers and I piled into six jeeps and took off.

After a short stop at their base, I was driven forty-five minutes up a steep road to the mountains overlooking Beirut. I was staying this trip at a hotel called the Al Bustan, one of Lebanon's most famous hostelries, an elegant, old-world relic of a more peaceful time. My room was cool, restfully decorated in shades of blue, and large enough to accommodate two double beds, a desk, and two easy chairs. I went onto the terrace and gazed at the sparkling night lights of Beirut, which seemed to meld with the starlit sky.

I felt grubby, tired from the heat, and still clammy with the cold sweat that had covered me at the airport. I took a long, cool bath. Minutes after I emerged, there was a knock on the door.

It was Bashir, with Alfred beside him. "Boys!" I called delightedly. *"Boys?"* Bashir repeated quizzically. Alfred walked in first, laughing, and kissed me on the cheek, while Bashir sat on the bed.

"Bashir said yes," Alfred sang out from across the room.

"Just a minute," I said. "Where the hell were you, Alfred?"

"You know I can't go to the airport. It's much too dangerous."

"You told me you'd be there."

He shrugged. "We sent the soldiers. You got out all right."

"No thanks to you, kid."

"Never mind that, Barbara. The important thing is, everything is arranged for the film. While you're here you can talk to anyone you want, even Sheikh Pierre, Bashir's mother, and of course his wife, Solange."

It was a funny thing, but in all the weeks of thinking about and planning the film, it had never once occurred to me that I would have to interview Solange. Of course it was unavoidable. But I put off thinking about it, and turned to Bashir. "It means I'll have to come back," I said.

"I'm afraid so," he answered, and laughed.

Alfred left after half an hour. Bashir turned to me. We kissed with our eyes open, not to lose a moment's sight of one another.

A few hours later we ordered dinner and ate on the terrace. Bashir ordered steak, french fries, and a Coke; I had a sandwich with a glass of white wine. I felt very good, very relaxed and happy; Bashir, the same. I was thinking about the film.

"What do *you* think shaped you?" I asked him absently, almost as I would a colleague.

"That's your job to find out," he answered, and I heard an eagerness in his voice, a quick curiosity.

"But what do you think?"

He paused for what seemed a long time. "I love my father," he said, "but all my life I have had to oppose him, and to bear the brunt of his opposition. He taught me self-control and keeping my feet on the ground; but it's also true that everything I hoped to be, he opposed."

"What about your brother? I want to meet him, by the way."

"I don't know if he'll receive you."

I smiled. "Want to bet?"

It had grown quite cool. After dinner we moved inside. Bashir sat in an armchair and we went on talking. I asked him why he had agreed to the movie.

"I made a mistake not caring about our image," he said. "But in the beginning there was no time to worry about images. We had to worry about surviving. Now that we are past that point, I can see that it does matter what people think of us."

He looked into my eyes, and although there was six feet between us, I felt as if we were touching. Bashir smiled and said, "Do you know, Barbara, when you first came here, I couldn't figure out why you were interested in us. I didn't know if it was because you saw the injustice and were affected by it, or because the Israelis asked you to."

"You thought I was working with them?"

"The possibility occurred to me. But it didn't matter. Whatever the reason, yours was the first team that ever gave us time to tell our side of the story."

I didn't even try to keep the hurt out of my voice. "How could you think I would let anyone tell me what to do or believe? Don't you know me?"

"Yes, I know you now. But in the beginning it was hard to understand why you cared."

But it still bothered me, and I stayed mad until I remembered, for the first time since meeting Bashir, what

I'd thought when David Kimche first told me about him: I suspected that Bashir was in Israel's pocket. It made me laugh to remember it. I thought of telling Bashir, but decided against it.

Early the next morning, I called Bashir's brother, Amin, in his Beirut office. In addition to his duties as a member of Parliament and a leader of the Phalange party, Amin was also a businessman who had married into one of the wealthiest families in Lebanon. On the phone, I told Amin that I was an American reporter and that I would like to interview him. He agreed with alacrity, and invited me to come to his office later that morning.

One of Bashir's bodyguards picked me up from Al Bustan at nine and drove me to Amin's office in a spanking new building. I was ushered through the anteroom, in which a number of notable-looking Lebanese Moslems sat waiting, and into Gemayel's office. The building was replete with sophisticated computer equipment and technological razzle-dazzle. Amin's office was comfortable, coordinated, and plush, in great contrast to the undecorated severity of Bashir's. Amin told me with some pride that the building itself was an international convention center, to which he hoped to attract a lot of business. I thought that only lunatics would hold a convention in Beirut.

They looked a lot alike, the Gemayel brothers, but what I saw were the differences. Bashir's face was naturally vibrant and reactive, except when he chose to mask his emotions; Amin was guarded and reserved. He never answered a question without pausing to consider, and his answers seemed tailored to please. Amin was taller and slimmer than Bashir, with finer bones and thick black hair trained backward Travolta-style. Though he was only five years Bashir's senior, he seemed to belong to an older generation.

Amin said he had great hopes that Lebanon's political parties would reach an accommodation satisfactory to all sides—that is how he talked, as if what was going on outside his air-conditioned office was some kind of labor negotiation instead of bloody chaos. He looked bored, as if even he didn't believe his own words.

"I hear you and your brother don't get along too well," I said.

"Not at all," Amin said quickly. "We are good friends. Why, only last week we went out together with our wives." Bashir had told me about this meeting, their first in months. Despite the presence of the wives, it had been not a social gathering but rather a semi-official meeting.

When Amin walked me out, he saw Bashir's driver sitting in his antechamber, instead of downstairs in the car where I had told him to wait. Amin recognized the man at once, and gave me a very searching look and a curt good-bye.

On a lovely, sunny morning, Alfred Mady drove me through the winding hills of the Metn, the Christian heartland and the region that Amin represented in Parliament.

After about an hour's drive northeast from Beirut, we reached Bekfaya, a little jewel of a village in the Metn area where the Gemayel family had its 300-year-old ancestral summer home. Bekfaya is very close to the demarcation line for Syrian-dominated Lebanon, and Syrian troops were stationed just over the mountain from the beautiful little town known as the "city of flowers." Small, well-kept shops and vegetable stands heaped with produce lined the main thoroughfare, and the streets were spotlessly clean. There was a peaceful, romantic aura about the village, a sense that time did not flow at quite the usual speed here. Despite the rumbling of Syrian military vehicles, it seemed as if the war were far away.

We drove to the iron gates outside the Gemayel house and the Phalange guards waved to Alfred and let us in. Besides the armed guards at the gates, there were more all over the grounds; I saw about a dozen in all. The house contained about fifteen large rooms and was built of massive gray stones that kept the interior naturally cool.

I was very curious about Pierre Gemayel. Bashir had told me that his father was the most formative influence in his life and I believed him, but I knew there was more to the relationship than filial respect and paternal love. Just one year had passed since Bashir united the Christians, thus reducing all the elders of the community, including his father, to a secondary role. Pierre had bitterly opposed the attack on Danny Chamoun's militia, which paved the way to unification. Bashir gave his father no warning about the operation, which was actually carried out while Pierre Gemayel was lunching with Danny's father, Camille Chamoun.

I had also heard of a meeting between some American congressmen and Sheikh Pierre that had taken place the previous April, just after Bashir's forces engaged the Syrians in Zahle. Bashir's father doesn't speak any English, so Bashir, who had insisted on attending the meeting, offered to translate. He then "translated" precisely what he wanted the congressmen to hear. When one of the Americans who understood French pointed out that Bashir's translation bore no resemblance to Sheikh Pierre's words, Bashir replied frostily, "Excuse me, sir. I know what my father wants to say."

People who know them both told me that even after Bashir superseded his father, he went out of his way to solicit his advice and approval. But when they disagreed, Bashir went his own way.

Several years earlier, Bashir's intelligence people had imprisoned four people from the Bekáa Valley who were caught trying to sell three kilos of heroin in East Beirut. One of the four jailed was a good friend and political

supporter of Sheikh Pierre. Sheikh Pierre called one of Bashir's intelligence staff, Paul Ariss, and demanded that he release the man. Ariss replied: "Sheikh Pierre, if it was hashish I wouldn't care, but this was heroin. It kills people. And they've been dealing in kilos."

"They were exporting the drug," Sheikh Pierre replied. "It's not our problem." Ariss said he would check with Bashir, which infuriated Pierre Gemayel. He shouted: "You don't have to check with Bashir! I'm telling you to release him!"

Ariss called Bashir and recounted the conversation. Bashir told Ariss to keep the smugglers in prison and to ignore his father.

Sheikh Pierre received us on an outdoor terrace. I was struck by how tall, thin, and ascetic-looking he was. His austere appearance and imposing manner made me feel uncomfortable. While a servant served cakes and coffee, Alfred translated as I conducted an interview that was one of the strangest of my career.

The subject of the interview was Bashir Gemayel. Every question I asked was about Bashir. And yet every answer was about Pierre Gemayel.

I asked when the family began to realize that Bashir had leadership qualities; Sheikh Pierre responded with a dissertation on his own struggles to free Lebanon from French dominion. I asked how he felt about the talk in many circles that Bashir could be the next president; the sheikh answered with a rundown of how he had founded the Phalange party. I asked if he thought Bashir could unify Lebanon as he had the Christians; Pierre Gemayel talked about his unification of the Christians under French rule. I looked at Alfred in amazement, but his face was blank; he was the compleat translator, nothing more.

The only time Sheikh Pierre mentioned his younger son was when I asked what Bashir had been like as a child. The old man paused, and then he said, "He was a naughty boy."

"Were you close?" I quickly asked.

"He used to follow me around the house. Wherever I went, he was underfoot. When he wasn't underfoot he was making trouble. I got reports. The phone would ring at night. Once," Pierre said, and a trace of animation came over his stony features, "I had six calls in one night. All complaints about Bashir, all from different places, far apart. When Bashir came home I called him to me.

" 'Did you do this?' I asked him. 'Yes,' he said. 'And this?' 'Yes.' 'And this?' Yes, yes, yes, to all of them." Sheikh Pierre sighed. "A naughty boy," he said.

Bashir's mother, Genevieve Gemayel, was first-cousin to her husband. She had been out when we arrived but came home two hours later. We sat in the living room, which was decorated with ornately carved wooden furniture and heavy fabrics. Genevieve Gemayel was short and stocky, dressed all in black, with gray hair pulled back in a bun and no makeup. But she had laughing eyes like her son and the same direct speech and intensity of gaze. Unlike Pierre, she openly adored her youngest child.

Bashir was close to his mother. He still called her "Mommy" and spoke to her every day. He had told me that his mother was his best friend in the family. Having met his brother and father, I could see his need for one. I asked Genevieve what Bashir had been like as a boy.

"Lonely," she said. "He missed his father. Once, when he was sick, I sat beside his bed, reading to him. All of a sudden he burst out: 'I wish my father was a mailman.' 'Why, Bashir?' I asked him. 'At least then he'd be home more,' he said."

"Your husband told me he was a hell-raiser," I said. Alfred translated. She laughed, and her eyes took on a warm glint of love.

"He was terrible. I had one friend he couldn't stand, and he used to hide under her chair and poke her with my knitting needles. Once, when he was really angry, he went

all through the house pulling electric wires out of their sockets."

He had too much energy, his mother said, and until he was well into his teens he could not control himself. But she understood him and helped him, and she always told him that he was destined to do important things.

"Bashir believes in destiny," I said.

"Of course." She shrugged and leaned toward me. "When Bashir was born, the doctor in Beirut looked at him and said, 'This boy is going to be very special.' From birth it was written."

The doctor was being kind to the wife of a powerful politician, I thought. Nothing is written. But because she chose to believe him, she had imbued Bashir with the belief as well.

"I've heard that Bashir didn't have many close friends," I said. "Why not?"

"What did he need friends for?" she asked me in amazement. "He had me."

I had to see Solange.

I dreaded the meeting. Bashir never said so, but I thought she must know about us, because so many people did. Bashir's secretary, Isis, was a close friend of hers.

11 Solange and their infant daughter Youmna were staying in a small house at the beach. We arranged to meet in a large group for dinner at a nearby restaurant—Bashir, Solange, Alfred Mady, myself, and several close friends and advisors of Bashir's whom I also needed to interview for the profile. I went early for a private talk with Solange.

We sat facing each other on a sofa in the cramped living room of the beach house. A large photo of Bashir sat on the coffee table. When I mentioned that it would be a good one to show Los Angeles producers, Solange held it out to me. "Here. Take it," she said.

But I couldn't. I already felt as if I were there on false premises.

The interview got off to a slow start. It was a stiflingly hot day. The back door was open to allow the ocean breeze in, but the room was still uncomfortable. Or at least I was; and so was Solange, who, though calm, did not look entirely unaffected.

Hiding behind my job, I launched into a series of questions, trying to act as if this interview were no different from any other. I asked Solange whether she took an active part in Bashir's work.

"He doesn't talk to me about business very much," she said. "Bashir always wants me to be home, to be able to give lunches for his friends whenever he wants. He calls and says ten people will be arriving in one hour for lunch, and I always have to be ready."

She worried about him all the time, she said, always fearing that something would happen to him.

As gently as I could, I led her to talk about Maya. Her composure faltered; she could not speak directly of the baby's death. "Afterward," she told me in a low voice, "Bashir was very good to me. He stayed with me every moment, and he told me we could have as many children as I wanted."

I looked down. I couldn't write. No questions came to me. That was when Solange in her sweet little girl's voice said, "Do you have to spend so much time with Bashir?"

I raised my head. Her face did not amplify. She waited for my answer. The heat in the room was getting to me. I stammered, "Yes, to do the film, I have to spend a lot of time with him."

Finally, the doorbell chimed and Solange ran to answer it. Bashir came in. A hush filled the house. She spoke to him in whispers. A few minutes later, a nurse came in holding the baby and placed her in Bashir's arms. He cooed to the infant and played with her for a few minutes, then the nurse took her away.

If Bashir felt strange about this meeting, he didn't show it. I felt like an intruder and duplicitous to boot, and it wasn't a feeling I was used to or liked. I couldn't wait to leave for the restaurant.

I knew that Bashir was irrevocably married. Solange was his childhood sweetheart, the mother of his children. She had suffered terribly on his account. He would never leave her, and we both understood that from the start. It was no one's fault but my own if I got hurt; but Solange was another matter.

She seemed to me a sweet woman cast in the Middle Eastern mold of womanhood, raised to be exactly what she was. She cared about clothes, about looking good, about her children and her family. She adored her husband and in no way saw herself as his equal. She thought that this was what he wanted her to be, and perhaps that is so.

A few minutes later we left for dinner at a restaurant on the beach. Colored lights were strung up, illuminating the area like the lights of a carnival. Now that the sun had gone down there was a delightful, cooling breeze from the sea. Bashir sat outside on the terrace with Alfred, Solange, and a few friends. I went inside with four or five of Bashir's advisors.

In the few months that I'd been away, Bashir's political standing had grown tremendously in Lebanon, even as it had in the United States. Consequently, after years of chronic shortfalls, Bashir's treasury was nearly full. The Lebanese Forces collected taxes at the Beirut port that they controlled and from the residents of East Beirut. Businessmen had also begun making voluntary contributions to Bashir's cause. Bashir had told me that he knew he was going to succeed when the business community began to court him. "Those people," he said, "are great survivors. They do it by betting on the winner years before governments know which end is up. Right now they're betting that we can bring the stability they need in order to make money."

The revenue went to paying for services normally provided by the state: civil services, defense, even the foreign ministry. The foreign offices of the Lebanese Forces had in many respects superseded the Foreign Ministry of Lebanon, and now had offices in the capitals of the United States and many European and Latin American countries.

With millions of dollars running through his treasury, Bashir was forced to turn to business advisors for help in administering the funds. One of my dinner companions was Bashir's financial aide.

"How do you like working with Bashir?" I asked him.

The man spread his hands, palms up. "Bashir tells us what he wants done. We say impossible. He says, 'Enough, that's it. I don't want to hear your problems, I just want results.' And somehow he always gets what he wants.

"He's killing us," the businessman said. "But we know he's our only hope for the future."

As soon as dinner was over, we went outside. Bashir looked at me with a smile. Solange was at his side. Without making a show of it, she was watching us closely.

"Did you enjoy your dinner, Barbara?" Bashir asked.

"Yes, I did," I said politely, holding out my hand. "Thank you for inviting me, Sheikh Bashir."

" 'Thank you for inviting me, Sheikh Bashir!' " he sputtered the next day, as soon as we found ourselves alone.

"Well, what was I supposed to do, kiss you good-night?"

Bashir laughed. I wondered what his wife had said about our interview, but I didn't like to ask. We were in a small office on the floor below his own office in the Lebanese Forces headquarters.

"I heard you made an interesting phone call earlier," Bashir said.

"There isn't much you don't know, is there?" I teased him.

"No," he said seriously.

While I waited for him to arrive, I had asked one of his

aides to get me a line to the United States. He dialed a number and handed me the phone. Feeling very daring, I called the private number of the Israeli press attaché in Washington, a friend of mine named Nachman Shai.

"*Shalom*, Nachman," I said. "It's Barbara. I bet you can't guess where I'm calling from." The aide rushed out of the room, looking sick to his stomach.

"I knew that guy would run to you," I told Bashir. "I was only kidding, you know. Did I commit a capital offense?"

"No," he answered, looking a bit abashed. "It's just that we have our own means of communicating with the Israelis. If you want to use it anytime, you may."

Bashir, I thought, was drawing closer to the Israelis all the time. I knew they were supplying his men with uniforms, weapons, and training. The day would come when Bashir would be asked to pay the piper, and I wondered what would happen then.

Then Bashir settled himself on the corner of the desk and a look of great though rather fearful anticipation came over his face.

"We didn't get a chance to talk about it yesterday," he said. "Tell me what my father said to you."

I gave him the gist, but he wasn't satisfied until he heard every word Sheikh Pierre had said. It was clear to me that although Bashir had overtaken his father politically, he was still boyishly hungry for his father's approval. He pointed to a picture of his father that hung on the wall. "Without that man," Bashir said, "I wouldn't be what I am today. He taught me everything."

That morning Bashir was scheduled to visit a Lebanese Forces training camp outside Beirut. We drove up there together, Bashir behind the wheel. As I studied his profile, I knew the time had come for a discussion I'd been postponing.

Several weeks before my trip to Lebanon, I was visited in Washington by a top Israeli official with close ties to Bashir. He had seen our "20/20" piece and praised it highly. But then he added, "There's a lot you don't know about Bashir Gemayel."

"Like what?" I said.

"Tony Franjieh," he said.

I remembered the name. Tony Franjieh was the son of Suleiman Franjieh, a former president of Lebanon and head of the powerful Franjieh clan. Tony was the leader of the family's militia. He had been assassinated in June of '78, together with his wife and daughter and a number of guards. Because the killing occurred at about the same time as the Syrians began shelling Christian East Beirut, the news of the young warlord's murder was quickly passed over by the American media.

"What about Franjieh?" I said.

"Bashir had him killed," the Israeli said. "He sent his men to Franjieh's summer home, where they slaughtered everything that moved, including the maid, the chauffeur, and the family dog."

"Bashir wouldn't have done that," I said calmly. "That's against everything he believes in."

"Everything he believes in *now*," he corrected me.

He words hung in the air long after he was gone. I discounted them, but they wouldn't go away. Why would the Israeli tell me this, I wondered, if it weren't true? What reason could he have? And despite myself, I connected the dots between the July 7 wipeout of Danny Chamoun's Tigers, the elevation of Elie Hobeika, and the assassination of Franjieh. The picture that emerged was of a young Christian warlord ruthlessly mowing down anyone who stood in his path.

But that was not the Bashir I knew; and I knew him, I believed, as well as anyone.

Now, as we drove together through the mountains, I recounted what the Israeli had told me. Bashir listened in silence, his face drawn and grim. And when I had done, he said tersely, "I didn't order Tony's death, much less his family's. You ought to have known that."

"Who did it?" I asked.

He was silent so long I began to think he would not answer.

"What you heard is partly true," he said at last. "Tony Franjieh had threatened my life, and he was killing my men. He was also deep in the drug trade, and you know how I feel about that.

"I warned him over and over that we would be condemned to live in this zoo forever unless we could rise above feudalism. We tried all the traditional channels of influencing him. Even the Maronite patriarch tried to make peace. The last straw was when they killed a Phalange leader, held the body, and refused to allow him a church burial."

"So you had him killed."

"*No.* We had intelligence that the killers of our men had taken refuge at Tony Franjieh's house, and that Tony and his family were away. I sent our troops to the family's summer house as a show of force and to arrest the killers of our men."

I said, "But when they found Franjieh there, why did they kill him if they didn't have orders to from you? And why did they kill his wife and a three-year-old baby and the maid? They're animals, whoever did that."

The car phone started to ring and Bashir grabbed at it, almost hitting himself with the force he used. He barked a few words into the receiver and hung up.

"Look," he said. "I don't know who is telling you these things. I didn't order Tony's killing and I didn't approve it after the fact, either. It's a perfect example of what's happening in Lebanon, and what will continue to happen on all sides, even by our boys, until we create peace and order and responsibility here." His voice was very calm, but the words flew out of his mouth. "You've seen the pictures of the bodies at Damour, the priests killed in their own churches, the women raped and mutilated. You've been to our orphanages and you've met our guys who've lost arms and legs and eyes. You've seen our women dressed in black, in mourning for the rest of their lives. And what did our friends in the West do? They offered us green cards.

"We are not emigrating," he said. "We have as much right to be here as any other Lebanese. It's the outsiders who've come into our country and disrupted our peace and started this savagery."

"You're justifying . . ."

"I'm not justifying anything. What our guys did to Franjieh was wrong. Look," Bashir said, "do you remember Geraldo's interview with the Syrian who admitted torturing el-Louzy to death? Geraldo asked him if he was a man or a beast, and he said, 'If a man is in a situation like a beast, he becomes a beast.' It's true—and that's what we are trying to stop."

I said, "Did you punish the ones responsible?"

"We have had our problems for a long time with the group that did this operation. They're an independent force and they're more loyal to their leader, Samir Geagea, than they are to us."

"Did you fire their leader?"

Bashir's eyes were steely. "He was wounded at the beginning of the operation. Our intelligence was bad and everything went wrong. Geagea's one of my best and bravest fighters. It's a problem to control him, but I can't afford to fire him. We need him and his men; we need every man willing to risk his life for the cause."

We drove on in silence for a while. Then I said, "'Why do the Israelis think you did it?"

"Because they gave me the green light to do it," he said fiercely, slowing the car and glaring at me. *"But I didn't,* because apart from everything else, it would have been stupid. The last thing you want to do in the Middle East is to kill the son of a headman, because then the blood feud goes on forever. During the July 7 operation, Danny Chamoun was in our hands, and we let him go."

I believed him because I knew him, and because his

explanation made sense. I had sensed all along, in the strength of Bashir's hold over his men, the necessity for that strength, and I knew that savagery evoked savagery. Since then, I've turned up an independent eyewitness to Bashir's briefing prior to the Franjieh operation. My informant was Charles Chartouni, then a friend of Samir Geagea and now one of his top aides.

"Bashir told us that Tony and his family would not be home," Chartouni told me. "He said to use whatever force we needed to arrest the guys who'd murdered our man. But what happened was that Franjieh's men didn't wait—they opened fire immediately, and Samir was wounded in the first round. After that our guys went wild. Bullets were flying everywhere, and it didn't stop until nothing in the house was moving. Bashir didn't order it," Chartouni repeated. "And when he found out, he was very, very angry."

On my last night in Lebanon, Bashir took me to an outdoor café for dinner. We met in his office at about ten P.M. I felt very sad to be leaving him, not knowing when I would see him again. I put my arms around him and laid my head against his chest.

"Don't go," he said, holding me.

"I have to. I have another story to do."

"Stay here. We need your help with our radio and television stations. You could make our amateurs into professionals."

I didn't say no right away. I thought about it. A very big part of me was tempted, and it wasn't my job that held me back, but Penny. Even so I began to think that perhaps I could stay in Beirut, going back frequently to be with her. Being here with Bashir made me realize how important it was to take my life into my own hands, because the future was never secure. But in my heart, I knew that to have Bashir I would have to give up my daughter. By that point, there was no other sacrifice I wouldn't have made for Bashir.

"I can't," I told him, and he nodded sadly and said, "I understand."

After that we went to eat, and later Bashir drove me back to my hotel and stayed for an hour or two. I let him think I was asleep as he gently kissed my forehead and started to leave. Then I called out to him urgently: "Bashir, wait. I don't want to go away. I'm frightened."

He came back and sat beside me on the bed. "What are you frightened of? That something will happen to you?"

"No—that something will happen to you, while I'm away."

"Barbara, I've told you before. I believe in destiny. What is meant to happen will happen."

"I love you," I said.

"I love you, too. You know that. This is your home, and we are your family. If you come here, we can take care of you. And you can bring your daughter, too."

I looked into his eyes and something very deep and very old welled up in me. I spoke without knowing what I was about to say. "Bashir," I said, "your enemies are my enemies."

His eyes were inexpressibly tender and sad. "You'll have a lot of enemies," he told me. Then he kissed me one more time and left.

The plane stopped in Jidda, Saudi Arabia, to pick up passengers and refuel. I stayed on board, nursing a bad cold I'd caught from Bashir and gazing about at the

heavily veiled women and robed men. When the passengers reboarded for the last leg of our flight, I noticed that I was the only white person aboard.

We arrived in Khartoum, the capital of the Sudan, long after dark. The plane rolled slowly down the runway of the tiny, rickety-looking Khartoum airport to a floodlit area where we came to rest. As I descended the stairs from the plane, a living wraith walked up to me, a giant: 6'5", swathed head to sandaled toe in flowing white robes, with coal-black face and hands. The huge white turban draped around his head gave him an extra five inches. Even in heels I barely reached his waist. I began to wonder if the fever from my cold was causing me to hallucinate. The apparition spoke. "Miss Bar-ba-ra?"

"Yes?"

The giant introduced himself. He worked for government security and had been sent to help me through airport customs and escort me to my hotel.

The road from the airport to Khartoum was unpaved. The Grand Hotel had been built by the British when the Sudan was a part of the British Empire. It was a graceful building with traditional colonial veranda and enormous, light, airy rooms. As soon as I got to my room, I hung a picture of Bashir on the wall. Looking at him gave me a sense of security.

I needed one. I was feeling very alone.

Since "The Unholy War," ABC had become noticeably less supportive of my proposals. When I first suggested a story on the surrogate war being played out by Libya and Chad on behalf of the U.S.S.R. and the U.S., Av Westin said in a voice of utter incredulity, "Chad? Who's going to care about Chad?"

Grudgingly, he allowed me to follow up anyway. I flew to Paris to meet with intelligence operatives working for a leading French magazine, *Jeune Afrique*. They gave me contacts deep within the Sudanese political and intelligence establishments, and helped flesh out my skeleton of a story with hard information on the workings beneath the surface of what appeared to be no more than a border skirmish.

The Chadian government had been overthrown by a Libyan-backed regime, which was also supported by the Soviet Union. The Chadian rebels against the new regime were supported not only by the United States, but also by Israel. Despite the formal break of ties following the 1967 Six-Day War, Israel had kept up good relations with most African countries, including Chad. Thus, when Libya took over Chad through a puppet regime, Israel was motivated by both its friendship with Chad and its enmity toward Libya to get involved. France, too, was monitoring the Chadian rebellion carefully, for it still had strong ties to its former colony. But it refrained from actively supporting the guerrillas because the guerrillas had, the previous year, kidnapped a female French anthropologist and held her for ransom.

I already had permission from the Sudanese government to enter the war zone on the border of Chad and the Sudan, to interview Hussein Habrè, leader of the mobile guerrilla forces of the Chadian rebels. Habrè was a bit of a rogue elephant: an intelligent, cultured man, a French-educated lawyer, he was also responsible for kidnapping the French anthropologist. I had wanted to take along an assistant, but Westin insisted that I go to Africa alone. When I was ready to film, he said, he would dispatch a crew to join me.

I had coordinated my visit with the government of Sudan, through its ambassador in Washington, Omar Eissa. Urbane and intelligent, Eissa was well connected; his brother was the personal physician to President Nimeiry of the Sudan. In addition to allowing me into the war zone, the Sudanese had also agreed to give me access to intelligence information and to defectors from the Libyan troops supporting the Chadian regime.

The government of Sudan was exceedingly efficient. The day after my arrival, I was told that a C-130 American-made army transport plane was ready to take me and my crew to the Chadian border, where Habrè was based. Despite Habrè's predilection for taking Western hostages, I was all ready to go; I knew the story was important, and so far it was all mine. I called ABC and asked for a crew. All the crews were busy now, they told me. During the next few days I kept calling, trying to reach Westin. I used the enforced delay to interview President Nimeiry and several Libyan defectors, who gave me fantastic information. One of these defectors was Mohammad Mugarieff, who recently led a coup attempt against Libyan ruler Qadaffi—but that is a different story.

The Chad-Sudan frontier kept heating up. The Sudan shot down a few Libyan planes that had been strafing Sudanese territory in hopes of hitting the rebel forces. A

Bashir at military exercises of the Lebanese Forces.

Bashir with Arzi Gemayel, his favorite sister, at the Convent of the Cross in Deir el-Salib, north of Beirut.

Moments before his death, Bashir mounts the steps of the Phalange headquarters in Ashrafiyeh.

September 15, 1982. Bashir's soldiers cling to his coffin as he lies in state in East Beirut.

A view of the Bekáa Valley.

An aerial shot of Zahle, capital of the Bekáa Valley and headquarters for Elie Hobeika's dissident Christian forces.

Barbara Newman with Pierre Yazbeck, filming in the Bekáa, overlooking the terrorist stronghold in Baalbek.

The Roman ruins at Anjar, now a bastion of Syrian intelligence and Kurdish terrorists.

Elie Hobeika and his bodyguard, code-named Cobra, watching an Israeli surveillance plane flying near the Syrian border in the Bekáa.

This marijuana in the Bekáa will ultimately be sold to finance terrorist activities. Lebanon's hashish is said to be the most potent in the world.

**Interviewing Hobeika in his
heavily fortified stone bunker in Zahle.**

Syrian hegemony in Beirut today is vividly exemplified by this scene of a Beiruti ordered by a Syrian soldier to deface a poster of the Ayatollah Khomeini.

series of guerrilla clashes between the Libyans and the Chad rebels were reported in the international press. Such incidents draw reporters like honey draws bees. I still had the inside beat, but I could feel the hot breath of competition on my neck. I kept trying to get a crew. Finally, some two weeks after I arrived in Africa, a crew was sent from Paris. But when they heard that we were going to the front, they turned around and went back to France: too dangerous, they said. Many more frantic calls to ABC at last produced a second crew. This crew was less worried about the fighting than about their health. When I could not guarantee them an adequate supply of bottled water, they too departed.

Meanwhile, the news organizations in America had begun to report that a war was imminent between the Sudan and Libya over the Sudan's support of Habrè. I knew from the high-level Libyan defectors I'd interviewed that this story was a red herring. Libya had no intention of attacking the Sudan; the only war in the area was the one I was trying unsuccessfully to cover; the clandestine, undeclared guerrilla war between Habrè's commandos and Chadian government troops with their Libyan allies.

After more than a week, I finally got through to Westin. I told him that the rumors of war between Libya and the Sudan were off the wall. He brushed that aside and told me that the "Nightline" program was sending over a correspondent and a crew to cover the expected flare-up between Libya and the Sudan.

"What about my crew?" I said.

"And since you're over there," Westin continued as if he had not heard, "you'll produce the report for 'Nightline.' "

"What report?" I yelled. "It's a nonstory."

"Don't embarrass me," Westin warned.

The "Nightline" crew and correspondent arrived. Our collaboration lasted one day. When I saw that they were bent on making something out of nothing, I blew up. "This is the stupidest report I've ever heard," I yelled at the correspondent. "We're covering the wrong goddamn story!" More calls to New York, and again I was overruled. But this time, I refused to play along. "Nightline" had to send another producer to do their story.

The rumor of war remained a rumor. The expected war never materialized. "Nightline" aired its story, which was instantly forgotten. But my mutiny was remembered.

ABC finally sent a third crew, this one from Cairo, for my Habrè story. But by this time, CNN and other correspondents had gotten into the war zone ahead of us. What started out to be a world-class story, an ABC exclusive, was lost. The real story about this surrogate war in Africa would not be told until several years later.

It was the last straw for me and ABC. I was finished there and I knew it. Bashir had asked me to return to Beirut before I went back to the United States, and I had half-promised to do so. But now I needed to clarify my position at the network. I went straight from Kennedy Airport to ABC's offices.

It didn't take long. As soon as I walked in the door, Av Westin said, "You embarrassed me."

"You let a great story die," I retorted.

"We're not going to renew your contract."

"I think that's best."

He glared at me. "Clear out your desk by the end of the day," he said.

"I don't have a desk," I told him, and with that I left Westin and ABC.

I took the next flight to Washington. I couldn't wait to tell Penny. "Guess what," I said, the moment I saw her. "No more traveling. No more ABC. You've got a mom again."

First she was speechless. Then, looking very confused, she said, "What do you mean?"

"I left ABC. I'm not going to be traveling so much anymore. I'm going to stay right here, and we can be together, just like we always talked about. I'll be here when you get up in the morning, I'll help you with your homework, and I'll tuck you in at night."

"But how will we live?" asked my daughter, practical beyond her years.

"Don't worry," I said. "I'll still be paid by ABC for a few months and meanwhile I'll find a different job. We won't starve." My firing had not exactly come as a surprise; the writing had been on the wall ever since my colleagues lined up against "The Unholy War." In the back of my mind was the idea of working on Capitol Hill as an investigator. Many of my friends were there, the work was interesting, and best of all, as far as Penny was concerned, there would be no traveling.

Finally the news sank in. Penny whooped and gave me a big hug and kiss. Within a few days, I began in that late fall of 1981 to work for the Senate Judiciary Committee as an investigator. My mandate was to dig up interesting subjects for investigations within the Justice Department. Since I had always done my own research as a television producer, this job was very easy for me, involving just one small aspect of what I used to do routinely to put a piece together. Best of all, the day ended at five—not A.M., but P.M.

It was an ideal job. I should have been delighted.

But I wasn't.

I missed Bashir. I missed journalism. Life felt just a little flat, a little too safe. I was restless and lonely.

I put photographs of Bashir all over my house. Two were on the dressing table beside my bed. In the den I hung a poster, and in the living room I placed an enlarged snapshot in a silver frame on the mantle of the fireplace, beside a picture of Penny. People who visited my house said it looked like a shrine, but I didn't care. I needed his presence.

It was during this season of discontent that Jack Anderson and I became friends. I liked Anderson as soon as I met him. He was irreverent and self-confident, and one hell of a reporter. His column, which he had inherited from Drew Pearson, was published in eight hundred newspapers in the United States and around the world, far more than any other journalist.

A reporter since the age of twelve, Anderson has contacts everywhere, and there wasn't a major story in the 1970s that he didn't have a hand in breaking. He had won the Pulitzer Prize for his reporting on Henry Kissinger's foreign policy. At heart, he is a muckraker and a loner who dislikes the Washington establishment. Tall and imposing, with a massive head of white hair, Anderson pursues his own brand of journalism, skewering the powerful and championing the underdog.

During the Watergate years, the Nixon administration had instigated Project Mud Hen, an FBI investigation of Anderson. The surveillance was so shoddy that Anderson's nine children could easily spot the FBI agents sitting in their cars and would often go out to offer them cups of coffee.

Anderson was planning an investigative television show, one that would get behind the headlines to show the news from the inside. One cold day in December 1981, we sat together in his office in a Washington townhouse that had once been the most select brothel in the nation's capital. As I gazed out the window at the White House, Jack offered me the job of producer.

Before accepting, I talked it over with Penny. "It would mean less money and more traveling, though probably less than I had with ABC," I said. "That's really why we need to discuss it. I haven't forgotten my promise to you when I left ABC."

"But you really want to do it," Penny said.

"Yes," I said. "I really want to do it."

I saw her struggle. She suppressed a sigh and put on a smile and gamely said, "Sounds like a great job, Mom. Go for it."

I kissed her and called Jack to accept.

It was a grand partnership. Jack and I had the same approach to the news. We wanted a sparkling program that didn't imitate the networks, and did what they could not. We wanted a show that would reflect our own deep concerns, dig deep enough to show how things really worked, and present stories that the public couldn't see elsewhere.

Within several months we started with a terrific station lineup: eighty stations located in all the major markets. The budget for the show was so low, about $50,000 a week, that I couldn't afford to hire anyone with television experience. I used Jack's print reporters and did most of the work myself.

Bashir and I spoke on the phone several times a week. Because his phone was monitored, we had to avoid talking about anything personal or sensitive. Bashir was now being courted seriously by the United States, an exciting but demanding suitor; and he was growing particularly close to Philip Habib (whom Reagan had sent to the region as U.S. ambassador plenipotentiary). I could hear in his voice that he wanted to talk about this to me but couldn't.

It was frustrating, and I badly missed seeing him. In January of 1982, I took a few days off from my preparations for the new show and flew to the Middle East.

I found Bashir changed. He was thinner and he dressed more carefully, frequently wearing suits and ties. He had also begun to moderate his words. It was unsettling. At dinner the first night, I asked him, "Are events moving too fast for you? Are you losing control?"

"No," he said, looking very determined. "They can't move fast enough." Spoken, I thought with a shiver, as if he felt he was running out of time.

There was a quiet about him like the proverbial calm in the center of a storm. Everyone in Lebanon was predicting a cataclysm in the region. The country had been too unstable for too long, and Israel was crouched at the border like a panther waiting to spring at the throats of the Palestinians. The upcoming presidential elections in Lebanon could well unleash that force.

The Americans, who favored Bashir for president, kept warning him to keep his distance from Israel lest he permanently alienate Lebanon's Moslems. Bashir was caught in a bind. He coveted the political support of the Americans, but he also needed Israel's military backing to stave off the threat of Syrian-Palestinian hegemony over Lebanon.

"Israel's going to invade," he told me. "It's a question of when, not if."

"Uh huh," I answered skeptically.

Bashir lowered his voice. "Sharon himself told me."

"That's nice. Has he told his government yet?" Arik Sharon was the Israeli Minister of Defense.

"What Arik wants," Bashir said, not without admiration, "Arik gets."

Bashir was utterly confident in his ability to take advantage of the coming events. He had already started planning for the election, which he insisted he would win democratically and not, as some of his advisors were suggesting, through a coup by the powerful Lebanese Forces. Winning the election was going to take some doing, because it was expected that many Moslems would boycott the election in order to deny him a quorum. Bashir had started to court votes and to change his image.

"Bashir," I asked when we were alone, "are you becoming a politician like all the others?"

"No," he said. "But I don't feel the same necessity all the time to defend our cause. Many more people understand now why we're fighting."

"You mean you're getting what you want, so now you feel more secure?"

"It's not a matter of feeling; we *are* more secure now. Finally, we can plan for the future instead of fighting every moment for our lives." Bashir looked at me intently. "Once I'm elected, I'm going to invite all of the Lebanese living outside the country to come back and help in the reconstruction."

"Even the ones you called traitors? Even your enemies?"

"Especially them," he said. "I will offer them amnesty. We need their help to repair the damage here."

"You know, Bashir, if you become president, you will have less power than you do today."

"That's fine," he said. "Our goal is not to solidify the power of Bashir Gemayel; it's to set up institutions that work and a sense of continuity, so that everything doesn't depend on one single man."

I laughed incredulously. "Do you know the saying that power corrupts, and absolute power corrupts absolutely?"

A big grin came over his face. "I will not become corrupt, because I'll always have you to keep me in line."

We laughed and I kissed him, and for one brief moment I had a vision of the two of us continuing on into a shadowless future, a future limited only by our mortality. And with that fleeting vision came the certainty that if such a future could be mine, I would willingly forsake all alternatives.

My visit was too short, whetting a thirst it could not satisfy; but I had to get back to work.

We wanted to open the show, which was to be called "Jack Anderson Confidential," with a real blockbuster. We had a lot of good stories in the pipeline. To demonstrate the lack of safeguards against terrorism, we planned to hire a helicopter and fly over facilities where nuclear bombs were assembled. We shot an exposé of Special Operations and CIA drug experiments on unwitting civilian guinea pigs; and we filmed the first piece uncovering the Bhagwan Shree Rajneesh cult in Oregon. Another story we planned to cover was sexual harassment in the Pentagon.

But good as they were individually, none of these stories had the power and urgency we wanted for our first show. As we cast about for something earthshaking, an event took place that made our decision easy.

Israel invaded Lebanon.

Bashir had predicted it, but I hadn't believed him.

On June 6, 1982, Israeli troops streamed into Lebanon. It wasn't the first time. Over the years, elite Israeli units  had often crossed the northern border in retaliatory raids against the PLO. But this was different. Now the whole Israeli army had been mobilized in an all-out war against the PLO. Tens of thousands of Israeli troops poured into Lebanon, fighting their way northward toward Beirut.

The immediate provocation had been the attempted assassination of the Israeli ambassador to England, Shlomo Argov. Argov was shot in the head on June 3, 1982, as he left the Dorchester Hotel in London following a banquet. One of his attackers was wounded and captured by a British security man. Israeli intelligence quickly concluded, largely on the basis of the weapon used, that the would-be assassins—Argov survived the attack—were probably from the rejectionist Abu Nidal terrorist group, a bitter rival of Arafat's Al Fatah. When this was brought out in an emergency cabinet meeting in Jerusalem, Israeli Prime Minister Menachem Begin reportedly shrugged off the distinction, saying, "Abu Nidal, Abu Shmidal, they're all PLO."

In retrospect it seems clear that Begin seized on this opportunity to do what he was already convinced needed to be done for the security of Israel's northern border settlements and the Christian population in Lebanon. The attack on Argov had also played directly into the plan of Israeli Defense Minister Arik Sharon.

Bashir told me that Sharon had been frustrated by the failure of Israel's repeated small-scale incursions into Lebanon, particularly the Litani Operation of March 1978. During that limited operation, Israeli forces succeeded in clearing PLO guerrilla bases out of southern Lebanon up to the Litani River. But no sooner had Israel left the region than PLO fighters began trickling back in. The U.N. forces stationed in southern Lebanon were useless against this kind of infiltration, and there were cases in which members of the U.N. force had actually supplied the PLO with intelligence. Lebanese Major Saad Haddad, Israel's ally in the border area, found it impossible to keep the PLO out.

Bashir said that Sharon wanted a government in Beirut willing and able to make peace with Israel and to expel the Palestinian fighters from Lebanon. Bashir thought that his unification of the Christians in 1980 had convinced Sharon that Bashir was the man to do it. But Bashir had always maintained to anyone who would listen that Lebanon's real enemy was not the PLO but Syria. In fact, in April 1982, when Israeli plans for a war in Lebanon were well advanced, he shocked a few high-ranking Israeli officers when he told them, "If you don't intend to take on the Syrians, don't come." (This was a divergent opinion from that held by the Israeli political leadership, which supported only a limited incursion of some 25 miles.)

As early as a year before Israel invaded, Bashir told me that they would enter Lebanon to engage in a full-scale war. "One day," he said, "you will see Israeli troops on the streets of Beirut. Sharon wants me to be president of Lebanon, and he'll go as far as he has to to make that possible."

I never spoke to Sharon about this, but my good friends Israeli military correspondent Ze'ev Schiff and Ehud Ya'ari, Middle East affairs correspondent for Israel Television, wrote in their book, *Israel's Lebanon War*, that Sharon shared Bashir's view. They quote Sharon saying to political activists of his Likud party that, "Israel's objective is to see to it that Lebanon becomes an independent state that will live with us in peace and be an integral part of the free world, as well as to solve the problem of the Syrian presence in that country. . . . And a government of that kind cannot come into being as long as the terrorists control southern Lebanon and two-thirds of the city of Beirut and as long as the Syrians control whole sections of Lebanon. In other words, it is impossible to deal with this subject without taking care of the Syrians."

This was Bashir's very thesis, and the Schiff-Ya'ari account squares with what Bashir told me about Sharon's intentions long before the invasion. Despite Sharon's denial of any plan to meddle with Lebanese politics, Schiff and Ya'ari quote him in a speech to military personnel saying that, "to establish a government of that kind, you need sixty-six out of the ninety deputies to the Lebanese Parliament, and a list of deputies will be prepared."

Schiff and Ya'ari assert that Sharon's ultimate goals were to establish "a new political order" with Bashir at the helm in Beirut and to drive the PLO out of Lebanon and into "a gilded cage" in Damascus. That accomplished, the Palestinians in the Israeli-occupied West Bank and Gaza Strip would be orphaned, and moderate Palestinians would be able to accept Israel's terms for peaceful coexistence (or, more precisely, would be unable to reject such terms.) "Sharon explained to his aides," Schiff and Ya'ari write, "that in his estimation, a successful operation in Lebanon would ensure unchallenged Israeli superiority for thirty years to come. . . ."

It's not known to what extent Sharon shared these ideas with Prime Minister Begin. It is clear, however, that Begin's commitment to the Maronites sprang from his own identification of the embattled Christian minority with the Jews of Europe under the Nazis. That he saw the PLO as Nazi equivalents is obvious from his rhetoric. But it appears that he, along with the rest of the Israeli political leadership, initially supported only a small-scale war in Lebanon; in fact, Begin told U.S. Ambassador Habib that he expected it to last only seventy-two hours.

The issue of the war's goals and the Israeli objectives became intensely controversial in both the United States and Israel. I never understood why, because it seemed to me that Israel's intentions had been a very open secret. In the early spring of 1982, several months before the Israeli invasion, I helped Alfred Mady, as Bashir's representative, to meet with the high-powered, politically connected public relations firm of Gray and Company. Bashir had decided to improve his image in the United States. Neil Livingstone, a vice-president on Gray's international staff, attended the meeting and later told me what happened. When asked why the Lebanese Forces needed help, Alfred's answer was that very soon Israel would invade Lebanon and Bashir Gemayel would become president.

As soon as I heard about the invasion, I called Bashir.

"Bashir," I almost shouted at him, "I can't believe it's happening!"

"I told you it would," he said. "Didn't you believe me?"

"How far will the Israelis go?" I asked.

"As far as they have to," was the cryptic reply.

"We're coming over," I told him. "We've decided to

make the first show of 'Jack Anderson Confidential' a report on the Middle East. I'll see you within a month."

But first, early in August, Jack and I flew to Israel.

I had never been there in the midst of a large-scale war. My friends looked harried and unshaven, as if they hadn't slept in weeks. There was a frenetic pace and a sense of insecurity; by July, Beirut was under siege. Israeli troops had surrounded the city and Israeli artillery was bombarding Moslem West Beirut in an effort to persuade the Palestinian fighters to leave.

Close to a year before the invasion, Bashir had told me that when it came, he expected to link his troops with the Israelis, and that the Lebanese Forces would attack the PLO fighters in West Beirut. According to Schiff and Ya'ari and other published reports, Sharon had banked heavily on his promise to do so, for he knew that the Israeli public and the cabinet, which was already bitterly divided over this war, would not abide the kind of casualties that would inevitably result from hand-to-hand fighting in the close quarters of West Beirut.

Israel had brokered Bashir's new, close relationship with the United States, but now that the match was made, the matchmaker felt left out in the cold. Since the spring of 1982, Israeli-U.S. relations had become frosty. Although Israel and the United States had the same strategic goals, they also had tactical differences in their approach to the Middle East. The United States envisioned Lebanon under Bashir as a pro-West Arab nation, a moderate counterweight to the pressure of the pro-Soviet revolutionary regimes surrounding it. They cautioned Bashir against siding actively with Israel during the fighting; if he did that, they said, he would cast himself as just another Christian warlord and thereby ruin his chance of uniting Lebanon under his leadership. Lebanon was part of the Arab world, the Americans argued, and Bashir, if he became president, would be president of an Arab country. The United States warned him that they would not support his presidential bid if he unleashed his forces against his fellow Arabs.

Reluctantly, Bashir heeded this advice and resisted strong, almost unremitting Israeli pressure to bring his troops into the fray. Official Israel was divided on the subject of Bashir. The Mossad, the army brass, and especially Arik Sharon supported him; but Israeli military intelligence campaigned actively against Bashir. The Israelis we met, some of whom had supported Bashir in the past, viewed his refusal to fight with them as a betrayal. I was surprised that they had so badly misread the implications of Bashir's relationship with the Americans.

One who expressed anger at Bashir was my old friend Rafi Eitan, the prime minister's advisor on terrorism, who had been so helpful when I was working on "The Unholy War." Jack and I had dinner at a Chinese restaurant in Tel Aviv with Rafi, his wife Miriam, and Uri Dan. Dan, whom I had met on my first trip to Israel, was a journalist, and a confidant and press advisor to Arik Sharon. At the dinner, Rafi aired his misgivings about Bashir.

"From all I've read in the reports of military intelligence, Bashir is not reliable, and he's not a good candidate for Israel to back. He should be the strongman, the power behind the scenes. He should not be president."

"Why do you say that?" I asked. "Bashir is the only one capable of bringing peace to Lebanon; he's the only one with the integrity and vision to create a strong Lebanon. He's not corrupt like all the others."

Rafi looked utterly spent. He took off his glasses and rubbed his eyes. "He will never be accepted by the Moslems," he said flatly. "He will divide us from the Shiites just as we are starting to have good relations with them."

Rafi was spending most of his time in southern Lebanon, working to develop Israel's relationship with the moderate Shiite Moslems of the Amal party, who had at first welcomed the Israeli invasion. The past ten years, during which the PLO turned southern Lebanon into a staging ground for attacks on Israel, had taken a bitter toll on the area's residents. The PLO had terrorized the Shiite population, taking over their homes and displacing the population, many of whom fled to crowded refugee camps in the southern suburbs of West Beirut. Rafi believed that the Shiites would be better allies for Israel than the Maronites and Bashir.

"They will accept him eventually," I said vehemently. "You don't understand him. He has plans for an amnesty; he's going to bring back all the leaders in exile, Christian and Moslem."

Rafi curled his lip. "The Christians are not allies for us. Let me tell you something about the Christians. They are very, very, very good-looking."

"Oh, come on, Rafi."

"Tell me one time they ever fought effectively. Tell me one thing they have ever done in their own interest without us."

"I don't know about that," I said. "But I know Bashir, and you're wrong about him. The Americans are putting a lot of pressure on him to distance himself from Israel, and he's feeling his way. Personally, I don't think the Americans understand the region too well, and they've bitten off more than they can chew. But Bashir isn't rigid. He'll see how things are going."

"I see that you like him too much," Uri Dan piped in suddenly. He had listened quietly until now. After that there was nothing more I could say. Both Rafi Eitan and Uri Dan were long-standing friends of Arik Sharon. It worried me to see Rafi so skeptical about Bashir, so mistrustful of his character. A coldness came over me in that hot, crowded restaurant, and I wondered if Bashir was courting disaster.

The next night we drove to the Negev to interview Minister of Defense Arik Sharon on his desert ranch, which was cordoned off and guarded by haggard young soldiers. The pitch blackness was broken by wires of electric light bulbs strung on poles outside the house. When Uri Dan introduced me to Arik Sharon, Sharon shook my hand and stared fixedly into my eyes for a full minute, as if he were trying to X-ray my character. I returned his gaze. Finally, he removed his eyes from my face and asked us into the dining room to start the interview.

Tall and obese, Sharon sweated heavily under the television lights; nonetheless he exuded enormous self-confidence. As a general in the Southern Command, Sharon was considered even by his political enemies to be one of the most brilliant commanders in Israeli history. He was also a maverick who refused to follow orders he didn't agree with, a practice that his critics say he carried over when he left the army to take up a political career.

Sharon had come to the United States several months earlier to brief Secretary of State Alexander Haig on Lebanon. Press reports stated that the Israeli Defense Minister warned Haig that Israel would no longer allow the PLO to use Lebanon as a staging ground for forays into Israel, and Haig approved a limited operation designed to eliminate the PLO from a narrow belt along Israel's border.

Sharon told us that the invasion was to protect his country's northern settlements from bombardment by the PLO. Israel, he said, was not interested in interfering in internal Lebanese affairs, only in securing its own border.

After the interview, which took about an hour, Sharon invited us into his living room for coffee and cake. His wife (the sister of his first wife, who was killed in a car crash) served us from a table so low she had to kneel down beside it. Although this is a traditional Middle Eastern practice, it embarrassed me that we were all seated on a sofa while she was on her knees.

Early the next morning, we left for Beirut. For the first time, I was able to drive directly there instead of flying via Cairo or Greece. The Israeli Foreign Ministry rented a black Cadillac stretch limousine for us. We were driven by an Israeli soldier and accompanied by an army liaison officer, a businessman in civilian life who had recently been called up to reserve duty. Another member of our entourage was a colonel who was an expert on the Shiite population; he, too, was a civilian, a professor at Tel Aviv University's Center for Strategic Studies.

The Shiites, our guide explained, were a branch of Islam regarded as heretical by the majority Sunni Moslems. The schism dates back to 661 A.D., when Ali, the son-in-law of the Prophet Mohammad, was assassinated in a power struggle over succession. The Shiites (or Shi'a, literally *followers of Ali*) were for many years a disadvantaged minority under Lebanon's unwritten power-sharing formula, which allocated to them little political power and almost no economic strongholds.

Recently, however, the Shiite population in Lebanon had grown to exceed that of the Sunni Moslems. When, in 1979, the Ayatollah Ruhollah Khomeini ousted the Shah of Iran and established a Shiite theocracy, the Shiites of southern Lebanon, already roused by the incursions of the PLO, woke to full political consciousness. But, as everywhere in Lebanon, the newly politicized bloc quickly splintered. There were now two main parties and accompanying militias: the moderate Amal, with which Israel was trying to reach an understanding; and Hezbollah, which advocates worldwide Khomeini-style Islamic revolution and theocracy.

Our car, though large, was not air-conditioned. The August heat was sweltering. I sat in the back between Jack and Dale Van Atta, one of Jack's associates on his column. A large man, Dale sweated so profusely that he had to mop his face periodically with a towel. Each time he did, his elbow poked me in the ribs.

We followed the same route northward along the Mediterranean that the Israeli army had taken a few weeks earlier, but to my surprise there was little sign of their passage. Everything seemed so peaceful. With the sparkling sea on one side and groves of cypress, olive trees, and orange orchards heavy with fruit on the other, the countryside was exquisite. Occasionally through our open windows we heard the bleating of sheep as they grazed. Passersby stared expressionlessly at our huge car with its Israeli plates. We passed graffiti written in black paint on white stones; "Welcome Israeli liberators," they said, in English and Arabic, but our Israeli professor-guide predicted that the Shiites would soon turn against Israel. "No invading army is welcome after a certain period of time," he told us. "The PLO treated the Shiites brutally, so now they welcome us. But this will pass and we are bound to inherit their antagonism. This war is going to turn them against us, and they will be our enemies."

But on the surface there was peace in the area and the people were content. Bashir was about to be elected president. I knew his plans to unify the country and to bind the wounds of the long civil war. I thought the professor was being unduly pessimistic.

We stopped in two seaside cities, Sidon and Tyre, to take pictures and interview local officials. Before the Israeli invasion, this had been a bastion of PLO activity; now, near the ancient port of Sidon, I saw dozens of posters of Bashir lining the streets.

As we continued northward up the coastal road, we came to a bombed-out shell of a town. Huge craters had been blasted through foot-thick stone walls by Israeli gunboats that still patrolled the harbor. Great piles of rubble littered the streets.

"Where are we?" I asked our young driver.

"Damour," he answered grimly.

Damour. I'd heard the name a hundred times or more. I heard it now in Bashir's voice, tinged with bitterness: Damour. Images flooded back. Once again I saw the survivors of massacres lined up at the door of my hotel room in Beirut, clutching worn photograph albums and boxfuls of sickening pictures. Here in Damour, before Bashir created the Lebanese Forces, 10,000 Christians had been butchered while the Lebanese authorities and army sat on their collective hands. Here, priests had been murdered, women raped, children slaughtered like calves and their bodies carelessly piled in heaps. Thirty thousand survivors were then forced out of Damour through the very port that Israeli gunships now patrolled. When the PLO took over Damour, they transformed this once vibrant city into an armed camp and set up a sophisticated training facility, complete with radar and an ammunition depot, in the heart of the city.

I asked the driver to stop and let us out, so Jack and I could walk inside the city.

"No," the driver said flatly. "It's not safe." Our army liaison officer supported him; the city had only just been cleared of PLO fighters, he said, but there were still booby traps and live mines around.

We persisted, and at last, reluctantly, they agreed. Jack and I walked silently up a hill toward a deserted church. The cross on the steeple made a plaintive sight, silhouetted against the barren landscape. Had I seen this church in the pictures?

Looking through the rubble in the center of town, we soon found signs of panicked flight: food left on plates, clothing and toys strewn about. In the area the PLO had made their own, we found among the debris mementos of the terrorists, including license plates from all over Europe, passports in one name from several different countries, street maps of European capitals on which red markings had been drawn, and coded notebooks. Several of the rooms had obviously served as barracks, with four or five mattresses to a room. From a journalist's point of view, it was a treasure trove; but as I walked through the ruined buildings, my mind played tricks on me. I thought

I heard people around each corner, speaking in excited Arabic, working, planning operations. . . .

Jack and I wanted to stay and film, but our escorts were growing increasingly agitated. "It's not safe," they kept telling us. "The whole place could go up. It hasn't been cleared." Still we lingered, turning over debris, looking for something I couldn't put my finger on. The place was ghost-ridden, a city whose agony was as layered as the dust beneath our feet.

From Damour it took only another hour to reach Beirut. There was almost no traffic on the coastal road, which was closed to all but Israeli army vehicles. We entered the  capital through the eastern suburbs. The city was buried under traffic.

Beirut's traffic had always been a problem, but now it was a nightmare. Israeli soldiers, jeeps, armored personnel carriers, and tanks crowded the streets. Israeli soldiers walked about looking wary but bewildered, obviously as amazed at being in Beirut as I was to see them. Other than the heavy presence of Israel, East Beirut bore no signs of the war being waged just beyond the Green Line.

We drove to the Israeli command post at Ba'abda, on the outskirts of East Beirut, near the Presidential Palace. The site had been well chosen; it overlooked the airport and three PLO refugee camps. Jack used the phone to telephone Yasir Arafat's press aide and received permission to interview Arafat almost as soon as he mentioned his name. The PLO had not been so accommodating when I was here with Geraldo, but Jack's reputation as the most widely syndicated columnist in the world was magic to the press-conscious PLO. Other reporters had waited for weeks to see him, without receiving even an acknowledgment of their requests for an interview.

In Israel, David Kimche and other people in the Foreign Ministry had warned me not to set foot in West Beirut. They said that I had been placed on an enemies list since "The Unholy War," and that if I went in, chances were that I would not get out alive. I decided to heed their warning and wait for Jack at our hotel in East Beirut.

The unfashionable Hotel Alexandre, long shunned in favor of the more accommodating Commodore Hotel, was now home to the entire Western press corps, which had been driven out of West Beirut by Israeli bombings. From a not-so-charming backwater inn it had turned into a swarming beehive. At the Alexandre, Jack found a taxi driver willing to make the hazardous trip into West Beirut for a hefty sum in American dollars, up front of course. Minutes after he left, Bashir called.

"Bashir," I said, "I can hardly believe what I'm seeing here. Israeli soldiers in Beirut!"

"Strange, isn't it?" he said. "The problem is, they may like it so much they won't want to go home."

"I doubt that. Bashir, we can only stay one day. We're scheduled to interview Begin in Israel tomorrow."

"Then we must make the best of the time," he said, his voice becoming very warm. "We will have dinner tonight. Naoum will arrange it." Naoum Farah was the chief of his de facto foreign ministry. "Do you mind if we eat in the office? My people don't want me to go to a restaurant with all the shelling going on."

"It doesn't matter," I said, "as long as I see you soon. Jack's gone to interview Arafat. I didn't go."

"I know."

"How do you know?"

"Because you're still here," he said. "You're still alive."

Jack came back from West Beirut deeply skeptical about Arafat. The PLO chairman had treated him to what Jack perceived as a set piece of political propaganda. He spoke vehemently against Israel, using a swagger stick for emphasis, but refused to stray outside the PLO orthodoxy. Jack was taken to a hospital to see children hurt in the Israeli bombing. When he asked Arafat, "Why do you put your headquarters right next to civilian dwellings?" Arafat pretended not to hear.

At dusk we went up to the roof of the Alexandre to film the Israeli bombing of West Beirut. As we watched, a number of F-16 fighter jets suddenly appeared streaking northward across the darkening sky, singly and in groups of two or three. We heard a faint whirring sound. As they approached, the planes emitted orange-red flares, decoys intended to attract the PLO's heat-seeking missiles. They came closer, and we saw them release missiles. The planes traveled incredibly fast; one moment they were dots against the southern sky, the next they were huge, menacing birds of war—swooping down upon the city, soaring up, and flying off.

The roof was crowded with Western press people, who for the most part watched in heavy silence as half the city burned. It was the worst kind of voyeurism, and I saw on the faces of my colleagues what I felt in my gut—a sense of horror and despair.

Not fear, though. At least not in my case. Although bombs were falling on the other side of town, East Beirut felt safe, or perhaps it was I myself who felt safe. In Israel I had heard about these optically guided missiles, considered ideal for urban areas because they were so precise they could level half a house and leave the other half standing. I knew the skill of the Israeli pilots. When I saw them traveling at such speed, it seemed impossible that they could distinguish one side of Beirut from another, much less one building from its neighbor.

But they did. With almost pinpoint accuracy, one by one the planes loosed their bombs on West Beirut, some no more than a mile from where we stood. We would hear a muffled thump, and someone would say, "There goes Shatila," or "That was Bourj el-Barajneh," or "They're going for PLO headquarters over in Fakahani now."

Although the planes were Israeli and we ourselves had witnessed their coming, it felt to me as if Beirut were exploding from within, like a pressure cooker kept too long on the fire. With every bomb that fell, people were dying almost at our feet, and for what? For the crime of being in the wrong place at the worst time, or of being too poor or too infirm or too hopeless to escape.

The shelling went on for about twenty minutes. When it was over, Jack and I went inside. We didn't talk on the way down from the roof. We went to the bar, and I ordered a glass of wine.

A few hours later, we were picked up by one of Bashir's drivers and driven to the Lebanese Forces headquarters in Qarantina, near the port. Naoum Farah was waiting for us in Bashir's office, but Bashir was at a meeting down the hall. After a few minutes I heard his familiar rapid step. He strode in, went straight to Jack, and shook his hand. He thanked him for a column Jack had written back in Washington, supporting Bashir's candidacy as the best hope for Lebanon. By coincidence it had appeared that very day in the *Washington Post* and several hundred other papers.

Then he turned to me. "Welcome home," he said, and kissed me on the mouth. It surprised me that he would, in front of Jack.

We had dinner at the same table at which Bashir and I had shared so many meals in the past. He sat at one end, with Jack and Naoum on his right and me on his left. Jack asked how his campaign was going.

"The conditions are not ideal," Bashir said. "But the time is right."

"I hear you're going to be president soon."

"It's difficult," Bashir said. "The members of Parliament are very establishment people, and I am not like them."

"I don't understand," Jack said. "You come from a leading family yourself, don't you?"

"But I'm nothing like our politicians." Bashir looked down at himself ruefully. "Their ties match their shirts, and their belts match their shoes, and their handkerchiefs match their socks. And they are very good at small talk. It's hard for me," he said.

"Bashir," I put in, "is it true what the Israelis told us? They said that when the French foreign minister called to ask if you needed help, you told him, 'No, don't send your troops to visit our whorehouses. We'll send ours to visit yours'?"

"Yes, I did," said Bashir in a lilting voice, like a schoolboy owning up to an infraction and challenging you to make something of it.

Jack, sometimes a little prudish, looked down at his food.

"The Israelis are angry with you," I told Bashir, abruptly I realized, but there was no time for tact. "They say you don't keep your deals."

"I always keep my deals," he said curtly, and it was clear that he wanted no more on the subject.

Bashir ate almost nothing. The old Bashir would have devoured his food with gusto. I asked him if he was feeling all right.

"Food is bad," he said, toying with a fork that in the old days would have been otherwise engaged.

"You've lost enough weight. You're going to get sick."

He made no reply. When I looked at him closely, I saw that he had aged over the past few months. He had lost so much weight that his watch flapped around his wrist and his wedding band kept falling down his finger. There were deep, dark circles under his eyes and crow's-feet etched at the corners. Although his hair had been cut very short, some gray was beginning to show at the temples. But one thing about him was unchanged: his luminous, burning eyes.

Jack asked about his agenda, if he was elected.

Bashir spread his hands. "Mr. Anderson, we have been fighting so long that we have forgotten how to live in peace. We must first teach our people how to live in peace with one another."

"How?" Jack said.

Bashir leaned toward him. "We are going to end feudalism in Lebanon, in the army and all the other institutions. We are going to establish institutions that function for the people, not for themselves. And we are going to remove terrorism from Lebanon. We will no longer be a base for terrorist attacks all over the world. Lebanon will be free."

"What about the Palestinians in Lebanon?"

"I pity the Palestinians," Bashir said, his eyes burning. "They are the victims of their own leaders and the Arab countries who perpetuate their misery and use them as pawns. But we are victims, too, and Lebanon is my first concern. Look," Bashir said. "When the PLO caused trouble in Jordan, King Hussein kicked them out. When they made trouble in Egypt, Sadat got rid of them. Then they came here, and they found a weak country, with an archaic structure of government by clan. They were able to divide the country on sectarian lines. Because people did not have a well-developed sense of nationality, the minorities, stirred up by outside forces, fought among themselves, as if they forgot that they were all Lebanese."

"But what are you going to do about the Palestinians?" Jack persisted.

"We have to solve that with the rest of the Arab nations, and I don't think anyone wants them. They are not," he said, "the best guests or neighbors. When Mr. Carter talks about a Palestinian homeland, I don't think he means Plains, Georgia."

"Would you kick them all out?"

"Those who wish to live in peace under Lebanese rule," said Bashir, "may stay. But their fighters must go, down to the last soldier. The PLO must move on to another station. It's over for them in Lebanon."

"That's a pretty big agenda," Jack said.

"We have no other choice," said Bashir. "Look," he said. "Last week I went to Saudi Arabia. I was invited by the king. He said, 'Bashir, we're with you; we will make you president. We'll get our people in parliament to vote for you. All we want in return is one small concession. Let fifty, just fifty Palestinian fighters remain, to allow the PLO to save face.'"

Bashir chopped the air with his hand. "'No,' I told him, 'not one will stay. And I will be president without your help.'"

It was nearly eleven by the time Jack and I left the office. We arranged to interview Bashir at eight the next morning, since we had to leave for Israel that afternoon for our interview with Begin. Bashir and I had no time to talk privately during the dinner. As soon as we arrived back at the hotel, I called him from the lobby.

"I'll pick you up in fifteen minutes," he said. "Would you mind waiting in front of the hotel? I can't go inside."

I ran upstairs to change into a dress, then hurried back down to the lobby. I hoped to slip out of the hotel unnoticed; instead, I ran right into Jack Anderson, deep in conversation with NBC's John Chancellor.

Jack grasped my arm and looked me up and down. "Where are you going at this hour?"

"Uh . . . I have to go over the format for tomorrow's interview with Bashir's people."

Jack glanced outside. The sky was lit with flares, and whenever someone opened the door, sounds like a small-town fourth of July drifted in. "Now?" he said incredulously.

I gave him a "duty calls" grimace and headed for the door. I could feel his eyes on my back. Our Israeli liaison officer spotted me leaving and followed me outside. "Now what?" I thought, but before I could devise a way to get rid of him, Bashir drove up. I got in. He put his arms around me and gave me a long kiss. "I missed you so much," I said, as I kicked aside a machine gun that lay on the floor.

We drove through the deserted streets for about ten minutes, until we reached an apartment house that I'd never been to before. "Sssh," he told me, holding his finger to his lips. "We must be very quiet," he said as he held my hand. The apartment we entered was very dark, except for two candles burning in the bedroom, one beside the bed, the other on the opposite side of the room. Bashir turned to me and took my hand again. We looked into each other's eyes.

"Did you ever think it would turn out like this?" I asked.

"About us, you mean?" he said, laughing. "You know how I have always felt about you."

"No, not that," I said. "I mean having the whole world come to you. In a few weeks you are going to be president of Lebanon."

"I *am* going to be," he said calmly. "Not my father, not my brother."

"Your brother wouldn't mind the job," I said.

Bashir laughed. He said, "Why are you surprised? You knew this would happen."

"I did?"

"You said it. What was that quote from Emerson?"

"If a man holds his place," I said, "and there abides, defying all odds, then the whole world will come around to him."

"You see?" he said. "You were right." Then he pulled me close and drew my head to his shoulder. I looked up at his smiling eyes. We kissed and lay down on the bed, and left the candles burning.

Later, I took a pendant from around my neck and held it out to him. "Look, Bashir. It's a coin from the days of the Jewish revolt against Rome. The inscription says 'For the freedom of Zion.' It symbolizes a people's struggle for freedom."

Bashir took it in his hand. "It's very beautiful, and very old. You should treasure it."

"I do," I said. "It's my prized possession. That's why I'm giving it to you. Because it's as much about your people's struggle as it is about mine."

He didn't speak for a moment, but his eyes were lit from within. He touched the medallion gently and looked closely at the inscription. Then, in a hushed voice, he said, "Give it to me after I'm elected president. Then I will deserve it." He added something in Lebanese.

"What is it?" I asked.

He shook his head. "I love you so much I can't tell you how I feel about you in English."

We held each other for a long time. Finally, he got up. He said, "After the election, Barbara, you will come back. It won't be long now. We have waited a very long time."

I didn't want to part from him. I felt unnerved, almost paralyzed, by a fathomless sadness that was not rational. At last everything we had dreamt of was coming true. Bashir was going to have the opportunity to unify Lebanon. He was going to show the world he was a peacemaker, not a warlord.

"What's wrong?" he asked.

"I don't know. I'm frightened. It's been my experience that goodness rarely wins in this life."

Bashir cupped my face in his hands. "I've told you, I believe in destiny. What is meant to happen will happen. There is nothing we can do about it."

"Yes there is," I said tartly. "I don't like this kind of talk, and I don't think you believe it, either. Why are you still driving yourself all over Beirut with no protection? Why aren't guards standing outside this door right now? Your security stinks, and you've got to change it."

"I am, Barbara," he said in a soothing voice. "I am making changes." As we drove back to the hotel, he kept his hand on my leg. It felt warm and reassuring, but I knew that Bashir's personal safety wasn't his first priority—or his second, or his third.

A beautiful, warm morning. We decided to do the interview in front of the Lebanese Forces headquarters. Bashir waited upstairs in his office while the crew set up the equipment. I stood in the sun, shivering. Last night's mood had not left me.

One of Bashir's assistants came down to get me. When I entered his office, I saw him standing near the table where we had eaten dinner last night.

"Barbara," he said, "I want to talk to you. I want to make sure that you're coming back after the election." He didn't wait for an answer. "And there's something else. About Israel: I am going to keep my deal, but not on their timetable. I want you to understand that. Do you?"

"Yes, but it's not important what I think."

"Yes it is."

"I mean it's more important what the Israelis think. Look, Bashir. I don't want you to become another Shah of Iran: first supported by the United States, then dropped like a ton of bricks. America is too big and has too much at stake to support you militarily. Only Israel will do that. If you back away from Israel, eventually you are going to be all alone. And once the Arab countries perceive that, they'll begin to blackmail you, and you won't have any independence left."

He sat down at the table and motioned for me to join him. He crossed his arms and said rapidly, "The Americans are telling me to distance myself from Israel. They want a moderate Arab government in Lebanon, one that can push the whole region toward the West. They don't want an outcast."

I spoke urgently, not knowing how much time we had. "Your guys are so enraptured by this sudden embrace from the U.S. that they're giving you bad advice. I argued with Alfred about this. He screamed at me: 'We can't depend only on the Israelis! We need a superpower!' He doesn't know what he's talking about, and you're going to pay a heavy price for that. Just look at the past if you want to see the future," I said. "Ever since Vietnam, when the stakes get high, we back off. We dump our allies when the going gets tough. It's not even bad faith; the U.S. is just too powerful to support allies when they become liabilities. Believe me, Bashir. If things get hot here, if it looks, for example, like Syria or the terrorists are going to involve the U.S. in fighting, the U.S. will leave. You know this," I almost shouted at him, "you've told me it yourself."

Bashir said, "I told the U.S. not to send the Marines here unless they understand the consequences. Barbara, I understand what you're saying, but I have to take this option now. Don't worry. I'm not closing off any others."

"Just so you understand. Your friends in Israel think you used them. They say you promised to link your troops with the army, and that once you snared them into coming to Beirut, you reneged. They don't know about the U.S. pressure; they think you just deceived them all along. I tried to explain, but they wouldn't listen; they think I'm too close to you."

An aide came into the room to tell us that the crew was ready to film. We went downstairs, and Jack interviewed Bashir. They talked about the same things we had the night before: the struggle in Lebanon and Bashir's plans for the future. The change in Bashir since I first interviewed him two years ago was striking. The charisma, the passion, and the courage were the same. But where once he had almost pleaded for understanding, he was now more polished and confident; he was no longer a supplicant, but a man whose time had come.

The interview ended. Bashir had another meeting. He shook Jack's hand and then he came to me. He stood in front of me for a few minutes. Neither of us spoke. I struggled to control my emotions. Bashir kissed me on both cheeks and whispered in my ear, "I will see you again soon." Then he walked to his car, turned around, waved to me, and drove off.

We piled into our stretch limousine and headed back to Israel. Jack was effusive about Bashir, even comparing him to Jack Kennedy. I kept thinking that I ought to be happy.

As we passed by Ba'abda and got onto the coastal road, I heard a loud thump. Almost at the same moment, the car lurched to one side and skidded across the road. "Sniper!" yelled our Israeli liaison officer, and someone grabbed my head and forced it down. I felt the car straighten, gather momentum, and surge forward.

"Okay now," the Israeli said after a few minutes. I sat up and looked around. Jack had gone white, and Dale was clutching his stomach. My whole body felt numb, but my voice came out very calm. "What was that?"

"Hand-held rocket," the Israeli replied. He shrugged apologetically. "There's still some terrorists around."

Strangely enough, I felt better. Our near miss gave shape to the awful, vague premonitions that had plagued me ever since my evening with Bashir. The danger, it seemed, had come and gone.

In Israel we met Prime Minister Begin, who greeted us effusively. "Jack Anderson!" he said. "You're famous! I'm notorious." Then he launched into a biblical analysis of Israel's claim to the West Bank, which he called Judea and Samaria.

Afterward, we left almost immediately for Washington to edit the piece. It was our first program, and it aired on August 16, 1982.

One week later, on August 23, Bashir was elected president of Lebanon.

The election by Lebanon's Parliament was moved, for security reasons, to an army headquarters protected by Israeli forces. It was democracy Lebanese-style; though not a coup, for Bashir opposed the idea of seizing political power militarily, neither was it an election utterly free of duress. For one thing, Bashir was the only candidate; for another, the electoral operation was assigned to Bashir's intelligence staff, and Elie Hobeika played a large role in ensuring the proper result.

Bashir's leadership of the Christians during years of sectarian warfare had made him many enemies among the Lebanese Moslems. Islamic leaders called for a boycott of the election. Had the call been unanimously heeded, the boycott would have prevented the Parliament from assembling a quorum, thus denying the election to Bashir. But Bashir had spent months talking to delegates, trying to convince them that as president he would strive to change the country for the good of all the Lebanese, not just the Maronites. Weary of war, occupation, and disunity, a number of Moslem delegates were willing to defy the boycott. In its dispatch on the election, UPI said that it was "highly significant that Shiites and some Sunnis voted for Gemayel despite opposition of religious leaders of both Moslem groups."

It was hopeless trying to tell Bashir how I felt over the phone. So I sent him a letter, by messenger. In it I quoted something Winston Churchill had said in 1941 to the young graduates of his alma mater, the Harrow School, during the height of the German blitz of England. Churchill told the youngsters: *"Never give in, never give in, never, never, never, never—in nothing, great or small, large or petty—never give in . . . except to convictions of honor and good sense."*

I knew Bashir would like it. I pictured him reading it and laughing with pleasure. I waited for a response. But it never came.

On the morning of September 14, 1982, Bashir Gemayel, president-elect of Lebanon, spoke at the convent Deir el-Salib outside Beirut, where his sister Arzi was a nun.

15 The convent, a cool and lovely stone edifice on a hill overlooking the sea, held both sweet and painful memories for Bashir. When Maya was alive, he used to bring her there on weekends. The child was fascinated by the tank of colorful tropical fish that stood in the entrance hall.

Bashir spoke to the assembly of nuns and other spectators. "We must always remember," he said, "that no one will do for us what we do not do for ourselves. This election, my presidency, is the beginning of the road; and it has come only because we prepared ourselves for it. The Americans did not make me president. The Israeli invasion did not make me president. They helped, of course. They created the conditions that allowed it to happen. But had not we ourselves been unrelenting, had we not been unshakable as a people, it never would have come to pass."

It was the last of a series of speeches Bashir had made since his election. Over and over, he had urged people to "put aside communal ties and instead support the legitimate central authority"; and he pledged repeatedly that he would not represent one party or one sect, but all of Lebanon. "The people of Lebanon must agree," he wrote in an article, "that force has no place in the inevitable disagreements that arise within any country."

Bashir's election had infused the country with hope. Even his enemies began to believe that Bashir's talk about unity and an end to the corruption and factional loyalty was more than campaign rhetoric.

Saeb Salam is a Sunni Moslem and former prime minister of Lebanon who had led the election boycott. After the election, which Bashir won with the support of a significant number of Shiite and Sunni Moslems, Salam paid a call on Bashir. In an intricate comedy of manners, Middle Eastern style, each man adopted the other's customary mode of dress for their first meeting. Salam, a very formal man, wore a sports shirt; Bashir donned a suit and tie. When Salam entered Bashir's office, he looked the younger man over and said, "Sheikh Bashir, you never cease to confuse us."

Salam then launched into an hour-long diatribe, demanding that the new president honor the long-standing, unwritten agreements that effectively divided the rule of Lebanon into separate fiefdoms. Certain sinecures were traditionally reserved for Sunni Moslems, others for Shiites, still others for Christians. Salam demanded assurances that, despite his radical bluster about reform, Bashir would abide by these unwritten rules.

Bashir listened with the cultivated patience that was so foreign to his character. He did not interrupt, but waited until Salam was finished. Then he said calmly, "I will follow the written laws to the letter; I will be bound absolutely by the constitution. But within that framework I will do as I see fit; and I hold myself bound by no deals. You are free to oppose me. I would welcome your support, but I will absolutely uphold your right to oppose me. What I will not do is compromise."

According to associates, Salam came away thoroughly impressed by Bashir, prepared for the first time to work with him.

Bashir had always railed against holders of no-show jobs who pocketed fat government paychecks while cheating the people out of services they were paid to provide. At eight A.M. the morning after his election, government offices were crammed with veteran employees who didn't have desks, didn't know the way to their offices, and had never met their fellow workers. They came to work faithfully every day thereafter until Bashir's death, and then they came no more.

After his victory, Bashir embarked on a series of speeches that, because they came after and not before the election, galvanized the country. Again and again he said that a new era had begun for Lebanon, and he told the people that their fate was once again in their hands.

Pierre Yazbeck, who heard many of the speeches, later told me that it was as if Bashir had attained a state of grace in which his words were not just words but things or events in their own right. He said that listening to Bashir in the days after his election was like seeing a vision realized before your eyes: a moment of fulfillment and a beginning combined. And this assertion was echoed many times by other people who were in Lebanon during Bashir's twenty-one day reign.

While Bashir was speaking in his sister's convent, a twenty-six-year-old Lebanese man named Habib Tanous Chartouni was performing one last check on the massive bomb—450 pounds of TNT—that he had planted the night before in a room on the second floor, directly above the central meeting hall of the Phalange party headquarters in Ashrafiyeh. The detonator was a highly sophisticated Japanese device designed to set off an explosion from a distance of several miles away. According to Lebanese intelligence sources, the device was supplied by or through Bulgaria, which often acted on behalf of the Soviets in such matters.

Chartouni, a Christian, encountered no difficulty entering the building. There was no reason why he should—which, no doubt, was why he was chosen. Chartouni used to live in an apartment on the top floor of party headquarters, and some of his family still lived there. The family had ties to the Gemayels; his uncle was a bodyguard to Sheikh Pierre, and his sister was the girlfriend of one of Bashir's aides. The Phalange guards and party members were used to seeing him around. As added protection, though, he carried in his pocket a safe-passage card signed by Elie Hobeika, chief of security for the Lebanese Forces.

After his speech, Bashir bid a warm farewell to his favorite sister, then left for Phalange headquarters in Ashrafiyeh. Despite the advice of friends, who urged him for security reasons to avoid following his routine, he insisted on attending the party's regular Tuesday afternoon meeting. This would be the last time because, as president-elect of Lebanon, Bashir was about to resign his party post. Not for anything would he have sacrificed, for nebulous considerations of security, the opportunity to say a personal thank-you and farewell to the branch where he had launched his political career ten years earlier.

Security was no tighter than usual at party headquarters that day. There was no need for body searches or identity checks, since only party members were invited.

Bashir's car drew up to the curb in front of Phalange headquarters in Ashrafiyeh. He was over an hour late, but they had waited for him before beginning the meeting. As he made his way slowly into the building, stopping to greet old friends and to accept their good wishes, Bashir was watched from a window above. When he entered the ground-floor meeting hall, which was packed with about four hundred party members, Habib Chartouni slipped out of the building and drove to an East Beirut neighborhood called Nasrah, less than a mile from Ashrafiyeh.

At approximately 4:00, Bashir began to speak.

At precisely 4:10 P.M. Habib Chartouni pressed the detonator.

The explosion was heard all over Beirut. The three-story building in Ashrafiyeh rose into the air, then collapsed into rubble.

The word went out all over Beirut, Lebanon, and the world that an assassination of Bashir Gemayel had been attempted—and had failed. The exact story was hazy, though, and no one seemed quite sure where Bashir was at the moment. Some said he was wounded in the left leg and taken to hospital; others, that he walked away from the blast unharmed. But no one doubted he had escaped, once again. Although the loss was great—twenty-six people would ultimately be found dead and over one hundred wounded—the relief was greater. Church bells pealed in celebration, and Lebanese Forces soldiers fired into the air. The Voice of Lebanon radio station exalted: "Today is the resurrection of Lebanon!"

But no one knew where Bashir was. No one could find him.

After several hours, the Phalange-run Voice of Lebanon station went off the air. The state-run station made no announcement, but switched to a program of solemn music. And then came a period of dreadful uncertainty until, early in the morning of the next day, Lebanese Prime Minister Wazzan read a statement. Bashir Gemayel, he said, in a breaking voice, had been killed.

This was the reason for the long uncertainty: Bashir's

body was unearthed early, in the first wave of rescue attempts. But his face was so badly crushed that no one recognized him. His body was taken with others to a hospital morgue, where it was identified only hours later, by his ring and a nun's letter in his pocket.

Habib Tanous Chartouni has not come into this story before and will not appear afterward, because he is nothing. He was the hand, not the mind, that did the deed. While Chartouni set and detonated the bomb, his control agent, Nabil Alam, waited somewhere in West Beirut. Both Chartouni and Alam were Lebanese Christians, but their loyalties lay elsewhere. It took me a long time to learn just where.

Chartouni wasn't meant to be caught, and would not have been had he not forgotten something important. He was not, by all accounts, the brightest of men. Although, at a press conference after his capture, Chartouni called Bashir a traitor because of his friendship with Israel, he also maintained—and to this day maintains—that he never meant to hurt anyone, and that the bomb was meant only to scare Bashir and teach him a lesson. It's noteworthy that at least some of his interrogators believe him. They say that Chartouni was just dumb enough not to have realized.

The thing that Chartouni forgot was that his sister was in the building.

He remembered at the last minute, just as he was about to set off the detonator. He called her and told her to drop everything and get out of the building at once. She ran into the street, screaming hysterically that something terrible was going to happen. Moments later, the building exploded.

She was picked up and interrogated immediately.

"How did you know something terrible was going to happen?"

"My brother told me."

"Where is your brother?"

"I don't know where he is now, but he told me to meet him later at . . ."

Chartouni was arrested at once. He confessed almost immediately, first to his interrogators and later publicly, at an emotionally charged press conference. When Chartouni tried to blame Bashir for his own death, by saying he had sold out to Israel, a woman journalist leapt up. "You haven't killed a man," she screamed, "you've killed a country!" At the insistence of the Lebanese government, the Lebanese Forces turned Chartouni over to the state. But he has never been brought to trial, even though Amin Gemayel, Bashir's older brother, succeeded his brother as president of Lebanon.

No one knows the reason why except Amin, and he hasn't told. Most informed sources say that Amin did not bring Chartouni to trial because he did not want to enhance Bashir's status as a martyr. They say that, had he been able, Amin would have eradicated all memory and trace of his younger brother.

Like all of Lebanon, I got the false news first.

In the early afternoon of September 14, I received a phone call in my office from Michael Ledeen, a special assistant to Secretary of State Alexander Haig. Ledeen knew of my friendship with Bashir.

"I just saw a wire report," he said. "Someone shot at Bashir Gemayel. He's okay—just a scratch—but they took him to the hospital. They say he's walking around joking with people."

Another escape, I thought. Bashir has more lives than a cat, fortunately for him. I was late for an interview with Senator John Glenn on Capitol Hill, so I decided to call Bashir's office in Beirut later to find out what had happened.

I left for the Hill with two reporters from the staff of "Jack Anderson Confidential." The subject of our report was nuclear safeguards, and Glenn, who was the chairman of the Senate Nuclear Non-proliferation Committee, was extremely forthcoming. We walked out of his office a few hours later feeling that great high a really good interview produces, and on our way back we stopped at the Monocle, a top political restaurant, for a celebratory drink. Then we drove back to the office in Bethesda, Maryland.

As soon as we walked in, at about eight P.M., someone bellowed from my office: "Newman, get in here right away!" Alex Sheftell, a businessman involved in the show, was standing behind my desk, phone in hand. I remember feeling a little annoyed to see him there.

"What is it?" I said. "What's the matter?"

"Gemayel is dead," he said.

I turned and left, registering without seeing the shocked faces of the two reporters. I walked past them and out the front door.

I got as far as the street, and then I collapsed.

The meaning of Bashir's death to Lebanon became clear two days later, when Lebanese Forces, under Israeli protection, entered the Sabra and Shatila refugee camps to  "clean" them of Palestinian fighters. Bashir had steadfastly refused to do this when he was alive. Maddened by his death and now unrestrained, the Christian soldiers carried out a massacre that even by Lebanese standards was horrific. Estimates of the dead ranged from three hundred to twelve hundred—mostly civilians, including many women and children killed at close range.

The field director of the operation was Elie Hobeika, whom Bashir had installed as chief of security after Maya's death, the man I had called Bashir's Iago. In their book *Israel's Lebanon War*, Israeli journalists Ze'ev Schiff and Ehud Ya'ari describe in detail Hobeika's role in the massacres. They write of an episode in which one of his men called him on the radio to ask what to do with a group of fifty women and children. Hobeika replied: "That's the last time you're going to ask me that question. You know what to do." The book describes people killed when live grenades were strung around their necks, and it documents cases of rape, dismemberment, and mutilation. Some Palestinian women were put on a truck and driven around Christian East Beirut, while soldiers called on everyone to look at the new widows they had just made.

This was Bashir's epitaph, and thus was he betrayed. Everything he had worked so hard to accomplish had turned to dust. He had strived so desperately to break the chain of violence and bring peace to his broken country. Now he himself was dead, a victim of violence, and the world was revolted by the cruelty of the Lebanese Christians.

For permitting Hobeika's troops to carry out a massacre that should have been anticipated, Israel also became the target of harsh criticism, from within as well as without. Ultimately this incident would turn the tide against Israel's controversial engagement in Lebanon. These massacres would also factor into the decision by the Reagan administration to deploy marines in Beirut—a decision that would prove fatal to hundreds of United States servicemen and highly detrimental to the United States' standing in the Middle East.

The killings in the refugee camps were not anomalous reactions to the pain of Bashir's death, but true harbingers. Everything Bashir warned about has come true. Each day's news confirms it. The Syrians have continued their destabilizing games, pitting faction against faction and making it impossible for any Lebanese government to exercise authority. The Lebanese army is powerless. The country is subdivided into warring sects. Lebanon is home, still, to the most violent terrorist groups, most of them headquartered in the Bekáa Valley, which is under total Syrian control.

The explosive disintegration of Lebanon after Bashir's death is a measure of the creative force of the man who held it together. During that narrow window of hope—the three weeks between Bashir's election and his assassination—Lebanon had a glimpse of a far different future. Freedom from Syrian domination, freedom from terrorist occupation, Lebanese Christians and Moslems working together to heal the wounds of civil war, and after a reasonable period of waiting, peace with Lebanon's southern neighbor, Israel—they were all, fleetingly, possible.

But that vision exploded along with the building in Ashrafiyeh. It is utterly, irretrievably gone. Lebanon has returned to the chaos and despair of the years before Bashir unified the Christians and, briefly, the entire country. The cycle has begun again, only this time the players are tougher and there is no hope on the horizon; there is no Bashir.

The meaning of Bashir's death to me took longer to make itself felt, because for a long time I denied it. Oh, I knew he was dead, all right. I couldn't walk past my telephone without thinking that it would never again ring with his call. And each time I remembered, my knees would buckle, my breath would come out in a sharp gasp, and I felt as if someone had kicked me in the gut. But I convinced myself that if his revolution could succeed, if Lebanon could carry on, somehow, along the path that he had cleared, then Bashir would still live.

I immersed myself in things Lebanese. What social life I had revolved around a small circle of Lebanese friends. We would see each other often and eat at each other's homes. We were the walking dead, and the company of others like ourselves was comforting. Penny says of that time that she felt more Lebanese than American.

But as the first hard months passed and the time stretched into a year, I began to watch events with clearer eyes. Amin's election was a terrible setback, for despite the lip service he paid to his martyred brother, Amin went his own way, which was the way of the traditional Middle East politicians. Amin believed in compromise and deception, and in playing one side against the other—everything Bashir had despised. It was clear within a year of his election that Amin had lost control of the country.

I saw Bashir's closest friends falling away, aligning themselves with this power or that, selling themselves to the Syrians or others, or emigrating to the West, giving up the dream of a united, sovereign Lebanon and settling for shackled lives of ease and wealth.

In the days following Bashir's death, I could not abide the sight of the medallion I had meant him to have. I gave it to Alfred Mady, saying that it was up to him to carry on Bashir's struggle for freedom. Alfred thanked me with tears in his eyes, but later I learned that he had the piece appraised.

When I understood that Bashir's friends had turned against him and that Lebanon had forgotten him, I grew very bitter. I cut my ties to the country and threw myself into my work in an attempt to expunge the past. Twenty times a day I told myself: "You've got to get on with your life." I went through all the forms of living, but I could not forget Bashir, nor could I shed the nagging sense of an obligation unfulfilled.

Like a festering wound, the pain of Bashir's death increased with the passage of time. I thought it was because I had never said good-bye to him. Two days after his murder, I attended a memorial service at St. Matthew's Cathedral in Washington, where I sat in the front pew with Geraldo and cried myself sick; but even so, I hadn't said good-bye properly.

In the summer of 1983, almost one year after Bashir's assassination, Penny turned thirteen. For her *Bas Mitzvah*, we decided that my present would be a trip to Israel and Lebanon. We would visit Bashir's grave. Several times we made reservations and canceled at the last minute because of shelling in Beirut; this time it was the Syrians bombarding the Christians in East Beirut. Finally, there was a lull in the fighting, and Penny and I boarded a flight to Beirut.

I fought despair when our plane touched down and I realized that Bashir would not be there, that he would not call me five minutes after my arrival as he always had, that we would not fall into each other's arms. For Penny's sake I covered my feelings and shepherded us through customs and passport control. But here, too, were reminders of Bashir. One of the porters, a Christian, recognized me. He seized my baggage claim tickets and retrieved our luggage for us.

This time no soldiers were waiting to whisk us away. We were staying with the mother-in-law of Charbel el-Khoury, who had replaced Alfred as head of the Lebanese Forces office in Washington. Odile Khashan, a small, pretty, blonde woman, was waiting outside the airport. She drove us to her little apartment in Ashrafiyeh, just a few blocks away from where Bashir had lived with his family. The weather was hot and humid. Our hostess apologized for the lack of air-conditioning in her apartment; the electricity had been knocked out by Syrian shelling and there was no telling, she said resignedly, when it would be repaired.

A short while after we arrived, we heard the dull thud of artillery shells. Though it didn't sound close to us, Mrs. Khashan sat down on her sofa and cried. "I'm sorry," she said when she had recovered a little. She lowered her voice so that Penny would not hear. "It's just that I've lost two good friends already to this shelling, and I never know myself, when I leave for work in the morning, if I will make it back home at night." The fact that the shelling was sporadic made it all the more unnerving, she explained, because you never knew when it would begin or where it would hit.

"But what about the Lebanese Forces?" I asked. "Why aren't they doing anything?"

Mrs. Khashan shook her head sadly. "You've been away

too long, Barbara. The Lebanese Forces don't have the same power. Sheikh Pierre made them turn over their treasury to the state, to Amin, but he does nothing to help us."

I felt so bitter inside, so very angry. Now I could see with my own eyes that everything Bashir had accomplished was destroyed—that his hard work and unstinting effort, and the deaths of Maya and all the other innocent victims, had been in vain.

We visited Lebanese Forces headquarters and were warmly welcomed by Fadi Frem, a close friend of Bashir's and mine who had taken over as head of the Lebanese Forces. His office was in a separate building from Bashir's, which had been turned into a shrinelike museum. I couldn't bear to look at it. I found the headquarters greatly changed, and not for the better. When Bashir was alive it had been tautly run, filled with a sense of excitement. Now I saw signs of slackness and disorder that Bashir would never have tolerated.

The streets were full of gigantic posters of Bashir, songs about him played constantly on the radio, and every home I entered contained his portrait. But despite the cultlike following, I saw that Bashir's essence had been forgotten. His image was revered, but his cause had been utterly abandoned.

The next day, a girlfriend of Alfred Mady named Samia Toutounji drove us to Bashir's burial place, a small family sepulcher on a grassy knoll near the Gemayels' ancestral summer home in Bekfaya. Chairs had been set in front of the mausoleum but no one was there. Several bunches of wilting flowers lay against the stone crypt.

I knelt and leaned my head against the cold stone. I saw Bashir's face clearly before me, and a year's worth of unshed tears welled up. I covered my face. Penny pressed my arm. "Leave me," I told her. "Let me be alone with him." She kissed me and walked away.

"I told you I'd be back," I said. I didn't exactly like my tone of voice, but it was out of my control. I hit the hard stone with my fist. "You couldn't wait? You had to get killed? Bashir, you had no right," I cried. "Now look what's happened."

Birds chirped in the trees around the crypt. The air was sweet with jasmine and rose and the untamed scent of wildflowers on the hill. Slowly my tears abated and, with them, my anger. "You knew I'd come, didn't you?" I said. In my mind I heard his voice: "Barbara, you will tell our story." We made a deal, Bashir and I, and his death didn't end it. Now, at last, I understood my restlessness this past year and why the pain of Bashir's death had grown worse instead of healing.

I had to tell his story, but in my way. I'm a professional, and in my world stories have beginnings, middles, and ends. Bashir's end was still a mystery.

Oh yes, they caught the hit man—the drone Chartouni—but he was nothing. Who activated him? Who really killed Bashir?

I remembered what the Lebanese journalist had screamed at Habib Chartouni: "You haven't killed a man," she'd cried, "you've killed a country." It was true. Lebanon had teetered on the verge of redemption and fallen back. Only memory remained, and soon even that would fade.

Suddenly I heard the muffled thump of artillery shells, and with a sharp clatter of heels over stones, Samia came racing up the hill. "Quick, get in the car," she yelled. "The Syrians are shelling from over the mountain."

We ran back to the car. Penny was huddled in the back seat. Samia took off like lightning. One shell hit the road just behind us; another fell on a field to our left. "Bastards, bastards," Samia muttered as she drove.

I put my arms around Penny, so frightened for her that I had no fear left for myself. "Are you scared?" I whispered.

"No," she said. "If I die, at least I'll die with you."

"No one's going to die," I said, and held her tight all the way to Beirut.

As the years went by, I tried many times to write about Bashir, but I could not. Lebanon was too saddening a subject, and every time I started writing about Bashir I

17 would become bogged down by a great weariness. I lacked the energy, perhaps the courage, to let myself remember.

I tried to put Lebanon out of my mind, to move on to other things and a new life. When "Jack Anderson Confidential" closed down after disputes among backers, I started my own production company to make films, documentaries, and docudramas. The company succeeded, and after a while I became very busy.

But my unfinished business with Bashir gnawed at me. I wanted the world to remember him, and I wanted to be equal to the trust he had placed in me. Most of all, I wanted to do what those charged with the responsibility had failed to do: discover and expose his real killers.

One story leads to another, as I have said before. When information about the Middle East found its way to my door, it was natural for me to follow up on newsworthy reports. But I think it was also that sense of unfinished business that drew me back to the region time and again. I never went without developing all the information I could about Bashir's death.

Within the Christian community I heard charges and countercharges. I had learned to discount information from these sources, whose motivating force was all too often personal grudge. But there was one report that came to me repeatedly from many sources, including some top-ranking Lebanese intelligence people. I was told that although Bashir's assassin and his controller were Christians, they were members of the Syrian Popular Party. This political party believes in a Greater Syria and opposes the existence of Lebanon, Israel, Jordan, Iraq, and Cyprus—a view diametrically opposed to Bashir's. Chartouni and Alam were also said to have worked for Syrian military intelligence.

With no contacts in Syrian military intelligence, there was no way I could check directly, but this was not unduly discouraging. I have found that with patience most questions can be answered; and that kind of patience I have.

In the summer of 1987, I undertook a commission from Central Television, part of ITV in London, to produce a documentary on Hezbollah. Not a single group but rather an umbrella organization for radically fundamentalist, pro-Iranian Shiites, Hezbollah holds most of the Western hostages in Lebanon. To do the job I needed to get inside their territory, the Syrian-controlled Bekáa Valley, where the most ruthless groups in the world lie together like lambs in a terrorist paradise. It was here that the Islamic Jihad, a faction of Hezbollah, rehearsed the attack on the U.S. Marine headquarters and the U.S. embassy that killed over 250 Americans and wounded hundreds of others. Few journalists had entered the Bekáa, and fewer still had emerged. For a Western journalist, and especially for me, it was the most dangerous place on earth.

The Bekáa is a long, deep rift valley produced ages ago by the shifting of ancient land masses. Forty-five miles long and ten miles wide, it is bisected lengthwise by the Litani River; the valley is bounded on the north by the city of Baalbek, on the west by the Lebanon Mountains, and on the east by Syria. One-fifth of Lebanon's territory, but a much larger proportion of its fertile land, is in this green valley. Once the breadbasket of Lebanon, much of the Bekáa has been given over to more profitable crops: marijuana and opium poppies. Throughout history, the Bekáa Valley's fertility and strategic location have made it a much contested area. The people of the valley are fiercely loyal to local warlords, and they know from generations of experience how to live under occupation.

Hezbollah's presence in the Bekáa was created by Syria, which runs the area like an ecological experiment in terror. Starting in 1979, several thousand Iranian Revolutionary Guards, the shock troops of the Khomeini regime, entered Lebanon under Syrian protection. These soldiers formed the nucleus of Hezbollah, whose charge is to export the Islamic revolution worldwide. Though Syria, a socialist state, is no proponent of theocracy, it allowed the Revolutionary Guards into Lebanon to use them for its own ends. The Syrian aim was to radicalize the Shiite population and block Israel's attempt to create a *cordon sanitaire*, or security belt, in South Lebanon, which would be jointly patrolled by Shiites and Christians.

The Bekáa Valley butts up against the Syrian capital, Damascus; and it was clear to Syria's leaders—no one's fools—that if you're going to raise terrorists in your backyard, you'd better keep them tightly penned. And so they have. There are more than eighteen Syrian army troop concentrations in the Bekáa, including units of the most elite Syrian commandos working with Syrian intelligence. *Nothing* happens there that the Syrians don't know about.

Lately, though, Hezbollah's successes in taking hostages had begun going to its head. The group, which numbers about 3,000, had begun flexing its muscles, acting independently of Syria. It wasn't the terrorist activities of Hezbollah that irritated the Syrians, but the lack of approval and coordination for these activities. However, they preferred—and still prefer—not to take large-scale military action against Hezbollah. Such action would certainly result in a great many Syrian casualties; it would alienate Syria's own fundamentalist population and incur the risk of a backlash, as well as jeopardize Syria's friendship with Iran.

Syria had another reason for clipping Hezbollah's wings. Around 1987, Syria started trying to break its dependence on the Soviet Union. In order to shed its outlaw image in the West, Syria was using its leverage with Hezbollah and Iran to act as middleman in freeing some of the hostages.

It seemed to me that, under the circumstances, Syria might be amenable to the program on Hezbollah that I wanted to do. But I needed a way to ask them.

I thought at once of Elie Hobeika.

The fact is, I'd been thinking a lot about Elie Hobeika during the past year.

He came up a lot, Elie did, in conversations about Bashir's death. The year before the Hezbollah program, in the summer of 1986, I had gone to East Beirut to research a documentary for Home Box Office. While I was there I looked up a man named Pierre Rizk, whose *nom de guerre* is Akram. Akram was a member of Elie Hobeika's inner sanctum and now serves as head of Lebanese Forces intelligence under Elie's rival, Samir Geagea. It was Akram who first told me that Elie Hobeika, acting on behalf of Syria, had participated in the plot to murder Bashir.

I was not, at first, especially impressed. Akram and

Hobeika were former allies who were now at each other's throat. Akram had plenty of reason to lie about Hobeika; but what possible reason had Elie to kill Bashir, whom he had worked so hard to establish as president, just as they were at the point of success? Elie had bet on a winning horse. If not out of loyalty then out of self-interest, it made sense for him to stay the race.

Akram arranged for me to be driven to a half-finished palace perched high above the Mediterranean. Five stories tall, it was blasted into sheer rock, towering over and commanding the sea. The floors were marble, the rooms enormous. It was a palace fit for an Ottoman potentate, complete with a shooting gallery on the lowest level.

I stood on the veranda, gazing out to sea. Later, in a briefing in his office, Akram said, "That was the home Hobeika was building for himself and his family, before he had to leave so suddenly. You know, Elie comes from a poor family. Before he took over the Lebanese Forces he had no money of his own. This house was built entirely on money stolen from the Lebanese Forces while he was the head."

"But I've heard that Chartouni and Alam were Syrian agents," I said.

"Of course." Akram sounded surprised. "Who did you think Elie was working for?"

I stared at him. "I don't buy that. I know he's living in Syria now, but that's just since Geagea kicked him out of office. When Bashir was alive he worked for him."

"No," Akram insisted, "Elie has served the Syrians secretly for years. Two days after Bashir's murder, Hobeika did Sabra and Shatila for Syria."

"Come on," I said.

"Think about it," Akram replied. "The massacre accomplished three things. It embarrassed the Israelis, it discredited the Christians, and it killed a lot of Al Fatah men—Syria's enemies in the PLO camp. All three Syrian goals, and all three accomplished by Elie's operation. And there's another thing." He moved his chair closer to mine and lowered his voice. "The night before the massacres, just a day after Bashir's death, we know that Elie met with a Syrian intelligence agent."

I didn't believe Akram. For one thing, the Sabra and Shatila story was just too pat. For another, I didn't know of any reason for Hobeika to betray Bashir. And yet the more I thought about Elie, the more questions I had. Even his enemies said that Hobeika was not only the best security head Bashir ever had, but the best in the country. Yet he allowed Habib Chartouni, a known Syrian agent, to live on the top floor of a building that Bashir regularly visited. It didn't jibe. Neither did the report that when he was caught, Chartouni had a safe-passage card from Hobeika in his pocket.

I couldn't forget my conversation with Bashir about Hobeika. "You've got a tiger by the tail," I'd said, and Bashir had answered, "Better than letting him run loose."

His aides used to tell me about terrific fights between Bashir and Elie, who chafed under Bashir's tight rein. Elie had wanted to run his own operations autonomously, without interference, briefing Bashir when they were over. Bashir insisted on knowing and approving every detail in advance. Elie wanted to handle his own budget; Bashir demanded strict accounting in weekly meetings.

I wondered: Had the tiger bitten Bashir?

That summer in Lebanon, I developed enough information on Hobeika to have a pretty clear picture of his activities after Bashir's death. He had become a close friend of Rifat Assad, younger brother of Syrian President Hafez Assad. Rifat was notorious in Lebanon as a ruthless drug smuggler. Several people had pointed out the curious fact that immediately after the blast, the entire Phalange and Lebanese Forces leadership had rushed to the scene to dig for Bashir, except for one man: Elie Hobeika. Bashir's chief of security had emerged from his office only after Chartouni's flukish capture, to take personal charge of the prisoner's interrogation. It was also odd that, although the identity of Chartouni's controller emerged early on in the interrogation, somehow Alam was able to escape from Beirut to the Bekáa Valley, where he remains to this day under Syrian protection.

Bashir was succeeded as chief of the Lebanese Forces by Fadi Frem, with Hobeika ensconced as the powerful and now far more autonomous head of security. Several years later Elie led a coup that established him as leader.

While head of the Lebanese Forces, Hobeika carried out a reign of terror. He used his position to enrich himself. If he or his people wanted a certain property, they would force the owner to sell at their price. They demanded protection money from businesses operating in East Beirut and, if refused, they resorted to kidnappings.

Had Elie Hobeika confined himself to extortion and kidnapping, he might have had a long reign as head of the Lebanese Forces, but his overweening ambition led him on to the fatal mistake of getting involved in politics.

Upon Bashir's death the Israelis began pulling back from their involvement in Lebanon, rebuffing the many who tried to replace Bashir in their scheme of things. Hobeika, once close to Israel (he even honeymooned there), was shunned after his involvement in the Sabra and Shatila slaughters. Hobeika, clearly a man of mutable loyalties, then openly turned to Syria. It is to be supposed that a certain amount of pro-Syrian sentiment would have been well tolerated by the new Lebanese regime, which was itself pro-Syrian. Eventually, however, Hobeika went too far. He pressured the Lebanese leadership to sign an agreement granting the Syrians hegemony over Lebanon. The attempt failed; Elie was accused of treason and shortly thereafter was replaced in a coup by Samir Geagea, leader of the infamous operation against Tony Franjieh. (Akram, Hobeika's confidant at the time, took the winning side and thus remained as Geagea's security chief.)

After the coup, Elie fled with a hard-core group of about four hundred fighters, mostly veterans of Sabra and Shatila. He surfaced in Damascus as the Syrians' top Christian-in-exile. His men were quartered in the Bekáa Valley, where they called themselves the real Lebanese Forces.

I said before that Elie Hobeika was a man of mutable loyalties, but I think that was wrong. He was, rather, a man of unshakable loyalty—to himself. Although I had come to believe him morally and logistically capable of arranging the assassination, his own self-interest ought to have bound him to Bashir, who never let loyal men down.

Just before I left Lebanon that summer, Akram told me that he had proof of Hobeika's complicity in the killing, including tapes of Hobeika's interrogation of Chartouni. He agreed to send me copies. But despite numerous reminders the tapes never came. This reinforced my suspicion that Akram was just blowing smoke, trying to discredit Hobeika.

Although the accusations against Hobeika were unproven, my questions remained. I wanted badly to talk to Elie, but I needed a reason, a legitimate cover.

The program on Hezbollah provided a perfect opportunity to kill two large birds with one stone. I contacted Hobeika in Damascus through an intermediary. He remembered me and agreed to a meeting in Paris.

On a warm July evening in Paris, I met Elie Hobeika in the cocktail lounge of a hotel near the Paris Opera. I had seen him only once before, six years ago, but I recognized him immediately.

I've met killers who, off duty, seemed charming, intelligent, even cultured men. You would never guess what they did for a living if you didn't know. Elie, on the other hand, looked as if he'd been typecast for the part of chief gangster: a dark and brooding face; black hair cropped in the shape of a helmet; wary, restless, clever eyes without a mote of compassion.

During our meeting, Hobeika boasted about his connections to the Syrian high command and intelligence. A television program about Hezbollah, he told me, would be very acceptable to the Syrian government at this time, and he promised to obtain the necessary permission for me to enter the Bekáa Valley, receive intelligence information, and interview former Hezbollah operatives about the group's plans.

The more accommodating Hobeika was, the more I felt like the fly who was invited into the spider's parlor.

"What about my connection to Bashir?" I said. "Don't the Syrians know about that?"

Hobeika shrugged. "Bashir is dead," he said. "No one cares anymore. Leave it to me," he said.

A few weeks later, I received word that the Syrians had given the project a green light, and that Hobeika himself would be my guide into the Bekáa. There was one catch. Since Elie could not safely enter Beirut, we would have to meet in Damascus.

I was intrigued by the idea of going to Syria, but very wary. Syria has one of the most ruthless governments in the world, for whom torture is a norm of interrogation and terrorism of diplomacy. Most recently, Great Britain broke diplomatic relations with Syria when it found irrefutable evidence that Syrian intelligence had masterminded the attempt to blow up an El Al flight from London's Heathrow Airport. In 1982, the Syrian regime revealed its true face in an incident that was widely reported in Europe but not in the United States. Threatened with a rebellion by Islamic fundamentalists in the two major cities of Hama and Homs, the government stationed its big guns outside the cities and then leveled them, killing thousands of their own civilians in order to rid themselves of the insurrectionists.

I weighed Hobeika's proposition carefully.

On one side of the scale was the fact that I was an American, Jewish, a known friend of Bashir's, a journalist who had reported stories against Syrian interests, and who was now being asked to enter Syria under the protection of a man who may or may not have been responsible for Bashir's death, but was certainly responsible for many others.

On the other side was the fact that I knew Syria was

trying to improve its image and denigrate Hezbollah—
neither aim would be served by killing me. I had the
chance to break a top-notch story on one of the most
pernicious terrorist groups in the world and at the same
time to interrogate Hobeika about Bashir's death.

It was a calculated risk. I decided to take it. The hardest
part was telling Penny.

She cried. She raged. "How can you do this to me?" she
demanded. "If the Syrians don't get you, the terrorists
will. You'll get killed. And then what's going to happen to
me?"

I said I had to go. I said I owed it to Bashir. I said that
I was the only one who could do what needed to be done,
and I told her all the reasons why the Syrians and Hobeika
should protect me.

The whole conversation was like a replay of fights I had
had with Bashir, when I taxed him for taking too many
risks and he answered that he had no choice. Only this
time, I was saying his lines and Penny was saying mine.
It's true that you never really understand someone until
you stand in his shoes.

Hobeika's people were to arrange for a visa to be sent
through the Syrian embassy in Washington. Several weeks
later, by the time I was scheduled to leave, it still had not
arrived.

I called one of Hobeika's agents. "No problem," he said.
"Elie will meet you at the airport and we'll get you a visa
on the spot." It made me wonder what I was getting into,
when the most reassuring aspect of my trip was that I
would be met by a man who had more innocent blood on
his hands than most surgeons see in a lifetime.

I brought along Schiff and Ya'ari's book, *Israel's Lebanon War*, to look over during the flight. I had read it before,
but now I combed it specifically for mentions of Elie
Hobeika. I found plenty. The book described his role as
field commander during the Sabra and Shatila massacres,
which I had already known. Minutes before we landed, I

read that during the Israeli invasion, Elie was involved in a liquidation campaign that targeted Syrian and PLO agents in Sidon and Tyre, the coastal cities I had visited with Jack Anderson in 1982. My God, I thought, Elie's protectors now are his victims of a few years ago. Did the Syrians not care about the past, or did they not know? I ran to the bathroom and threw the book down the towel chute.

Despite all my reassurances to Penny (and myself), I had a moment of panic when the plane touched down in Damascus. I sat in my seat until all the other passengers had disembarked, while images of dark, dank cells, chains, whips, and electric prods played through my head. I had told no one in the State Department about my trip, for they would certainly have tried to block me. Without a visa, there was no official record of my visit. For all I knew, I was stupidly walking into a trap.

I pulled myself together and walked through the passageway leading directly into the terminal. Elie Hobeika was sitting close to the gate, waiting. He shook my hand and we walked together toward passport control. A hand-lettered sign on the wall, written in English and Arabic, caught my eye. It said, "No one can leave the cuntry [*sic*] without first clearing customs authorities." The sign looked old, and the misspelling of "country" must have been on the wall for years. I started giggling and couldn't stop. Hobeika looked at me and said, "Sssh! All these men standing around are security agents." That shut me up.

From the VIP lounge, Hobeika called Syrian Vice-President Khaddam to sort out my visa problem. But it was early afternoon, and Khaddam was having his siesta. The head of security at the airport, a burly man in his thirties dressed in civilian clothes, treated Hobeika with great deference, backing out of the door and apologizing for every delay. Coffee was served. After twenty minutes, Elie reached Khaddam and the problem was resolved.

I sat beside him in a black, bulletproof Mercedes that

the Syrians had provided him. The door was so heavy I could hardly close it. There were scratches on the windshield and the driver's door from bullets fired a few months ago when Elie attempted a comeback in East Beirut. The Syrians, he told me, had saved his life.

Just outside the airport, Hobeika pointed out an impressive hillside complex. "President Assad's new residence and office," he said. The city looked modern, clean, undistinguished. We drove for about fifteen minutes to Hobeika's apartment, located on a cul-de-sac in a modern neighborhood of balconied high-rises and smaller multifamily residences. Several armed soldiers and plainclothesmen guarded Hobeika's duplex apartment on the first and second floors of a two-family house. The upper floors, Elie told me proudly, were occupied by the son of former President Bhutto of Pakistan. Bhutto was killed by his successor, General Zia, who himself died in a plane crash in the summer of 1988. Obviously this was the quarter of Damascus where Syrian President Assad stockpiled his favored exiles. Once, Elie and others like him had been important political figures in their own countries. But politics is fickle, and now they lived by the largesse of Syria.

Across the street from Hobeika's house stood a huge mosque, and the chanting of Moslem prayers was broadcast loud and clear into the apartment. Elie turned on his stereo to drown out the sound.

We sat in the living room, a far cry from the one planned for his Beirut palace. Small and crowded, it was a combination living room, dining room, and office. Over more coffee, served by one of his servants, we discussed the television shoot. I had not wanted to bring my own crew on this dangerous trip, so Elie had lined up a cameraman and soundman from Beirut, who would meet us in the Bekáa Valley. I said that I wanted to get as close as possible to areas where hostages were being held. No problem, Elie said. He would show me the Sheikh Abdullah barracks in Baalbek, where four or five hostages were reportedly imprisoned by Hezbollah.

It was getting late, and we had a drive of about an hour ahead of us. But before we left, Hobeika called me into his bedroom. "Look at these," he said, unwrapping six or seven magnificent old Russian icons. Several were gilt-encrusted. "The Syrians gave these to me," he said, gazing down very proudly at his collection. I wondered how the icons had got into Syrian hands. Had they come from the pillage of Lebanon? Whatever the source, Elie clearly had no qualms about accepting them.

As we drove through the night, Hobeika behind the wheel and classical music on the radio, we talked of many things. In the darkness he seemed more expansive, as if he were in his element. I brought the conversation around to Bashir.

"The way things turned out," I said, "I think Bashir died for nothing."

"He did. He died for nothing."

"Who killed him?" I said.

Hobeika looked straight ahead at the dark ribbon of road. "Syrian military intelligence," he said without hesitation. "But we don't know how far up the ladder it was authorized."

"People tell me you killed him." I tried to say this in a tone of disbelief, not accusation. But I shocked myself by saying it at all.

Hobeika was unruffled. "*I* killed him, they say that?" he replied. I saw a flicker of something that looked like amusement pass rapidly over his face. Then he turned up the volume of the radio and said no more.

Why didn't he deny it, I wondered. You'd expect an innocent man to deny it. Of course, you'd expect a guilty man to deny it, too. But if a man were guilty of a thing he was proud of, why then, I thought, he might say nothing.

We came to a Syrian checkpoint close to the border with Lebanon. Elie turned on the light inside the car and stopped only long enough for the guards to see his face. Then he arrogantly pumped the gas and sped off into the darkness. Looking back, I saw several men scurry toward a parked car. They raced their motors and quickly caught up with us but stayed just behind. "My bodyguards," Elie said, turning his face and looking at me with a contemptuous expression. I got the feeling that Hobeika was not enamored of his hosts. On the other hand, from what I had seen even in the short time I'd been in the country, Elie was very important to the Syrians. Not just anyone can order the vice-president awakened from his nap. And I could see in the look of the Syrian officials at the airport and the officer at the checkpoint that Hobeika was someone to be handled with kid gloves.

It was an eerie, unforgettable ride through a moonlit wilderness, with Hobeika's coiled, brooding presence beside me. He was clever and merciless, and he probably did murder Bashir, I thought, but a moment later I dismissed the idea, which sprang more from fear than from conviction.

We were going to Zahle, where Elie's forces were headquartered. Zahle had been the site of one of Bashir's greatest triumphs. I felt that he was with me, sitting next to me in Elie's car and giving me the courage to do what I had to do.

Ever since my question about Bashir's death, Hobeika's silence had been deafening. Questions were rising in my gorge. Why hadn't Elie, Bashir's brilliant head of security, learned about the Syrian plot to kill him? Why hadn't he known that Chartouni, who had access to the building where Bashir spoke every Tuesday, belonged to the Syrian Popular party? If Hobeika was as smart as everyone said he was, and I believed he was, how could he not have known?

But Bashir's shade notwithstanding, I knew that this wasn't the time to ask those questions. Not while we rode through this valley of death, trailed by a carload of Syrian agents who would, I had no doubt, do anything Hobeika commanded, from gravedigging by moonlight to burning off the hand that offended them.

We arrived at Elie's headquarters in pitch darkness. As we drove up the steep and narrow mountain road, the only illumination aside from our headlights was the full moon. A few soldiers in MP Lebanese Forces uniforms, which they had taken with them into exile, manned a makeshift gate. They straightened to attention and saluted when they saw Elie, and quickly raised the gate. We drove a little farther to his mountain hideout, a windowless bunker. We got out, and I stretched and took a deep breath of fresh air. The city of Zahle lay at our feet. As we entered I noticed that the stone walls of Hobeika's office were as thick as the walls of a crusader castle. A single bed covered with a sheet stood in the corner of the office. For security reasons, Hobeika slept in here whenever he spent the night.

I was introduced to Elie's key staff. Once, it seemed so long ago, they had been Bashir's men. As I looked at them, I wondered if these were really the "heroes" of Sabra and Shatila. Some of them looked so young. Every one of them carried a pistol in his belt. What a shame, I thought, what a waste.

These young soldiers knew I had been a friend of Bashir's, and they seemed ashamed when they spoke of their alliance with Syria. They were very polite and friendly, and because of their extreme youth, I almost made the mistake of forgetting the world they lived in—until a small misunderstanding on the second day of my stay reminded me.

"I'm going out to shoot some people in Zahle," I said to Hobeika's young assistant as I walked out the door with my camera crew.

"No, you can't do that," he said.

"Sure I can. I want to shoot some people. What's wrong with that?"

"No," he said.

"Yes," I said, in a very firm voice. "What do you think I came here for?"

My determination cowed him. "Okay," he relented. "But call us before you shoot anyone."

Elie stayed at his headquarters in Zahle the first week I was in Lebanon. I saw him every day, but getting him to talk about what I wanted to talk about was like trying to open a clam with your teeth. One day, he came into an office where I was talking to several of his soldiers about Bashir. Elie placed his face close to mine. "You know," he said, "some people think Bashir should have been buried in Israel."

"No!" I said in horror. "You knew him. How can you say that?" As I looked into his hard, cold eyes, I saw hatred and jealousy. Hobeika had clearly made a decision not to discuss Bashir with me at all, but he was unable to control his anger. I had heard that slur against Bashir once before, and it bothered me that I couldn't recall when. Then I remembered. When the prisoner Chartouni was displayed on television, he said that Bashir had betrayed Lebanon through his friendship with Israel.

One hot afternoon about a week after my arrival, we took a break from filming to drive to a swimming resort about forty minutes from Zahle. Along the way we passed a cultivated field that stretched as far as the eye could see. Beside the field stood a Syrian sentry. The crop looked to me like wheat.

"What is that?" I asked Elie.

"Hashish," he said.

I knew at the time that the Bekáa was one of the world's biggest drug producers, and that many terrorist groups used the proceeds from the drug trade to finance their activities. I had been told that Hobeika was among them.

Bashir had despised drugs, ordering his troops to destroy any found in Beirut and jailing anyone caught trafficking. He established an organization to counsel people with drug problems. Ironically, the head of this group had allied himself with Elie and was driving with us now, pointing out fields of marijuana plants and poppies.

What I did not know then, despite the Syrian sentry, was the extent of Syrian involvement in the drug business. Although nominally part of Lebanon, the Bekáa is completely controlled by Syria and has been for years. In 1982, Israeli tanks challenged the Syrians in the Bekáa, but now nothing moves there that the Syrians do not know of, nothing happens that they do not profit from. After I left Lebanon, I supplemented my own observations with information from Lebanese intelligence and other sources.

The United Nations has a budget, of which 60 percent comes from the United States, earmarked for the destruction of drug sources around the world. Starting in 1972, Lebanon received $25 million for the eradication of hashish and opium-producing crops in the Bekáa Valley. Since 1985, that amount has been raised to $90 million— including $54 million from the United States—which despite the impotent protests of the Lebanese government is now paid directly to Syria.

And what does Syria do with the money? It takes the $90 million and extorts more from the growers of the cannabis and poppies. It shares profits with the merchants who operate the eight factories in the Bekáa Valley that turn the cannabis into hashish and the poppies into heroin. (The three main factories are in Baalbek, Hermel, and Shmistar.) The processed drugs are then shipped either from the airports in Damascus or Beirut, which are under direct Syrian control, or from one of the three Lebanese ports controlled by Syrian proxies: the Sunni port of Sidon, in the south; the Shiite port of Ouzae, in Beirut; and the Druze port of Khalde, also in Beirut. According to Lebanese intelligence sources, the drug traffic in the

Bekáa Valley is worth, conservatively, $500 million a year—which makes the U.N.'s unwitting subsidy of $90 million (and the U.S. taxpayers' $54 million) just a drop in the bucket.

On this drive through the Bekáa, I made our convoy stop and wait while we filmed the marijuana fields. I stood in it, to give proportion to the picture; the lush green plants were taller than I was. Then we continued on our way to a swimming club that looked like the set from the back lot of a Hollywood studio. It seemed as if a square mile of astroturf had been brought in to cover the ground surrounding a large swimming pool and tennis courts. People were sunbathing, and the air was filled with the sounds of splashing and squealing children. The appearance of Hobeika's gun-toting bodyguards fazed no one.

We were in Chtaura, close to the site of heavy fighting between Syrian and Israeli tanks during the invasion of 1982. Chtaura is now a garrison town for the Syrian army and the headquarters of Syrian intelligence in the Bekáa. It is also the headquarters of radical PLO factions—the Abu Moussa group and the Popular Front for the Liberation of Palestine—and the more moderate Amal, a Shiite militia now working with the Syrians to contain Hezbollah. Because of its strategic location beside the Beirut-Damascus highway, Chtaura also serves as the drug trafficking capital of the Bekáa.

We sat on a terrace looking down on the pool. Elie toyed with my Betacam, taking pictures of the swimmers. He knew a bit about photography and obviously enjoyed playing with the equipment, and he looked more relaxed than he had since I arrived. "Elie," I said casually, "what were you going to do when Bashir assumed the presidency?"

Before he could answer, one of his aides said, "Elie was going to leave the country."

"Why?" I said, swallowing my surprise.

Elie scowled fiercely at the boy, who did not notice.

"Because he didn't want to embarrass Bashir. As head of intelligence he was in charge of many operations that could have been controversial. Elie *offered* to leave," the boy said proudly, "after Bashir won."

I turned to Hobeika, who had deserted the Betacam and was glaring at me with heightened color. "Bashir was going to let you go, Elie?" I said.

"Yes," he said, and somehow he managed to look both wary and sullen.

I kept quiet. The conversation quickly turned to our filming, but I didn't join in and neither did Elie. His aide had just handed me one large piece of the puzzle, and I was trying to fit it in.

The story I had just heard made no sense. Hobeika was just not that altruistic, and Bashir would never have let him go—he would have needed him more than ever after the election.

There was only one possible meaning to what I had just learned. For some as yet unknown reason, Bashir had lost faith in Hobeika.

The Syrians kept a tight rein on my project. Because of their anxiety about any incident with the Shiites and Hezbollah, especially one involving an American journal- ist, we were not allowed to move outside Zahle without an armed Syrian escort composed not just of soldiers but of their toughest comman- dos. Any filming outside the city had to be scheduled and approved.

I was eager to see as much of Zahle as possible, not least because Bashir had never had the opportunity to come here himself—it was far too dangerous. This Christian enclave of about 20,000 had been heavily shelled by the Syrians in 1981, when a few dozen of Bashir's men were holed up in the city, and again in 1984. Now, ironically, it was protected by the Syrian army, which had established numerous sandbagged checkpoints in the city. Troops roamed the streets as freely as if they were in Damascus. Through a translator I talked to one Syrian soldier, who said that he felt very much at home in Zahle.

Many shops were closed, and those that were open were full of expensive consumer goods and empty of customers. Lebanon was experiencing 1,000 percent inflation, and Zahle's Christians were isolated, cut off from the mainstream economy. Here and there I saw several old, weathered posters of Bashir, faded remembrances of another age. The façades of the buildings were scarred by the Syrian shelling, as the residents were by the occupation. One seventeen-year-old girl told me about an incident in 1981: "I was buying bread," she said, "and I saw a Syrian soldier shoot a little baby, two years old, and then he killed the father."

"What's it like now," I asked her, "with the Syrians here?"

"Awful," she whispered. "There is no freedom."

I interviewed a young, articulate woman in her early twenties, a Shiite who strongly opposed Hezbollah. She worked as a stringer for a Beirut weekly magazine. After we spent two hours filming the interview, she phoned Elie Hobeika, who had introduced us, to protest that she had just discovered that I was a Jew. She would never have cooperated if she'd known, she said, and didn't want us using the interview.

Services had broken down in Zahle, as they had throughout Lebanon. Though the marijuana fields outside the city were well irrigated, water to the city was cut off except for an hour or two each day. There was rarely electricity. Trash went uncollected, littering the streets and attracting swarms of insects and rats that spread disease. Typhoid, tetanus, Maltese fever, and diseases unknown since the Middle Ages were rampant.

One day the crew and I, with our ubiquitous Lebanese guards, were parked near a gas station, filming the enormous queue of cars waiting for gas. A Syrian soldier sauntered over, rifle over his right shoulder, and shouted something. Suddenly I heard the roar of thirty motor engines starting at once. As if by magic, the queue evaporated.

"What happened?" I asked our interpreter.

"The Syrian told everyone to move or he'd shoot them." He shrugged, as if to say, "Big deal; it happens every day."

One of our guards was a new recruit, fresh from East Beirut and not yet inured to the sight of Syrians lording it over Lebanese. This boy jumped out of our car, ran over to the station, and leaped onto the back of the Syrian soldier, knocking him over.

His friends reached him in a moment, pulled him off the Syrian, and hustled him back to the car. The Syrian stood up. His hand went to his gun and he walked toward our car. The Lebanese soldiers began to shout. I heard Hobeika's name, twice, three times. The Syrian stopped. He let go of his gun, raised his empty hands, and shouted something.

"What'd he say?" I asked.

"He apologized," said the interpreter, bursting into laughter.

I mentioned the incident at dinner to Hobeika, who smiled proudly at the courage of his recruit and also at the Syrian's apology. "You know," he said expansively, "someday we may have to fight the Syrians."

This was the opening I'd been waiting for. "Elie," I said, "you're in bed with the devil. If you ever cross the Syrians they'll kill you, just like they killed Bashir. You're their pet Christian, but as soon as you start becoming independent, they'll cut you down."

Elie stared at me. He said nothing.

"You yourself told me they killed Bashir. You interviewed Chartouni. How did they do it?"

Elie did not reply. Unheeding, his intelligence chief, Assaad Shaftari, code-named Asso, spoke. "It was planned for three years. Chartouni got his orders the day before the operation from his Syrian control in Paris. It was a very sophisticated operation."

Elie moved in his seat. Still he had not said a word. We stared at one another. Asso looked at Elie's face, excused himself, and hurriedly left the room.

"Three years is a long time," I said.

Hobeika stared. I could almost see the emanations of his dammed-up emotion shimmering in the space between us. He was, in his own way, as passionate a man as Bashir. But Bashir's passion had been focused outward, while Elie's was turned inward to some dark and secret place where it burned him. Bashir's drive came from his love of Lebanon, but Elie's came from love of power. It struck me then that Elie Hobeika was Bashir's shadow, his other side, his image in a warped mirror.

"Three years," I said, "is a very long time."

Elie's eyes narrowed. He opened his mouth as if to speak. Then he got up and walked away.

I couldn't sleep. I was living on nervous energy. Finally, I became very sick, with a form of pneumonia. I lost my voice and was overcome with nausea and paroxysms of coughing that left me faint. Sometimes, my energy would evaporate. My head would grow light and my imagination played tricks on me. I felt outside myself, as if it were someone else in Lebanon, with the Syrians on one side and Elie Hobeika on the other. Sometimes, when my fever rose, I thought it was all a dream. But inevitably the fever would recede, and I would be forced to accept reality.

Hobeika's men brought a local doctor who examined me and prescribed some medicine. I felt that if I took it I would surely die. I refused, and recovered.

One day, a Syrian intelligence officer drove me and the crew across the Bekáa Valley to West Beirut. The three-hour trip seemed to me like a voyage of a thousand years.

Lebanon's ugly, virulent civil war, which had resumed in the wake of Bashir's death, had left its mark everywhere. I had seen the ravages of war in Beirut and Damour; but now I saw it throughout Lebanon. And there could be no doubt about the victor. Every few meters there stood a Syrian tank or troop emplacement.

There was no more Lebanon. Lebanon was a fiction. We were in Syria.

I had been promised a drive through the teeming Shiite suburbs south of West Beirut, where several hostages were being held. Syrian troops ringed the Shiite strongholds. They had orders not to enter, but they controlled access to the terrorist warrens.

But the Syrian intelligence officer refused to allow us to enter the suburbs, saying that even with our truckload of Syrian soldier-escorts it was too dangerous. After much prodding, he finally allowed us to take pictures from a Syrian military checkpoint on a hill overlooking the suburbs. The crew began setting up. My cameraman was a young Frenchman, just starting out as a freelancer based in Beirut. The soundman was an Armenian. They were still unpacking their cases when the bullets began to fly.

I heard a sharp whine, and suddenly I was stretched out on the ground, half crushed under a lummox of a soldier.

"Get off me, you idiot," I yelled, pummeling him.

"Snipers," he gasped, trying to protect himself from my fists without hurting me. "Stay down," he warned, as he let me go.

The Syrian officer shouted a command and sullenly, the troops obeyed: they hunkered down and held their fire.

I was furious, not so much at the snipers who were firing at us as at the Syrians who were trying to protect us. "This is all your fault," I yelled at the uncomprehending soldier who had flattened me. By killing Bashir, the Syrians had unleashed this chaos. Hezbollah, the taking of hostages, the bombing of the U.S. Marine barracks and embassy, the Syrian hegemony over Lebanon—none of it would have happened if Bashir had lived. But that is precisely why he had to die. He had been the only person capable of uniting Lebanon, and thus he was the greatest impediment to total Syrian control.

Since the Syrians steadfastly refused to let us continue filming, and my own crew was eyeing me rebelliously, we packed up and drove into West Beirut. The Syrian officer led us to a restaurant on the waterfront in the midst of what used to be, in halcyon days, a carnival. Out front, a long-abandoned Ferris wheel shook in the breeze, and the sound of its creaking and moaning could be heard inside. It was like a macabre piece of giant pop art, a testament to the madness that had overtaken this once magnificent city.

The Syrian officer sat opposite me in the middle of a long table, our interpreter by his side. I asked the officer how he liked being in Beirut.

"Not much," he said.

"Well, what did you think of Bashir Gemayel?"

"A very impressive man."

"Then why did you kill him?"

The interpreter glared at me. "I'm not translating that," he said.

"Why not?"

"Because I value my life. Because you don't talk like that to Syrians. Because they don't exactly have the best sense of humor, especially these intelligence types."

It's one thing to label a country "terrorist," another to eat lunch with one of the flesh-and-blood implementers of that policy. The man sitting opposite me, sharing wine with me, had a wife and children in Aleppo, Syria. He showed me their pictures and said he was homesick. He was rather likable. The restaurant specialized in a certain type of fish. When I said that I wanted it grilled, not fried, he went into the kitchen to make sure they prepared it the way I liked.

I didn't want him to be considerate. I didn't want to feel

that he was human. It was more comfortable to think in terms of black and white, good and evil. Because it was certain that this man would not have attained the position he had without carrying out harsh orders ruthlessly.

Just before we left, when we had finished our wine, I asked him, "So, do you like the U.S.?"

"Not very much," was the reply.

"We're not wild about your country, either."

The lunch ended on this sad note.

A few hours later, I returned to Zahle to find Paul Ariss sitting alone in Hobeika's office. I knew Ariss from way back. When Bashir was alive, he had overseen the finances of the Lebanese Forces intelligence group. He lived in Paris now, and I had met him there when I was on vacation. A big, tall bear of a man, he is very likable and friendly. I was glad to see him, and not just because he was like a breath of fresh air in Elie's dank, dreary bunker. Ariss had been close to both Bashir and Elie in the old days. He probably knew as much as anyone about what had happened.

"Where's Elie?" I asked.

"In a meeting."

I closed the office door and sat beside him. Questions were burning in me and I didn't know how much time I had before Elie would bust up our tête-à-tête. But, much as I wanted to, I couldn't plunge right in. I was very much afraid of what Elie would do if he discovered my true motive.

I told Ariss about our day in Beirut, described the ubiquitous Syrian presence and the sniping incident, and didn't hide my emotions when I talked about my "if only" feelings—that if only Bashir had lived, none of this would have happened.

Paul agreed sadly. We shared a moment of silence. I sighed and shook my head and said, "Everyone says the Syrians did it."

He nodded absently. "The Syrians and the Soviets," he said.

"The Soviets?"

"That detonator was a sure sign," Ariss said. "Only the Soviets could have supplied that. And they had plenty of motivation. It's no secret that Bashir was getting help from the CIA and the Mossad. With him as president of Lebanon, the whole region could have tilted toward the West. Besides," he added, "we know for a fact that Ali Duba was involved."

"Who's he?"

"Head of Syrian military intelligence, but also the Soviet Union's man in Syria. He was in charge of the plan to kill Bashir."

"By using that Christian agent of theirs, Chartouni."

"That's right."

"That's the one thing I've never understood. How could you have let this Chartouni so close to Bashir, if he was a member of that Syrian-backed group? Why wasn't he checked out?"

"He was," Ariss said without hesitation. "We knew all about Chartouni. He joined the SPP when he was a student in Paris. Elie found out about it and told Bashir."

"What happened?"

"Bashir called Jean Nader and gave him the information. Nader told him, 'Look, I've raised these kids,' and gave his personal guarantee that they were loyal to Bashir. The thing is," Ariss said, "Nader was having an affair with Chartouni's sister, and it was very convenient having her in the building."

Jean Nader, the head of the Ashrafiyeh branch, had died with Bashir in the explosion.

"And Elie just accepted this?"

Paul threw open his hands. "He wanted to get the family out. But Bashir wouldn't go against Nader's word."

"So Elie just gave up? That doesn't seem right. He's much too tough to allow himself to be overruled on a security matter. Everybody knew Bashir went to Ashrafiyeh every Tuesday afternoon. He was a sitting duck."

"You know Bashir," Ariss said ruefully. "He did what he wanted."

He was right: I did know Bashir, and I knew he would never ignore these facts. True, he was sometimes inattentive to his personal security; but he was much too smart to close his eyes to real danger and too tough-minded to allow friendship to deter him from taking action in a matter of life and death.

And how could Nader vouch for Chartouni's loyalty when he had just been told that Chartouni was a member of a revolutionary group run by Syrian intelligence? Aside from the fact that Nader was unfailingly loyal to Bashir, his own death was a good indication that he had no inkling of the danger posed by Chartouni. And wasn't it convenient to pin the blame on a man who was no longer around to contradict anything?

I believed Ariss when he said that Elie had the information on Chartouni. But I doubted that either Nader or Bashir had ever heard a word of it.

The puzzle was coming together.

The climax of our shoot, and subsequently of the one-hour television program, came the next day, when we drove to Baalbek, headquarters of Hezbollah and the terrorist capital of the Bekáa Valley.

I had interviewed a deserter from the ranks of Hezbollah, who told me that while he served in Baalbek, several Western hostages were kept there in prison beneath the Sheikh Abdullah barracks. Syrian intelligence agreed, but they argued strenuously against my filming there. In the end, since they had known from the start that Hezbollah and the hostages were the subject of our program, they had to agree. But they sent a small army with us.

But before going to Baalbek we planned a preliminary trip: a drive through the Shiite village of Mashghara in the southern Bekáa Valley. Three cars loaded with Hobeika's soldiers, dressed for war with flak jackets and heavy arms, escorted us to a nearby Syrian army garrison, where we picked up seven carloads of Syrian commandos wearing the pink camouflage uniforms of the Syrian army. They, too, were combat-ready.

The villagers stared sullenly at our convoy as we entered Mashghara, past walls covered with anti-Western and anti-Israeli slogans in English and Arabic, banners, and posters with the pictures of Shiite martyrs. Our car broke down, but our guards would not let us get out. In the ten minutes it took to restart the car, I listened to the eerie silence that lay over the village. No children playing, no women gossiping in the market; unlike every other Lebanese village I had visited, there were no men sitting in cafés, whiling away their time drinking Turkish coffee and playing backgammon. The only sound was the amplified wail, calling the faithful to prayer, that descended from a towering minaret and echoed through the village. Mashghara seemed to me a village under siege, but a siege imposed from within.

The day after visiting Mashghara, we picked up a contingent of Syrian commandos who escorted us northward, in a convoy of ten army vehicles, through the length of the Bekáa toward Baalbek. The first sign that we were approaching the city's outskirts was the sight, very jarring in Western, fashion-conscious Lebanon, of women in chadors, the long robes that women wear in Khomeini's Iran. Hobeika's security chief, Asso, turned and thrust a scarf at me. "We don't want Hezbollah to see you in the car. Here, cover your Jewish blonde hair."

"This Jewish blonde hair cost me a lot of money," I said.

We passed the bombed-out ruin of what used to be Hezbollah's headquarters, which was destroyed by a French air raid in 1983, in retaliation for a suicide car bomb in Beirut that killed fifty French soldiers. The closer we came to Baalbek, the more nervous our escorts grew. Here, too, we were allowed to film only from the car.

On a hill just outside Baalbek, our convoy stopped at a Syrian army position. Our tough Syrian commandos were so unnerved that their hands shook; and when Asso tried to take a picture, he had to balance the camera on another man's shoulder. This was as far as they could go, the officer in charge told me. I would film from there.

I was ordered to stay in a filthy pit that must have been the outpost's garbage dump, out of sight and line of fire from Hezbollah sentries. Baalbek lay below us, quiet and ominous. I could see enormous murals of the Ayatollah Khomeini gazing into the distance, communing, it seemed, with Allah. High on a hill on the opposite side of the town, clearly visible through a high-powered lens from our position, was the compound of the Sheikh Abdullah barracks, which in happier times had been a resort hotel complex. My cameraman used his long lens to get excellent pictures of the radio tower that allowed Hezbollah to keep contact with Iran independent of the telephone system, and of the three-story building in which, we had been told, the Western hostages were kept. It was in Baalbek that CNN correspondent Jeremy Levin was held until he "escaped" from captivity. It was hard to see how escape from Baalbek was possible; indeed, a Syrian intelligence officer told me that the escape was staged after Levin's employer paid a ransom.

Hobeika had arranged for a local official to use our Betacam to film the Sheikh Abdullah barracks up close. The official invited me to come along. "With a chador," he said, "all women look the same." I declined.

The operational chief of Hezbollah was a Lebanese Shiite named Hussein Mussawi, who was also called Carlos after the famous Argentinian terrorist. Mussawi had distinguished himself as a commander of the Hezbollah faction called the Islamic Amal, when he helped direct the devastating bombings of the French military headquarters and the American embassy and barracks in Beirut. The Ayatollah Khomeini himself chose Mussawi to head the unified security command of Hezbollah, a position of enormous power for a man who started out as a chemistry teacher. If Khomeini answers only to God, Mussawi answers only to Khomeini. It is he who implements Hezbollah's policy of hostage taking. Through some Lebanese connections I received permission to interview Mussawi—the first interview he had granted since taking over as Hezbollah chief of operations.

This was a gift horse with teeth. Just a few months before, a former ABC news reporter named Charles Glass was taken hostage right after he interviewed the Ayatollah Fadlallah, spiritual head of Hezbollah. Glass was snatched near a Syrian checkpoint, virtually from under the Syrians' noses. Interpreting this action as a deliberate affront to their power, the Syrians threatened military action unless Glass was released. Hezbollah backed down and let him go.

But British Anglican Bishop Terry Waite has not been as fortunate. He was trying to negotiate a hostage release when he was taken prisoner by Hezbollah on January 20, 1987, and he is still being held. Elie Hobeika told me that he will be the last of the hostages to be released, because the Syrians will not intercede unless Great Britain agrees to resume diplomatic relations, severed when the head of Syrian Air Force intelligence was found to be involved in the attempt to blow up the El Al jet leaving Heathrow Airport. Mrs. Thatcher, the strongest of all the Western leaders in her determination not to deal with terrorists, has refused to pay this price to repatriate Waite or any of the other British hostages.

Since I could not go into Baalbek, I hired a Lebanese journalist to conduct the interview and gave her a list of questions. As soon as they met, Mussawi asked her who she was working for. When he heard it was me, he conveyed an offer: if I chose to do the interview myself, Hezbollah would guarantee safe passage in and out.

Terry Waite and Charles Glass had been promised safe

passage, too. The words are without meaning in Lebanon. I would have loved to meet Mussawi on safe ground, but I declined his invitation to Baalbek.

The interview was a scorcher. Mussawi did not deny Hezbollah's involvement in abduction, nor did he apologize for it. Rather, he justified it by claiming that the abductees were American or European intelligence agents who were being held to pressure the governments to change their anti-Islamic, anti-Iranian policies. He excoriated the West for its degeneracy, called Israelis and Jews "microbes who need to be exterminated," and ended with a prepared statement that he read in English. Addressed directly to the people of the West, it called on them to overthrow leaders who obstructed the Ayatollah Khomeini's revolutionary mission or else to suffer the consequences. "Which will it be," he asked, in the tone of a strict but kindly schoolteacher, "our love and collaboration, or the fires of Islam?"

I watched him later on tape. He didn't rant or foam at the mouth. He spoke in the cadence of reason. It made me shiver; it was like watching a thing that looked like a man and sounded like a man, but was not a man.

I left Baalbek with very mixed emotions; relieved to leave, of course, but deeply sorry for the hostages. Lebanon was not just a "story" for me, and I could hardly remember a time when it had been. Through Bashir, I had come to love this land, and I grieved to see what it had become. Hostage taking is the most cynical story I have ever covered. To me, it marks the culmination of Lebanon's long death rattle.

My piece was finished but for the editing, which I would do in London. The night before my departure, Elie, Asso, and I drove to a restaurant in a high-priced housing complex near Zahle headquarters.

There is a kind of high that invariably accompanies the end of a shoot, when you've gotten what you came for and maybe a bit more. Elie and Asso shared the feeling, no doubt because they, too, thought they'd got what they hoped for. That feeling of release and a little wine loosened up Hobeika.

I used a reporter's ploy, stating something as fact instead of asking a question. I said that Bashir had been killed on orders of President Assad of Syria. Asso readily agreed. This time, so did Elie, and without reservation.

They confirmed that Bashir's assassination had been ordered at the highest level, and talked knowledgeably about the trepidations the Syrians and Soviets had felt about his election as president. They were not precise about the Soviet role, and my impression was that they did not have first-hand knowledge. But they were very precise about the setbacks to America's Middle East policy that resulted from Bashir's death. Once Israel withdrew its support, the United States was drawn directly into the fray; one year later, it was forced out in humiliation. With Bashir gone, Lebanon's soil became a fertile ground for the cultivation of young terrorists, and operations against American and other Western targets began to be planned and executed in Lebanon.

But before leaving the next day, I cornered Paul Ariss alone in Elie's office.

"Paul," I told him, "I've been thinking about what you told me, about Elie calling Bashir to warn him about Chartouni. It just doesn't make sense. Bashir wouldn't have let it pass; and even if he had, Elie is much too strong to have tolerated it. He would have moved that family himself."

"Not after Bashir ordered him not to," Ariss said. "Besides," he said defensively, "it wasn't his job anymore. Elie wasn't responsible for Bashir's security at the end."

"Oh, no?" I said.

"Bashir created his own personal security system, headed by Abbas-Abbas and Poussy Aschkar. Elie had nothing to do with it." With that, Ariss walked out.

I went for a walk in the hills outside of Zahle and

wandered aimlessly among vineyards withering in the sun. In the distance I could hear gunfire, but I paid no attention; it was only Elie's soldiers practicing. Ariss had given me the last piece of the puzzle and I saw it now, as clearly as if it were spread out on a table before me.

Bashir would never have removed his security from Elie's hands unless he had reason to distrust him. He must have found out about Elie's Syrian connections, which were in place long before his death. How would he have reacted? Knowing Bashir's loyalty to his men, I thought he would have allowed Elie to leave Lebanon quietly.

Elie had said that he chose to leave, to spare Bashir embarrassment about past actions. From all I knew and had seen of the man—his love of power and luxury and his ego—such self-sacrifice was inconceivable. Elie had straddled the fence for years, keeping one foot in Bashir's camp, the other in the Syrians'. Now, just as his efforts on Bashir's part were reaching fulfillment, he was being sent into exile, robbed of the fruits of victory. I knew from his aborted castle how very much Elie had coveted those fruits. No, he would not have gone willingly.

Ever since I heard of Elie's planned departure, I had suspected that he had been forced out. Ariss's information that Bashir had also removed his personal security from the hands of the best security man in Lebanon confirmed my suspicion.

I had always known that Hobeika had the logistic capability of setting up the assassination, and that the safe-passage card in Chartouni's pocket was evidence of a linkage. But I had resisted drawing the obvious conclusion, because I could see no motive. Now it had become clear that Elie had everything to gain from Bashir's death. If Bashir lived, Elie would go into exile. If he died, Elie would eventually replace him as head of the Lebanese Forces.

Syria had planned for three years to kill Bashir. Throughout those three years, Bashir was a constant thorn in its side. What stayed Syria's hand? Did it have an asset close to Bashir, whose information was worth delaying Bashir's removal from the scene? Once he was elected president, they could wait no longer; by then their asset was blown anyway. Bashir was onto Elie.

I can't prove it. Truth is not a single thing; it's more like an onion, made up of layers. I think that I have penetrated most of those layers, if not all.

Hobeika drove me back to Damascus. This time it was I who remained quiet, and he who spoke. "I'm sorry I can't have dinner with you," he said as we sped through the grim valley. "My wife and I are dining with good friends." He mentioned the name of the head of Syria's air force intelligence, who functions as the overlord for all Syrian intelligence.

"That's all right," I said.

"Perhaps we'll meet again sometime, in Beirut." Hobeika turned and looked at me. "I'll be back, you know," he said. "It's only a matter of time."

I stared ahead, into the darkness.

Epilogue

I am a witness to something that almost was and now will never be. For many years I hoarded my memories, as if by holding them close I could keep them safe. But in this I was wrong.

Bashir's achievements died with him. Within a year of his death it was as if he had never lived, except for the added despair of people who know that their misery is not preordained, that things might have turned out differently. All that is left of Bashir is memory, and I have come to see that if those who love him do not speak out, then the only epitaph for this great man will be the one written in blood by the savagery of his fallen-away followers.

It has been painful—the writing, the remembering. But in a strange way I feel that it has brought me back to life, as if I were sleepwalking all these years since his death and have only just awakened. I have done what I had to do for Bashir; I have kept our covenant, told his story as best I could. In doing so, I find that I have also told my own.

Writing these words, finishing this work, I feel the greatest peace I have known since the day he died.

Bashir and I were raised in different worlds, but our love was sparked not only by chemistry but by passion and conviction. Loving him cost me everything. I jeopardized my job, my daughter's peace of mind, even my life for Bashir; and in the end I lost him.

I regret nothing. I am proud of him and of what we were to each other. I am proud of the work I've done. There are those who will say that journalists must avoid personal involvement that might compromise their stories, and to a large extent I agree. While I was reporting on Bashir, I resisted our mutual attraction. But I believe that taking an "even-handed," dispassionate approach to stories like terrorism and hostage taking is as wrong as covering Hitler neutrally. Reporters are human, whatever they may pretend. We all have opinions, principles, and beliefs that affect our work, and it's hypocritical to pretend otherwise. Reporters *need* to care, for it is that passion that drives them to uncover hidden truths, to write unpopular stories when necessary, and to go to bat for those stories.

Two promises compelled me to write this book. While Bashir lived, I promised him I'd tell the truth about him and his cause. And when I stood by his grave, I swore to expose his killers. I have achieved the second, to my own satisfaction. But my own satisfaction is no measure of the first.

Bashir had a generosity of spirit that I despair of conveying. I saw him make mistakes. It was part of his greatness that he was not afraid to take chances, to risk mistakes. But I never saw him do a petty thing or say a petty word. I do not say these things because I loved him; I loved him because they are true.

I've never claimed he was an angel. As gentle as he always was to me, Bashir had iron in his soul. It was his uniqueness that he never condoned wanton violence or revenge for the sake of revenge, but he was as strong as he needed to be. "You do not rule Lebanon with hugs and kisses," he often said. Recently I came across this, by Thomas Jefferson: "We are not to expect to be translated from despotism to liberty in a featherbed."

In his short lifetime Bashir accomplished many things. He was only thirty-four years old when the Israelis fought a war to see him become president and the U.S. government put its full force behind his election. But so much of what he was was still unfolding. How does one show what might have been? Yet that is my task, and it matters deeply that I succeed. Bashir's brief moment in the sun was to Lebanon as Arthur's reign was to ancient England—a splash of light engulfed by feudal darkness.

Bashir was a great beacon to his people, and the extinguishing of his light plunged them into a greater darkness than they knew before. But if he is truly remembered as he was, then someday, someone may blow on the embers and ignite a new beacon. This, then, is my remembrance, and may it serve the cause for which he gave his life.

This book was also born in anger: at Bashir for dying, at his killers, at the friends who forsook him before his body was cold. But in the course of writing, my anger was spent. I understand so much more now. Because of the risks I had to take to carry out my mission, I understand the risks Bashir took for his.

When Bashir died, the Christian community shed tears, but also heaved a collective sigh of relief. I have come to understand this, too. Imagine a tyro climber who's primed himself to scale a mountain far beyond his ability. When his climb is suddenly canceled owing to circumstances beyond his control, what does he feel? Disappointment, certainly—but also release.

Bashir was neither safe nor comfortable. His determination to overthrow the status quo of institutionalized corruption, drug dealing, and power-sharing arrangements in favor of an open political and economic system threatened many powerful people, including prominent Christians. While he lived he held them to his path, but the moment he died, the tradewinds of self-interest carried them away.

"Though a man escape every other danger," Demosthenes wrote some twenty-two centuries ago, "he can never wholly escape those who do not want such a man to exist."

And I understand, at last, how and why Bashir died. Chartouni pressed the button, but I believe it was Elie Hobeika who, through greed and envy and ambition, set Bashir up.

At the time of this writing, Elie Hobeika is still head of his breakaway faction of the Lebanese Forces, and he has burrowed even deeper into Syrian military intelligence. He's doing well, my sources tell me. He has a finger in the Bekáa Valley's drug industry, large enough to finance his troops and their car-bomb attacks against his fellow Christians in East Beirut; in recent years, hundreds of innocent people have been killed and maimed. He has another finger in the intelligence market. Elie sells intelligence gleaned from his Syrian friends to the intelligence services of Germany and France. In March of 1988, he flew secretly to the United States to try to trade information about our hostages, not for money but for political support.

Elie wants to return as head of the Lebanese Forces in Beirut and to be once again a king-maker in Lebanon. Right now it looks as if he may succeed. The Syrians intend to crush the Lebanese Forces, which function as an independent force outside their hegemony. To accomplish this, they would have to depose Samir Geagea as head of the Lebanese Forces. If Geagea goes, the way is cleared for Hobeika to return.

I would not have it thought that Elie Hobeika alone killed Bashir; I would not overstate his power. It took more than the malice of one greedy, earth-bound man to kill Bashir.

Bashir, like every other tragic hero, had one fatal weakness. He chose to elevate Elie Hobeika, a common if clever thug, to the position that allowed him to do what he did. And he made that fatal choice for a reason that wrings my heart, even now. Bashir made Elie his chief of security after, and because, Maya was killed.

Pierre Yazbeck told me, years later when we met in Paris. "It took Maya's death," he said, "to make Bashir realize that the rules of the game were dirty and hard. After she died he was crushed. He said, 'Why her? Why not me? Is she paying for my sins?' He was stoical with outsiders, but he wept bitterly on the breasts of those he loved. When I embraced him, he pressed my shoulder until I thought it would break. But then he buried his daughter. And he dried his tears and he said, 'Okay. Now we play by their rules. No matter how bitter, no matter how inhuman, we play by their rules.' "

And that was when Bashir brought Elie Hobeika into the fold.

I have mourned Bashir's child, whom I never knew, as if she were my own daughter. I have treasured my own child more for the knowledge that there but for the grace of God. . . . And here is what I think. I think that Bashir was a man who pulled himself out of a morass of destruction, despair, and cruelty; who rose above all the values by which he was raised and taught; who transcended his own impetuous nature and everything else that bound him, except the one thing that no one should ever have to transcend: the love of his own daughter. And if a man deserves to die for that, then God help us all.

INDEX

Israel (continued)
  intelligence agencies of, 4–5,
    9, 10, 17, 18, 221
  Lebanon invaded by, 151, 152,
    153, 154–158, 161
  Mideast objectives of, U.S.
    conflict with, 120–121,
    158–159, 175–176
  military support of Lebanese
    Christians by, 59, 106, 152,
    155, 157, 160
  Sabra and Shatila massacres
    and, 187, 188, 198
  Shiite Moslems and, 159–160,
    162–163
  Syrian confrontation with,
    108–110, 155, 156, 211
  uranium diversion by, 2–4
  West Beirut bombing by, 158,
    167, 168–169
Israeli Defense Forces, 82
Israel's Lebanon War (Schiff and
  Ya'ari), 156–157, 187–188,
  204–205

Jabar, Adnan, 11
"Jack Anderson Confidential,"
  153, 158, 177, 186, 194
Japanese Red Army, 11, 44
Jefferson, Thomas, 232
Jeune Afrique, 145
Jews, in Lebanon, 30
Jihad, Abu, 5
Johnson, Lyndon B., 3
Jordan, 21, 171
journalism, personal
  involvement and, 231
Jung, Carl G., 12

Kaa massacre, 52
KGB, 4
Khashan, Odile, 191–192
Khomeini, Ayatollah Ruhollah,
  162, 196, 224–225, 226
Khoury, Charbel el-, 191
Kimche, David, 17–19, 29, 30, 33,
  63, 128, 167
  on Lebanese politics, 19,
    20–23, 84
King, Jerry, 52, 73, 75, 76
Kuntar, Sammy, 13, 14

Labadi, Mahmoud, 75–76, 89
Lebanese army, 38, 125, 188
Lebanese Christians, 20, 120
  history of, 21–22
  Israeli support of, 59, 106, 152,
    155, 157, 160
  massacres and, 22, 31, 52,
    55–56, 65–67, 163–165
  political primogeniture
    among, 34, 49
  unification of, 23, 33–34, 71,
    105–106, 130
  Western press portrayal of,
    30, 31, 45, 50, 52–53, 57,
    139
Lebanese Forces, 20, 33, 45, 71,
  79–82, 197, 198
  under Amin Gemayel, 191–
    192
  as civil authority, 45, 81–82,
    100, 105, 136–137
  under Elie Hobeika, 200, 201,
    208–210, 233
  Israeli military support of, 59,
    138
  model for, 82
  offensive on "Tiger" militia
    by, 33, 105, 106, 139
  rise of, 105
  Sabra and Shatila massacres
    and, 187–188
  U.S. lobby for, 100, 191
Lebanese Information and
  Research Center, 100
Lebanese Moslems, 22–23, 162
  as Israeli allies, 159–160,
    162–163
  massacres of, 22, 52, 65–67
  presidential election and, 152,
    178, 180
  as pro-Iranian
    fundamentalists, 162,
    195–197, 212, 214, 222, 223,
    225–226
Lebanese War, 154–158
  immediate provocation for,
    154–155
  Israeli objectives in, 155–157,
    161
  Lebanese Forces during,
    158–159, 176

primogeniture, political, 34
Project Mud Hen, 150

Qadaffi, Muammar, 113–114, 146
Qarantina massacre, 22

Reagan, Ronald, 151, 188
Red Brigade, 11, 44
refugee camps, 89–90, 160
  massacres at, 187–188,
    198–199, 200, 204
Rivera, Geraldo, 6, 12, 14, 17, 25,
    30, 39, 89, 92, 96, 111–112,
    141, 190
  author on, 72, 77
  Bashir Gemayel interview by,
    77–78
  David Kimche interview by,
    18–20
  departure from Lebanon by,
    94–95
  in Lebanon, 73–79, 81, 83
  Mahmoud Labadi and, 75–76
Rizk, Pierre (Akram), 197–199,
    200, 201
Rolling Stone, 3

Sabra refugee camp massacre,
    187–188, 198–199, 200, 204
Sadat, Anwar al-, 171
Salam, Saeb, 180–181
Saudi Arabia, U.S. Mideast
    policy and, 120–121, 172
Sayaret Matkal, see Headquarters
    unit
Schiff, Ze'ev, 11, 156–157, 158,
    187–188, 204–205
Shaftari, Assaad, 216–217, 223,
    224, 226, 227
Shah of Iran, 162, 175
Shaked, Mano, 16–17
Sharon, Ariel (Arik), 11, 109, 152,
    159, 160–161
  Alexander Haig's meeting
    with, 161
  on Lebanese politics, 155,
    156–157
  Lebanese War and, 152,
    155–157, 158
Shatila refugee camp massacre,
    187–188, 198–199, 200, 204

Sheftell, Alex, 186
Sheikh Abdullah barracks,
    206–207, 222, 224
Shiite Moslems, 22, 67, 178, 214
  background of, 162
  Israeli relationship with,
    159–160, 162–163
  pro-Iranian, 162, 195–197,
    212, 214, 222, 223, 225–226
Shouf Mountains massacre, 31,
    56
Sidon, 163–164, 205
Silkwood story, 2, 53, 54
Six-Day War, 111
Soviet Union, 182
  assassination of Bashir
    Gemayel and, 182, 220–221,
    227
  Chad revolution and, 113–114,
    122, 145
  Syria and, 197
  terrorist groups supported by,
    10, 11–12, 17
Sudan, 144, 145–147
  Chad revolution and, 114,
    122
Sunni Moslems, 22, 162, 178
Syria, 22, 26, 31, 67, 82, 90, 104,
    197, 203–204
  assassination of Bashir
    Gemayel and, 195, 197–201,
    207, 208, 216–217, 220, 227,
    229
  Bekáa Valley controlled by,
    108, 195, 196–197, 211–212,
    214–216
  as destabilizer in Lebanon, 37,
    90, 188
  drug trade and, 211–212
  Great Britian and, 203, 225
  Hezbollah and, 195–197, 204,
    212, 225
  Islamic fundamentalist
    rebellion in, 203
  Israeli confrontation with,
    108–110, 155, 156, 211
  Lebanese views on hegemony
    of, 36–38, 45, 90, 104, 155,
    156
  Sabra and Shatila massacres
    and, 198–199

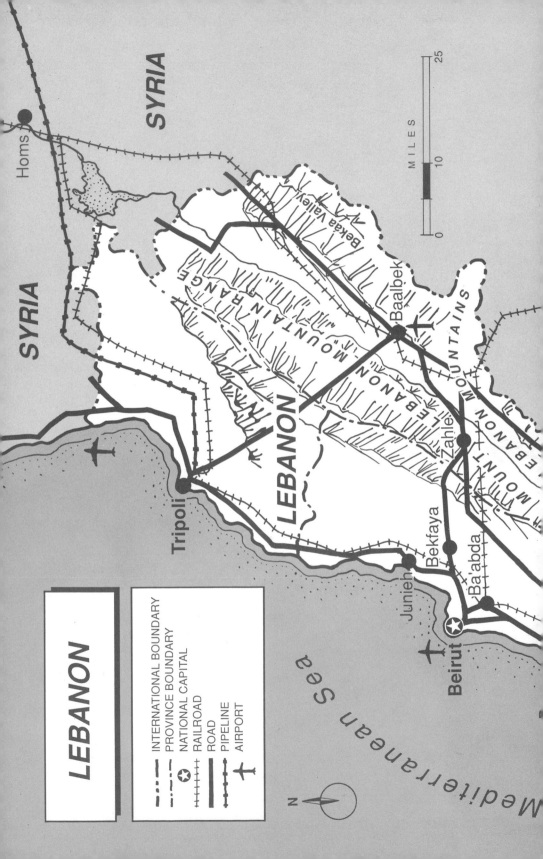

LEBANON

INTERNATIONAL BOUNDARY
PROVINCE BOUNDARY
NATIONAL CAPITAL
RAILROAD
ROAD
PIPELINE
AIRPORT

N

MILES

0   10   25

SYRIA

SYRIA

Homs

Bekaa Valley

ANTI-LEBANON MOUNTAIN RANGE

Baalbek

LEBANON

Zahle

LEBANON MOUNTAINS

Tripoli

Junieh

Bekfaya

Ba'abda

Beirut

Mediterranean Sea